WOMEN, SCHOLARSHIP AND CRITICISM

MANCHESTER
UNIVERSITY PRESS

Women, scholarship and criticism

Gender and knowledge c.1790–1900

EDITED BY JOAN BELLAMY,
ANNE LAURENCE AND GILL PERRY

MANCHESTER UNIVERSITY PRESS
Manchester and New York

distributed exclusively in the USA by Palgrave

Published by Manchester University Press
Oxford Road, Manchester M13 9NR, UK
and Room 400, 175 Fifth Avenue, New York, NY 10010, USA
http://www.manchesteruniversitypress.co.uk

Distributed exclusively in the USA by
Palgrave, 175 Fifth Avenue, New York, NY 10010, USA

Distributed exclusively in Canada by
UBC Press, University of British Columbia, 2029 West Mall, Vancouver, BC, Canada V6T 1Z2

British Library Cataloguing-in-Publication Data
A catalogue record for this book is available from the British Library

Library of Congress Cataloging-in-Publication Data applied for

ISBN 0 7190 5719 1 *hardback*
       0 7190 5720 5 *paperback*

First published 2000

07 06 05 04 03 02 01 00   10 9 8 7 6 5 4 3 2 1

Typeset in Goudy by Carnegie Publishing, Chatsworth Rd, Lancaster
Printed in Great Britain by Biddles Ltd, Guildford and Kings Lynn

Contents

Illustrations

Contributors

RICHARD ALLEN

Richard Allen is Dean of Arts and Senior Lecturer in Literature at the Open University. He has published articles on nineteenth-century British literature, and is currently researching post-colonial literature.

JOAN BELLAMY

Joan Bellamy was Dean of the Faculty of Arts at the Open University between 1984 and 1990, where she founded and directed the Women in the Humanities Research Group. She has published articles on nineteenth-century English literature, in particular the work of women writers. Her ongoing research is on the work and activities of Mary Taylor (1817–93).

CHLOE CHARD

Chloe Chart is a literary historian who lives and works in London. Her book *Pleasure and Guilt on the Grand Tour* was published in 1999 by Manchester University Press. Her other publications include an edited collection of essays *Transports: Travel Pleasure and Imaginative Geography 1600–1830* (Yale University Press, 1996, co-edited with Helen Langdon).

COLIN CUNNINGHAM

Colin Cunningham is a Reader in Art History at the Open University. He has researched and published extensively on civic architecture and applied design. He has published several books and articles on town hall architecture and the work of Alfred Waterhouse, including *Alfred Waterhouse 1830–1903: Biography of a Practice* (Clarendon Press, 1992), and articles on the relationship between gender and design in the eighteenth and nineteenth centuries.

LORNA HARDWICK

Lorna Hardwick is Senior Lecturer in Classical Studies at the Open University and Director of an on-line Research Project on the Reception of Classical Texts. She has published articles on Greek cultural history and the reception of classical texts in the nineteenth and twentieth centuries.

She is the author of *Translating Words: Translating Cultures* (Duckworth, 2000) and co-editor of *Homer: Readings and Images* (Duckworth, 1992).

CICELY HAVELY
Cicely Havely is Senior Lecturer in Literature at the Open University. Her research interests lie in Victorian and post-colonial literature and she has published extensively on Shakespeare and on nineteenth-century novelists, travellers and scholars.

ANNE LAURENCE
Anne Laurence is Senior Lecturer in History at the Open University. She has published extensively on religion and politics in the English civil war. Her books include *Women in England 1500–1760: A Social History* (Weidenfeld and Nicolson, 1994). Her current research is on the comparative history of women in the British Isles in the early modern period and on women and material culture.

SUSAN MUMM
Susan Mumm is currently a Lecturer in Religious Studies at the Open University after several years as Assistant Professor of History at York University, Toronto. She has published articles on women and religion during the nineteenth century.

ROSEMARY O'DAY
Rosemary O'Day is Professor of History at the Open University and Director of the Charles Booth Research Centre. She has published books and articles on early modern education and the history of nineteenth-century social investigation. Her books include *The Family and Family Relationships 1500–1900* (1994) and *The Professions in Early Modern England* (2000).

GILL PERRY
Gill Perry is Senior Lecturer in Art History at the Open University. She has published books and articles on early twentieth-century French and German art and eighteenth-century British art. She has a special interest in gender issues in the visual arts and her publications include *Women Artists and the Parisian Avant-Garde* (Manchester University Press, 1995) and *Gender and Art* (Yale University Press, 1999). Her forthcoming book *Flirting with the Muse* explores representations of the actress in late eighteenth-century British art.

MADELINE THOMPSON
Madeline Thompson was Research Assistant to the Women in the Humanities Research Group at the Open University in 1995–98. She was awarded an MA in Victorian Studies from Birkbeck College, London University in 1997.

Acknowledgements

This collection of essays arose from the shared interests of members of *Women in the Humanities*, an interdisciplinary research group of the Arts Faculty at the Open University, founded in 1987 by Joan Bellamy. Members of the group were drawn together by a common interest in gender studies and issues of women's history and 'feminine' practice, coming from the disciplines of history, literature, art history, religious studies, classical studies and the history of design. As academics working in different areas, we have tried to make accessible issues and debates which are specific to our own disciplines. In the process, we have learnt from one another and have found that collective interdisciplinary research and debate has much to offer a project concerned with gender. The editors would like to thank members of the research group for their continued support, criticisms of and suggestions for the content and development of this project. They would also like to thank the Arts Faculty Research Committee of the Open University for invaluable financial support, and Madeline Thompson for her diligent and intelligent work as research assistant on this project. Individual authors from different disciplines contributed greatly to the process of developing a coherent set of concerns, despite their many different starting points. Special thanks must go to Dr Joan Thirsk for her helpful comments on the original book proposal and to the editors at Manchester University Press for their enthusiastic support of the project. The editors would also like to acknowledge the contributions of Cathy Playle and Valerie Humphrey who patiently keyed in and revised drafts.

Introduction: gender and women's history

Gill Perry, Anne Laurence and Joan Bellamy

> Oh! my unenlightened country-women! read and profit by the admonition of Reason ... Let your daughters be liberally, classically, philosophically, and usefully educated; let them speak and write their opinions freely; let them read and think like rational creatures; adapt their studies to their strength of intellect; expand their minds, and purify their hearts, by teaching them to feel their mental equality with their imperious rulers.[1]

Thus wrote Anne Frances Randall (alias the writer and actress Mary Robinson) in a pamphlet on the rights of women in 1799. Her admonition to women to encourage the serious education of their daughters was a heartfelt plea for the need to give women access to intellectual study and to the achievements traditionally seen as a masculine prerogative. This collection of essays, drawn from different disciplines, explores the ways in which some of those very same 'daughters' actually engaged in forms of scholarly, critical or artistic activity at the turn of the eighteenth and during the nineteenth centuries, revealing some of the gendered views and attitudes encountered in both the production and reception of these works. Each of the essays explores the roles, public perceptions and self-images of women who engaged in forms of scholarly or artistic activity, many of whom are little known in canonical histories and reference books on the period. Many of the essays are also concerned with the different ways in which women who entered public spheres (for example in literary criticism, social reform or the theatre) negotiated or challenged prevailing notions of femininity, and with some of the misogynistic criticism which they encountered.[2] The collection represents the outcome of a significant body of new research in different subject areas which, it is hoped, will contribute significantly to – and help to redefine – the cultural map of the period.

Gender has become an increasingly important concern in the analysis of eighteenth- and nineteenth-century culture. The study of constructions of gender difference has provided insights into areas and questions previously hidden from traditional forms of historical, literary and cultural studies. As branches of gender studies, 'women's history' and the more broadly labelled 'women's studies' have grown and developed since the emergence of the feminist movement in the 1960s and 1970s. Women's history developed as a response to models of interpretation which 'denied women historical agency or dismissed women's activities and experiences as ahistorical'.[3] Political and social issues identified as causes of the subordinate position of women within society were traced to their historical roots, thus directly linking the concerns of the modern women's movement with those of women's history. As Barker and Chalus have written: 'Modern women's subordinate status was deemed the consequence of continuous historical oppression that stemmed from, and was represented by, the personalized domination of men over women within patriarchal society'.[4] With the growth of postmodernism and increasingly sophisticated models of cultural production, a broader category of gender studies has become well established. This category, with its emphasis on cultural constructions of femininity and masculinity, has allowed for more flexible and divergent models for viewing/considering relations between the sexes, and in the process has absorbed and helped to redefine the nature of 'women's history', established as a subject in the 1970s. This process of redefinition, in which the practice of 'women's history' has increasingly been reworked within the discipline of 'gender history' or 'gender studies', has been characterised by lively debate. In a paper given to a conference on the History of Women in 1990, the historian Louise M. Newman argued for the development of a 'merged practice':

> I will speak of women's history as a practice concerned with why specific groups of women share certain experiences, while gender history provides analyses concerning how gender operates through specific cultural forms. I am using 'gender' here to mean the set of meanings constructing sexual difference. When defined this way, gender may, at first glance, seem to have nothing to do with the experiences of men and women, but understanding how gender works to construct the meanings associated with 'male', 'female', 'masculine', 'feminine', 'womanly', 'manly', etc. is instrumental to understanding how and why specific groups of women share certain experiences.
>
> Although I am distinguishing between these two practices, women's and gender history, ultimately I believe that the two practices do and should converge: writing meaningful accounts of women's (and men's) experiences, I shall argue, cannot be accomplished without also examining the ways in which cultural meanings are gendered and otherwise represented. To state this another way, I am advocating that women's and gender history share a common goal – one that consists of articulating the history

of the interrelationships between 'experience' and 'representation' of cultural forms.[5]

The conception behind this collection of essays emerged from some of those debates which have characterised the relationship between women's history and gender studies, and is itself a product of 'a merged practice'. The project originated within an interdisciplinary research group based in the Arts Faculty of the Open University. Members of the group were drawn together by a common intellectual interest in gender studies and issues of women's history and 'feminine' practice, and represent the disciplines of history, literature, art history, religious studies, classical studies, and the history of design. It soon emerged that, despite the constraints of the academic boundaries between, and various analytical models favoured by, different academic subject areas, collective inter-disciplinary research and debate has much to offer a project concerned with gender. As a group we were able to share and develop our knowledge of some of the varied (and often inconsistent) interconnections and common economic, social and aesthetic constraints which characterised varied forms of women's production, greatly informing and enriching our understanding of the material under scrutiny. When practised by women, activities as seemingly diverse as journalism, translation, historical research, acting, interior design and literary editing revealed some shared (and complex) gendered structures of production, consumption and representation. The immense project of unpicking and seeking to understand those structures is, of course, part of the ongoing work of gender studies.

As will be evident from the essays which follow, the different contributors to this collection work with different methodologies and investigative strategies. The editors intended that these varied authorial 'voices' should develop approaches which they believe to be appropriate and intellectually valid. Thus while some authors approach their material empirically, others engage more directly with theoretical models or ideas associated with postmodern theory. All contributing authors, however, are committed to encouraging and enriching debate around the study and representation of practices by women. It is also the aim of this collection to interrogate the concepts of 'scholarship' and 'artist' across the different disciplines represented. We focus in each case on the historical evidence of women's lives, but we are especially concerned with the gendered associations and exclusions, and the implied structures of sexual difference which may (or may not) be revealed.

This book is thus underpinned by a dynamic concept of inter-disciplinarity, in which different disciplines are collectively involved in reflective critical analysis of key issues. But our attempt to combine the different methods which characterise different disciplines has on occasion required some conceptual self-awareness, and thus individual authors have sometimes provided explanations of ideas and approaches which are commonplace within their own disciplines.

Gender and biography

Our search for historical evidence has inevitably involved the accumulation and analysis of biographical material. The recovery and analysis of such material is part of an ongoing process of historical retrieval which has been central to both women's history and gender studies for several decades. However, the growth of gender studies has itself contributed to the continuing theoretical debates around the role of biography. Partly informed by these debates, our intention is not to produce a conventional series of biographical studies. Much recent feminist theory, the influence of which has been felt across the different disciplines which are represented in the collection, has critiqued such traditional forms of biographical study. It has been argued that within disciplines such as history, art history and literature, this form of study has tended to reproduce essentially masculinist narrative structures for recounting the lives and achievements of 'great' men. Such figures have been seen as individuals determining the path of historical and political evolution, or as 'geniuses' whose life stories are constructed to illuminate their artistic personalities and creative powers. Such traditional biographical conventions are ill-suited to frame the lives and activities of many women writers, artists, scholars and researchers who often worked outside – or on the margins of – dominant (and visible) intellectual and artistic activity. Biographies of 'exceptional' women (such as Wollstonecraft or Eliot) have proliferated and the work of these women is acknowledged within more canonical studies. However, further research remains to be done and biographical methods reworked if we are significantly to redefine the cultural map of the period.

Moreover, the biographical genre has been critiqued and reviewed with the growth of post-structuralist approaches to written and visual culture, which see social and historical culture as part of a broader framework of representational practice and political ideologies. Such debates have inevitably been fraught with contradictions, some of which will be reflected in the varying approaches to, and uses of, the biographical genres adopted by different contributors to this collection. With these differences of emphasis, each of the contributors has drawn on biographical material (some of which has not hitherto been published) in order to reconstruct a picture of how various women negotiated their professional and personal lives, and how those negotiating strategies could be seen to have affected their scholarly, artistic and intellectual work. As part of our ongoing research project we have used biography selectively, deliberately seeking out sources which will provide information both on the collective conditions (i.e. social, cultural, educational and legal) of women artists and scholars, and on the diversity of their experiences and strategies in negotiating a largely male-dominated professional culture.

We are well aware that the broad historical scope of this project, from the late eighteenth to the late nineteenth century, itself provides us with a complex and historically variable range of 'data'. Thus some of the professional ambitions and strategies adopted, for example, by the actress Sarah Siddons working at the turn of the eighteenth century (chapter 1) may seem at first sight to be far removed from the moral codes and professional religious culture negotiated by the preacher Catherine Mumford Booth nearly a century later (chapter 11). However, our interest in the study of gender has provided an analytical tool which, while acknowledging complex historical differences and the effects of diverse cultural contexts, can sometimes reveal unexpected similarities in the ways in which some women perceived and even exploited contemporary ideals of femininity and masculinity. The retrieval of evidence of actual lives has played an invaluable part in this difficult process of reconstruction.

The recent influence of psychoanalytic theory within feminist models of analysis has also encouraged a reworking of biography as an important source for gender studies, particularly within the disciplines of art history and literature. The study of 'identity' has become an important theme in the reconstruction of feminine and masculine subjectivities and in the analysis and understanding of sexuality. Although none of the contributing authors engages directly with psychoanalytic models, several address issues of feminine subjectivity and power which are informed by such approaches.[6] Moreover, most of the contributors are concerned (to a greater or lesser degree) to explore the ways in which gender difference could be seen to affect feminine identity and the *self-images* of the women in question. Thus different authors consider some of the strategies of self-narration and self-presentation adopted by women writers, artists and scholars, revealing how these may be ambivalently poised between the supposedly private and domestic – and the more public and professional – identities which women sought to negotiate.

Intellectual authority and identity

Most of the women who appear in this collection sought public recognition as authorities in their chosen fields of endeavour, achieving such recognition by various different strategies. Some used their own names or identities, even trading on them when they became celebrated. The actress Sarah Siddons used her apparently blameless moral reputation; the historian Agnes Strickland had a fine, perhaps exaggerated, sense of the value of her name to her publishers (chapter 7). A more common device was for a woman to present her work anonymously or pseudonymously, thus concealing her sex. Margaret Oliphant, the critic and writer (chapter 8), published most of her reviews anonymously. In journals such as Blackwoods, where reviews normally appeared without attribution, there were many open secrets about the authorship of long or controversial pieces. The convention of anonymity was exploited by women such as Oliphant in order to gain professional status.

Some women distanced themselves from their work by assuming fictitious identities or by relying upon the authority of a third party. The writer Maria Edgeworth (chapter 2) did both, adopting the identity of a male editor and using the apparatus of male scholarship. Anna Jameson (chapter 3) adopted the persona of a female traveller affecting love-sickness as a device for establishing her heightened sensibility. And the translator Anna Swanwick (chapter 10) relied heavily upon earlier scholarship and ancient writings, believing that any deviation from the original Greek text was 'a breach of trust'.

Other women, in contrast, used their own experience to validate their opinions. Strickland believed in the significance of the 'genius of place', referring to her own experience of sites of importance in the lives of those she wrote about. Writing about her travels, Sydney Morgan (chapter 3) replaced eyewitness testimony by an evocation of her emotions, because, as she claimed, such emotions could only have been elicited by a real visit to a real place. Spiritual experience might also be invoked: Jane Ellice Hopkins (chapter 11), the religious campaigner, towards the end of the century urged personal reinterpretation of the scriptures for new historical circumstances, and specifically rejected the absolute authority of the Bible in her religious campaigning. Some drew on their feminine sensibility or upon specifically 'feminine' attributes as sources of authority. Mary Wollstonecraft Shelley (chapter 4) used her moral discrimination as the test for her editorial work on Shelley's poetry, deriving her authority from her claim to possession, both as wife of the poet and as owner of the manuscripts.

Such identities were not mere disguises, but were used to help establish the authenticity of what these women were saying. That authenticity might be seen to derive from the intrinsic qualities of the work, its inner truth, or it might also be established by the authority of the eyewitness, or by reference to a third party or by the voice of God. But in all cases there was a common sense that an authentic truth was attainable, reference to which validated the work in the face of possible criticism.

Deconstructing scholarship

The idea of an authentic truth established by the intellectual or creative authority of the practitioner was used by many of the women discussed in this volume to have their voices listened to by audiences unaccustomed to regarding women's public utterances with respect. These women sought to earn respect by their scholarship, though the strategies they employed to display it differed markedly according to the conventions of the genre in which they were working.

The concept of scholarship is a complex and variable one, with different associations in different spheres of activity and genres of work, as the essays in this book suggest. Moreover, meanings of the term have changed between the nineteenth and twentieth centuries. In some essays it is applied to work which would not have been classed as scholarship in the nineteenth century, and even in the twentieth century did not necessarily conform to conventional definitions of the term. In this volume we have sought to enlarge the concept of scholarship beyond the recognised bounds of Victorian intellectual life and beyond that practised by men whose reputations rested upon their designation as scholar, artist or critic.

Many of the women considered here undoubtedly practised scholarship but even when they were working in areas, such as classical languages, where the use of the term 'scholar' is relatively unproblematic, they were rarely admitted to circles or networks where their claims to be scholars were treated on equal terms with those of men. Furthermore, critiques of their work normally referred to the author's gender, either praising her for manliness, or denigrating her for venturing into masculine territory where she was unfit to travel. Henry James disparaged Oliphant as a 'poor soul who had a simply feminine conception of literature', while Ruskin had little time for Jameson's art-historical judgements because of the 'feminine' manner in which they were delivered.[7]

Within nineteenth-century culture, 'scholarship' was widely perceived as an essentially masculine activity. Scholarly aspiration, ideals and achievements were often described in gendered terms. Prized and supposedly masculine qualities such as terseness were often contrasted with feminine qualities of emotion and moral sensibility, qualities which were believed to be incompatible with true scholarship because they impaired the capacity for objectivity. The positivist idea of objectivity was an essential element in the emergence during the nineteenth century of such subjects as history and political economy as discrete disciplines independent of literature. Women's supposed incapacity for objectivity may well have hindered their ability to advance in the academic study of such subjects.

Women were, however, regarded as uniquely fitted for such detailed meticulous work as translation from modern languages and the editing of plays and documents. But such activity largely served the work of (male) scholars, without being regarded as scholarship in its own right. Working in these areas, however, allowed women to engage in forms of scholarly activity by occupying new niches, conforming to the thesis articulated by the economic historian, Joan Thirsk, who suggested that when new openings in crafts, trades or academic specialisations have appeared 'women have usually been prominent alongside men', but only until the new venture has been firmly established, at which point men become predominant.[8]

Particularly important in the nineteenth century, was the opportunity afforded by an increasing, popular appetite for 'knowledge', which gave rise to a demand for non-specialist works on intellectual subjects. Many women used this niche as a way both of engaging in intellectual discourse and of earning money. Harriet Martineau, the Strickland sisters, Anna Jameson and Mary Somerville all wrote popular works on subjects in which academic specialisation was only just beginning and which, for the first time, were being taught in the universities (respectively political economy, history, art history and science).

Sages and men and women of letters

The idea of a sage, a public figure of intellectual authority, was the very antithesis of dominant ideas of femininity and the only recognised female sage was George Eliot. Yet objections to women constructing public personae perhaps weakened as, during the century, causes upon which they might speak with unique authority (women's education, the franchise, married women's property) entered the realm of public debate. It has been argued that women's claims to model themselves on the image of men of letters faltered for lack of the heroism which Thomas Carlyle identified in his essay of 1841.[9] However, women were considered to bring special qualities, derived from their femininity, to prose fiction and poetry, in which genres their authority seems to have increased during the nineteenth century. The status of 'men of letters' had more to do with moral standing arising from gender than from the genre of the writing itself. Many of the women who appear in this volume were women of letters in that they earned their living by the practice of writing, often in a variety of genres. Mary Cowden Clarke the writer, for example (chapter 6), was entirely typical in the variety of work she did: translations, essays, editions, biographical works, children's stories and a novel. The essays in this volume, then, suggest that far from simply engaging in what Deirdre David describes as 'passive elaborative work', many women were adept at engaging in a life of scholarship by their social and intellectual flexibility.[10]

Professionalisation, education and earning a living

A particular source of authority open to men was that of being 'a professional', a term which appears in these essays in a variety of senses. Sometimes it is used to describe the degree of competence with which a woman practised her calling (Siddons was undoubtedly a professional actress). Sometimes it relates more to an aspiration (Oliphant aspired to be a full-time paid editor because she felt that this conferred a status which recognised her literary standing). Often the term is used to mean little more than that a women earned her living by her *métier*. Professional status eluded many women, especially if, as in the case of the Shireff sisters, the educationists (chapter 5), and Haweis, the designer (chapter 9), many women were practising, in public, activities such as childcare and homemaking which were regarded as 'natural' for women.

Another source of authority for claims to scholarship was education. During the nineteenth century, the number of girls' schools increased and more women were admitted to higher education. But, broadly speaking, education for women was seen as an aid to women earning a living and being good citizens, not as a means of access to scholarly research or philosophical speculation. Henry Maudsley, countering in 1874 Emily David's arguments for women's education, set out the widely accepted biologically deterministic view that it was 'differences in their physical and mental natures' that rendered women unfit for the same kind of education as men.[11]

Although universities did, from the 1870s and 1880s, provide more opportunities for women to acquire an 'academic' education, 'the academy' itself remained inaccessible to women. Membership of such institutions as the Royal Academy and the Royal Society (association with which conferred high status upon the work of its members, identifying it as 'high' art or as serious intellectual advance, and members as professionals) remained largely closed to women. The simultaneous emergence of an academic profession, in which research and teaching were developed jointly, created posts with status, prestige and income, but few went to women. even in single sex institutions.[12] The addition of new subjects to the university curriculum, such as economics, literature and history, created further posts. Even so, the combined total of women teaching at Oxford, Cambridge and London in 1883/84 was only 17, increasing to 51 over the following ten years.[13] This figure may be an underestimate as there were large numbers of female supernumerary demonstrators and assistants. Not until the 1920s were university lectureships, readerships and chairs at Oxford and Cambridge open to women, and women's salaries in the universities were conspicuously lower than men's.[14] Professional appointments in history, literature and classics went predominantly to men, while the status of the independent scholar declined, thus reducing the opportunities for women to make a living as writers outside this institutional framework.

Much of the self-deprecation which appears in women's writings over the whole of the nineteenth century, and which is evident in several texts quoted in this collection, may be construed as a consequence of their need to earn a living. Many women asserted that they wrote for a general audience and, in the process, denied any claim to high-flown status. Such assertions must be seen in the context of their need to find publishers and acceptance with both reviewers and readers. Thus Jameson professed to write for women, for 'the fair, Pure-hearted, delicate minded, and unclass- ical reader', so as to forestall criticism for 'being neither critic nor scholar', while Swanwick was considered to have written for 'the general reader'.[15] They presented themselves judiciously as without the scholarly ambitions which might threaten or alienate their male colleagues.

The writing careers of many women were a product of their need to support themselves and, frequently, their families. The 1851 census revealed that the number of women of marriageable age exceeded the number of marriageable men, indicating that whatever sensibilities society might have about women, especially middle-class women, earning a living, many were forced to do so lest they starve. It is clear that those discussed here developed a whole range of adaptive strategies to ensure that their work could be published and find a readership. Often this meant both avoiding an overt challenge to patriarchal assumptions and colluding with the dominant view of women's intellectual capabilities and the worth of their public utterances.

On the other hand, the publication of popular journals, and the development of mass entertainment did provide more opportunities for women to earn a living. Whilst these women might have been regarded as on the margins of or outside the academy, which itself became more restrictive, they were able to take part in the commodification of some forms of scholarship as they sought to reach a wider audience. The contradictions inherent in the changing relationships between ideas of scholarly practice, the commodification of knowledge with the develop- ment of popular media, and the social roles of women in the nineteenth century form a central subject of this volume.

In an introduction to a collection of essays of 1869 discussing aspects of contemporary women's situation, the campaigner Josephine Butler (1828–1906), identified a disjunction between changes in the material world and the persistence of traditional ideologies, as a source of women's difficulties.

> The present distress [of women] must to some degree be reckoned among the phenomenon of a transition period in society; it is in part owing to the rapid advance in discovery, invention, expeditive processes, instruments of production, &c. which advances have been unequally yoked with our national conservatism of certain customs, conventions, and ideals of life and character. The great tide of an imperfect and halting civilization has rolled onward, and carried many triumphantly with it. But women have been left stranded so to speak.[16]

The issues and debates described by Butler came to be characterised as part of the broadly labelled 'The Woman Question'. From the late eighteenth and through the nineteenth century, these controversies generated justifications of customary ways of life against demands for change, each side appealing to ideologies which validated their positions. Whether or not they took part in the debates women were, nevertheless, surrounded by the conflicting messages about their roles, predispositions and abilities.

While some of the women discussed in this collection generated their own personal solutions in developing their work and achieving professional status, others found themselves caught up directly in broad ideological conflicts. More pragmatically, some identified with demands for specific reforms, such as access to education and training for the professions, improved property and legal rights, women's suffrage and joining the organisations to further such aims.

Sexuality and gender

The issue of female sexuality, how it was perceived by the women themselves, and how it was socially constructed in relation to desirable masculinity, features prominently in several essays in this collection which explore the problem of identity. Female sexuality is also implicated in debates on social and cultural power and professional status.

Several authors reveal that perceptions of a woman's sexuality could directly affect public views of her professional, creative or scholarly status and intellectual authority. Despite the shifts which occurred within discourses on femininity within nineteenth-century culture, attempts to define and evaluate the achievements of women were often explicitly or implicitly informed by widely held views on socially acceptable feminine sexuality. It is often argued that the development and expansion of industrial capitalism within nineteenth-century British society reinforced the sexual division of labour within the patriarchal family. A woman's responsibility for the well-being of her family was widely seen to come before her work in social production, a role which was seen to follow naturally from her biological status. Many studies have shown that within working-class society, the denial of access to socially recognised skills increased women's vulnerability to exploitative cheap labour markets, including prostitution.[17] For middle-class women, the culture of feminine domesticity and social (and sexual) subservience, was embedded in the economic and social structures – within laws and social policies. An assumption which underlies many of the contributions to this collection is that such sexual ideologies became intricately enmeshed in the institutional, legal, professional and intellectual cultures which we examine, and were often instrumental in shaping contemporary perceptions of femininity.

However, we are cautious about assuming a unitary Victorian sexual culture exclusively controlled and defined by middle-class males. Like all models of social behaviour, the Victorian model embraced some complex subcultures and dissenting groups – as well as certain 'conformist' movements. Many of these groups were mobilised in the public controversy which surrounded the passing of the Contagious Diseases Acts of 1864, 1866 and 1869. The laws were intended to control the spread of venereal disease among servicemen employed in garrison towns and ports. They introduced powers to arrest and to enforce regular internal examinations for women defined (vaguely) as 'common' prostitutes.[18] The Acts were chaotic and complex pieces of legislation, which generated powerful resistance, particularly among middle-class nonconformists and feminists, on the grounds of class and sex discrimination. As Judith R. Walkowitz has written: 'As a social experiment in the custodial treatment of poor "outcast" women, the acts provide a framework for examining some connections between ideology, public policy and social change.'[19] The controversy also provides a rich source of information on the history of gender relations in mid-nineteenth-century Britain.

The Acts could be seen to have institutionalised both the public control of (female) sexuality and state intervention in the lives of the poorest groups of society; they also generated a public debate in which political and gender issues converged. As we shall see, such debates and the ideologies which they reinforced or questioned could be seen to feed into a literary culture. They could also directly affect the strategies adopted by women writers, scholars or artists for publicising and representing their work. Thus (earlier in our period) actresses such as Sarah Siddons actively sought to promote themselves as respectable family figures, as morally upright wives and mothers, in an attempt to undermine the disreputable associations with prostitution and permissive sexuality which had blighted the profession of actress since the seventeenth century.

Although a few nineteenth-century feminists, among them Josephine Butler, the leader of the Ladies National Association, publicly identified the double standards operating within contemporary sexual culture as it was codified within the Contagious Diseases Act, many women negotiated more complex or contradictory strategies in their public roles. [20] In common with many women in pursuit of professional status, Margaret Oliphant positioned herself as a morally concerned journalist who was generally critical – or sceptical – of the representation in contemporary 'sensation novels' of women in the grip of sexual passion. As is suggested in Joan Bellamy's essay (chapter 8), Oliphant conformed to a dominant image of desirable Victorian femininity in her preference for female characters of untainted or uplifting moral stature. Her animosity towards Hardy's construction of the 'new woman' in *Jude the Obscure* exemplified these preferences. Similarly, Susan Mumm shows in chapter 11 that women preachers such as Jane Ellice Hopkins and Catherine Mumford Booth strategically identified themselves (in differing ways) with ideals of feminine purity and committed motherhood in order to counter the resistance which confronted women active in a sphere traditionally dominated by masculine values. Mumm argues that both women presented themselves as engaged with traditional female concerns, with sexual morality as a means of opening up debates on issues of female competence and capacity for religious authority. Hopkins became notorious as the leader of the male chastity group, the White Cross Army, which encouraged men to take responsibility for their sexual behaviour, thus countering the sexual oppression of Victorian women, which she identified as a religious sin. By emphasising the sexual exploitation of women and challenging the contemporary emphasis on subordinate and passive feminine roles, Hopkins could be seen to question some dominant views of desirable feminine sexuality while also maintaining a clear set of moral standards. As these and other essays show, the complex sexual ideologies which proliferated during our period are intricately tied to contemporary perceptions of gender difference and socially acceptable feminine sexuality.

Conclusion

The work of the women featured in this collection belies the claim that women showed a 'remarkable incapacity for independent intellectual labour'.[21] In many cases their endeavours to give their own work authority amounted to providing intellectual sustenance for men working in the same field. Few of the women who appear on these pages were transgressive to the point of overtly challenging patriarchal assumptions, yet within the restrictions under which they lived many of the women offered more subversive challenges, although not always consciously, through seizing practical opportunities. Few of these women saw their work in the broader context of women's position in society: both Strickland and Oliphant actually opposed the Married Women's Property Bill. Several wanted better education for women and worked for it in various ways, as Aikin (chapter 7), Swanwick (chapter 11) and Toulmin Smith (chapter 7), but attempts to secure professional standing, in the sense either of recognition by the academy or of permanent employment, to a large extent eluded them. It is we, interpreters of their work who, with hindsight, make stronger claims for their intellectual standing than perhaps they did for themselves.

Such women were acting outside the bounds of convention to the extent that not only did all have some form of independent intellectual life, they all gave it some form of public expresssion. They used whatever strategies might be necessary to get their work read, heard or seen, even, if necessary, adopting the guise of a man. They used such means as were at their disposal to make their work authoritative, for example, by meticulous attention to detail, by specific claims to authenticity, by a concern for the particular rather than the vast generalisations beloved of the sages. Many of our subjects conformed to the idea that women were not fitted for the philosophical. What Lorna Hardwick has referred to as the combination of 'challenge to and complicity with dominant traditions' runs through the work of virtually every woman discussed in this volume.

Notes

1   Reproduced in V. Jones (ed.), *Women in the Eighteenth Century: Constructions of Femininity* (London, Routledge, 1990), pp. 238–43.

2   For example, such criticism greeted the National Association for the Promotion of Social Science which was founded in 1857 and provided opportunities at their Congresses for women to read papers on matters relating to women's conditions. *The Saturday Review* (14 June 1862, p. 668) dubbed the Association 'the Universal Palaver Association' and attacked the women taking part. It reported scathingly, 'Lord Brougham's little corps of lady orators preaching strong-mindedness, gives a new aspect to the Association presence ... We heartily wish the strong-minded ladies happiness and success in their new alliance and do not doubt that they will remember to practice the precepts of one of their debaters "not in mind being thought unladylike". It is always better not to mind that which is inevitable'. (Cited in Hester Burton, *Barbara Bodichon* (London, John Murray, 1949), p. 66.)

3   H. Barker and E. Chalus (eds), *Gender in Eighteenth-Century England: Roles, Representations and Responsibilities* (Harlow, Longman, 1997), p. 4.

4   Barker and Chalus, *Gender*, p. 4.

5   Louise M. Newman, 'Critical theory and the history of women: what's at stake in deconstructing women's history?', *Journal of Women's History*, 2:3 (1991), p. 59 (this was originally presented as a paper at the Eighth Berkshire Conference on the History of Woman at Douglass College, USA, June 1990).

6   This relationship is addressed in different ways in essays which follow by Gill Perry (ch. 1), Lorna Hardwick (ch. 11), Cicely Havely (ch. 6) and Madeline Thompson (ch. 2).

7   Dorothy Mermin, *Godiva's Ride: Women of Letters in England 1830–1880* (Bloomington and Indianapolis, Indiana University Press, 1993), pp. 87, 98.

8   Joan Thirsk, 'The history women', in M. O'Dowd and S. Wichert (eds), *Chattel, Servant or Citizen: Women's Status in Church, State and Society* (Belfast, Institute of Irish Studies, The Queen's University of Belfast, 1993), pp. 1–2.

9   Quoted in Carol T. Christ, 'The hero as Man of Letters: masculinity and Victorian non-fiction prose', in Thaïs E. Morgan (ed.), *Victorian Sages and Cultural Discourse: Renegotiating Gender and Power* (New Brunswick and London, Rutgers University Press, 1990), p. 19.

10   Deirdre David, *Intellectual Women and Victorian Patriarchy* (Basingstoke, Macmillan, 1987), p. 4.

11   *The Fortnightly Review* 25, new series, 1, January-June, 1874 (London, Chapman and Hall), pp. 471, 468.

12   Reba N. Soffer, 'The development of disciplines in the modern British university', *Historical Journal*, 31 (1988), p. 936; Fernanda Perrone, 'Women academics in England, 1870–1930', *History of the Universities*, 12 (1993), p. 342.

13   Perrone, 'Women academics', p. 345.

14   Perrone, 'Women academics', pp. 347, 352.

15   Anna Jameson, *The Loves of the Poets* (London, 1829), p. 22; Dr Butler quoted in Mary Bruce, *Anna Swanwick: A Memoir and Recollections 1813–99* (London, T. Fisher Unwin, 1903), pp. 108–14, quoted in Hardwick (see chapter 10, this volume).

16   Josephine Butler, *Women's Work and Women's Culture* (London, Macmillan, 1869), p. xv.

17   These arguments are discussed in Sally Alexander, *Women's Work in Nineteenth Century London 1820–50* (London, Journeyman, 1983).

18   If found suffering from venereal disease such women could be interned in special hospital units for periods of up to nine months. Medical inspections were thus imposed on 'prostitutes' without comparable examinations being instituted for their male clients.

19   Judith R. Walkowitz, *Prostitution and Victorian Society* (Cambridge, Cambridge University Press, 1980), p. 1.

20   Under Butler's leadership the LNA denounced the Contagious Disease Acts as depriving the poorest of women of the constitutional rights and officially sanctioning and institutionalising male vice.

21   Hamerton, quoted in David, *Intellectual Women*, p. 17.

Musing on muses: representing the actress as 'artist' in British art of the late eighteenth and early nineteenth centuries

Gill Perry

Introduction: gender, art and 'the moral spirit of the Stage'

In July 1814 a feature in *The Theatrical Inquisitor* noted significant improvements over the last twenty years in what is described as 'the moral spirit of the Stage'. This improvement was partly due to Sarah Siddons (figure 1), seen as one of the greatest tragic actresses of her day:

> [Siddons] first showed the possibility of at once standing high in theatrical excellence, and retaining those purer distinctions, without which the glory of woman's talent 'lights only to her shame'. From that moment the Stage rose. From the period that honourable women found a reception, dramatic habits grew more deserving of public approval, and the Theatre refined from a place of fearful exposure, into a refuge for that genius and loveliness, which, within no other walls could be equally sure of protection and reward.[1]

There are many levels on which we can interpret this quotation. First, the (anonymous) writer is signalling the civilising or 'professionalising' of the theatre – in particular the London theatre – which had taken place throughout the eighteenth century. Second, and significantly, Siddons (1755–1831) is seen as the key figure in this process of professionalisation.[2] According to this view, her 'theatrical excellence' is at least partly constituted through her 'purer distinctions', a reference to her public image as a respectable and happily married wife and mother. These distinctions allow her talent to overshadow the 'shame' traditionally associated with actresses. The perceived sexuality of the actress functions

1 Engraving by Gardner after Gainsborough's *Portrait of Mrs Siddons*,
1785

here, then, as a powerful trope for the moral and professional status of the
theatre.

Throughout the eighteenth and well into the nineteenth century,
the discourse on the theatre and its players (both male and female) reveals
an ongoing struggle between the civilised ideal of theatrical decorum and
its professional, even 'academic',[3] potential, and the more widely accepted
idea of the theatre as a lower-class carnival or fair, as a form of marginal
or recalcitrant culture and transgressive sexuality.[4] Such negative and
class-ridden perceptions of the theatre had their origins in attitudes to the
'strolling players' of the seventeenth and early eighteenth centuries, before
significant attempts were made by the actor David Garrick (1717–79)

among others to reform and professionalise the theatre, in particular the established London playhouses of Drury Lane and Covent Garden.[5]

Issues of gender, as well as those of class origins, played an important part in this discourse. While the processes of professionalisation helped to legitimate the feminisation and sexual ambivalence involved in some male acting roles, it seems to have set into sharp focus some of the contradictions and struggles inherent in contemporary constructions of femininity. The perception of the actress as a public spectacle did not match easily with emergent notions, particularly at the turn of the eighteenth century, of the middle-class woman as domestic and private.[6]

In this essay I am concerned with some of the different ways in which contemporary representations of women performers (derived both from written and visual sources) contributed to, or helped to undermine, an image of the late eighteenth-century actress as an artist capable of creative and expressive interpretations of dramatic texts.

Although the narrowest notion of 'scholarship' was rarely applied to the work of actresses, around the turn of the eighteenth century a form of writing emerged which sought to represent their dramatic skills as forms of 'art' demanding intelligent analyses and imitative skills. As interpreters of classical, Shakespearean and more recent dramatic texts, actors and actresses alike were increasingly being represented as creative 'artists', the best of whom revealed creative intelligence and the ability to study and research a role, both skills which could be cited in any claim for intellectual authority. But, as I shall argue, such claims were often mediated by gendered assumptions. Contemporary views on creative artistic potential in the work of actresses were often directly linked to perceptions of their sexuality. The increasing power of a middle-class ideal of passive and domesticated femininity around the turn of the eighteenth century, with its associations of a respectable, subservient and modest female sexuality, did not match easily with any claims for intellectual authority. In this essay I will examine some of the different strategies adopted both by actresses themselves, and by their biographers and portrait painters, to reconsider – or reject – such claims and associations. In the process I will address the extent to which actresses were seen as agents of their own creativity, rather than passive interpreters of the work of others. Apart from Siddons, whose acting roles (and personal life) generated a debate about feminine 'genius', I will focus on representations of two actresses whose surviving writings provide some evidence of strategies of self-narration: the comic actress Dorothy Jordan (1761–1816) whose lengthy correspondence vividly describes her struggles within the profession, and Mary Robinson (1758–1800) who also became a writer, dramatist and defender of issues of Women's Rights.[7]

The late eighteenth- and early nineteenth-century discourse on the

2 Thomas Beach, *John Philip Kemble and Sarah Siddons as Macbeth and Lady Macbeth*, 1786

status and acceptable femininity of actresses is made up of much more than the critical debates in theatrical reviews and periodicals, the biographies, commentaries and so on. During this period a significant and rapidly growing 'discursive field' was that of *visual* representation in areas of both high and popular art. The so-called 'theatrical portrait' (figure 2) had been established as a respectable genre which, through the use of dramatic and historical references, could qualify as a sub-category of 'history painting', as for example in Reynolds's famous portraits *Mrs Siddons as the Tragic Muse* (figure 3) or *Garrick between Tragedy and Comedy*. And by the turn of the century a flourishing popular press had helped to represent many

3 Joshua Reynolds, *Mrs Siddons as the Tragic Muse*, 1789

prominent theatrical figures, and actresses in particular, as spectacular public spectacles.

What interests me is how these so-called discourses on the actress might be inscribed in – or mediated through – the visual arts, in particular through the practices of high art, a discipline which was also seeking to establish itself as a 'civilised' profession, as separate from what were seen as more 'mechanical' trades. But I am cautious about slipping too easily into a reflectionist mode which sees visual imagery as merely mirroring ideological, social or cultural forces in evidence elsewhere. In looking at visual representations of the actress, I will argue that some late eighteenth-century developments in 'academic' art may serve to complicate, rather than merely reinforce the dominant narratives on sexuality and female creativity. I will suggest that in visual representation the figure of the actress can become a potent metaphor for both the civilising of the theatre *and* the academic ambitions of portraiture.

Actress as muse

The different narratives on female creativity are often played out in representations of the figure of the Muse, a female embodiment of the source of artistic expression, derived from the nine sister goddesses in Greek mythology.[8] The literal and symbolic possibilities of this classical convention for representing (usually male) inspiration and creativity are multi-layered. It has been argued that within *written* texts the figure of the Muse was not always evoked as a female personification. For example, Rosann Runte has shown that in eighteenth-century literature the word 'Muse' was often used euphemistically to signify the arts in contrast to the sciences.[9]

However, it is in the visual arts that these linguistic ambiguities are mediated through the conventions of eighteenth-century painting, in which abstract ideas were often conveyed through a physical embodiment. I have argued elsewhere that in forms of visual representation the ambiguities of meaning are more often to be found in the roles of mythological or personified Muses, and the forms of feminine activity which they suggest.[10]

In terms of art-historical precedents, the personified Muse was most often used to signify passive creativity, as enabling the creative process by giving inspiration to the male poet or artist. In Poussin's famous seventeenth century *Inspiration of the Poet* (figure 4), for example, the mythological figure is passively present, as we focus on Apollo's moment of inspiration. And in eighteenth-century French portraiture a tradition developed of representing the female sitter in the disguise of a Muse – a convention which is sometimes called 'Muse portraiture'. Such appropriations of the Muse could, of course, be seen to reinforce the conventional associations of the theme – as the passive female object of the male painter's inspiration. But in some forms the figure of the Muse could also be interpreted to suggest creativity in the sitter herself. Some more positive representations of female creativity or achievement can be found in the

4 Nicholas Poussin, *The Inspiration of the Poet*, c. 1630

appropriation of the Sappho myth in female portraiture.[11] The figure of
Sappho, the best known female classical Greek poet, was often associated
with the Muses, and is sometimes referred to as the tenth Muse.

In painted representations of the actress from around the turn of
the eighteenth century some of these active and passive associations
actually elide, and allow for some different levels of meaning to be
attributed to the role of the female Muse. It could be argued that Reynolds's
portrait *Mrs Siddons as a Tragic Muse* is a reworking of the conventions of
French eighteenth-century Muse portraiture. But this personified Muse also
represented a creative activity on the part of the sitter, for Mrs Siddons
was renowned for her tragic roles, and appeared as Melpomene the tragic
Muse in Garrick's play *Jubilee* at Drury Lane in 1785. In an article titled
'Actresses' in *The Theatrical Inquisitor and Monthly Mirror* of 1815 the
author seems to acknowledge this elision of active and passive roles for
contemporary actresses, while also emphasising the qualities of female
performance which inspire (and one might argue sexually arouse) the
(male) viewer. The article is concerned to justify the modern addition of
women to the profession, wary perhaps of the moral backlash which this

development had provoked in contemporary criticism. The author quotes 'a late amiable writer' on this subject:

> It remained for modern times to complete their triumphs, by admitting female candidates into the lists; from that moment nature took possession of her rights; the finest feelings were consigned to fairest forms; the very Muse herself appeared in her own sex and person; beauty that gives being to the poet's rapturous vision, a voice that guides his language to the heart, smiles that enchant, tears that dissolve us, with looks that fascinate, and dying plaintive tones that sink into the soul, are now the appropriate and exclusive attributes of that all-conquering sex; in short they bind our nobles in chains, and our princes in links – of love.[12]

Through the dramatic skills of the actress then the Muse could appear as literally embodied in her own sex, and as a recognisable individual – albeit in the form of an enacted public spectacle. The painted image of woman as Muse, which is of course one stage removed from this physical embodiment, could suggest some further possibilities of meaning around the theme of female creativity.

Much has now been written about the art-historical sources and allusions which contribute to the 'grand' effect of Reynolds's large-scale portrait of Mrs Siddons (239.7 × 147.6 cms), which exists in two versions of 1784 and 1789.[13] The borrowing of Mrs Siddons's pose from Michelangelo's prophet Isaiah on the Sistine Chapel ceiling is now well established. The cup and the dagger, the traditional attributes of Melpomene the tragic Muse, are held by the two figures behind her. Although the specific identity of these two figures has been argued over in the nineteenth century, R. R. Wark has interpreted them as the Aristotelian figures of Pity and Terror.[14] The 'dignity' conveyed by such allusions is combined with visual clues which suggest an unashamedly theatrical subject. Siddons wears a theatrical costume which, as Aileen Ribero has written, conforms 'to the fashion of the early 1780s only in the fairly pointed bodice, and the slightly puffed out hairstyle'.[15] Her long false plaits and elaborately trimmed gown with a long train were part of a typical theatrical dress for tragic heroines during this period.

By the 1780s the theatrical portrait was well established as a portrait genre with historical or elevated possibilities.[16] And the representation of Sarah Siddons as a character of substantial mythological and scholarly importance (albeit one which she performed on stage) helps to give a particular elevated status to this portrait. She was widely acknowledged as the leading tragic actress of her day and, as C. R. Leslie has pointed out, Reynolds may also have been influenced in his choice of theatrical role for this work by a eulogistic poem by William Russel published in 1783 and titled 'The Tragic Muse: A Poem Addressed to Mrs Siddons'. Like Russel,

5 William Beechey, *Sarah Siddons with the Emblems of Tragedy*, 1794

Reynolds was contributing to the popular confusion of real and assumed roles which surrounded the very public lives of actresses, and in the process participating in a process of both elevation and professionalisation of the theatrical world. Moreover the establishment of this public role for Siddons was reinforced when other later portraits of her, such as William Beechey's

Mrs Siddons with the Emblems of Tragedy of 1794 (figure 5) continued this dramatic association.

Art, theatre and professionalisation

I am suggesting that late eighteenth-century attempts to create an 'academic' art practice, to root the discipline in more intellectual concerns, were closely related to contemporary efforts to professionalise the theatre. Debates about the status of art and the artist often intersected with the discourse on the role and status of the theatre. Sir Joshua Reynolds, as first president of the Royal Academy of Art (founded in 1768) sought in theory at least to raise the status of art, firmly establishing a notion of 'high art'. Although 'history painting' was traditionally seen as the most elevated, intellectual form of painting above portraits and landscapes, in most European academies, Reynolds's development of the sub-genre of 'historical portraits' was a pragmatic attempt to bridge the gulf between the strong demand for portraiture and the more respected 'history painting'. In such portraits sitters were often given pseudo-mythological or allegorical roles, replete with classical and art-historical allusions.

Moreover, this is an area in which feminine portraiture (i.e. portraits of women) features prominently in the attempts of Reynolds and some of his contemporaries to elevate the genre. Historical conventions for the representation of women were steeped in allegorical and symbolic traditions, themselves foreshadowed in the goddesses and female muses of ancient mythology. I have suggested in an earlier essay that the eighteenth-century fashion for allegorical portraits of women, especially middle- and upper-class women, was partly related to the fact that in comparison with their enfranchised male counterparts, who could be publicly identified in portraiture with their professional, political or military roles, women were more easily depicted 'in disguise'.[17] However, if the sitter was an actress, the disguise could be seen to belong both to an established allegorical tradition, and to her actual 'profession'. As such, the portrait of the actress enabled a natural elision between role playing and artistic representation; in one sense it provided an ideal form for Reynolds's historical portraiture.

Thus the portrait Mrs Siddons as the Tragic Muse was seen by some late eighteenth- and early nineteenth-century commentators as the paradigmatic 'historical portrait'. In 1823 Sir Thomas Lawrence famously referred to it as 'indisputably the finest female portrait in the world'.[18] Although Lawrence's praise is confined to 'female' portraiture it echoes some of the contemporary responses to the work when it was first shown at the Royal Academy in 1784. Concepts of the 'sublime' and 'dignity' are constantly deployed to describe the painting's effect in many eulogistic reviews which appeared in the British press of that year. For example *The Morning Chronicle* of 27 April 1784 commented: 'The Mrs Siddons is a grand picture, and approaches to sublimity', while *The Morning Post* and *Daily Advertiser* of 5 May 1784 commented on some of the previous criticisms of this work, claiming they were based on misunderstandings. The painting was seen to have 'proceeded from the most poetic mind' and 'The dignity of character, the sublime effect, the richness and harmony of colouring, are all wrought out with the highest degree of excellence.' [19] The language used here and in other reviews is more often associated with the critical discourse on *history* paintings. Notions of 'the poetic mind' are directly tied to contemporary attempts to raise the status of painting to that of poetry, to infuse the discipline with noble thoughts and ideas associated with historical scenes of civic, moral or political virtue.[20]

As I have suggested, the critical perception of this as a 'sublime', 'poetic' or dignified work is not exclusively derived from the pictorial means – the classical allusions, pose and compositional organisation, use of tone and colour, etc. It is not simply the elevated or poetic style which offer the spectacle of Mrs Siddons the possibility of 'dignity'. The actress Sarah Siddons, and the model of femininity which she was seen to evoke, were factors in the critical perception of the work. Put another way, the public spectacle of Mrs Siddon's femininity can stand as a metaphor not only for the professionalisation of the theatre, but also for the enhanced academic status and claims for intellectual authority of British art. This possibility is reinforced by the frequent juxtaposition in contemporary newspapers of reviews of Royal Academy exhibitions and theatrical performances which both feature Siddons. For example, *The Public Advertiser* of April 1784 features eulogistic reviews of both Reynolds's portrait and Siddons's performance as Sigismunda on the same page. References to Mrs Siddons as 'a glorious Actress' and 'transcendent Artist' in this play are a column apart from references to Reynolds outdoing all his artistic 'Performances' in 'the great Principles of his Art' in this portrait. It is significant that while Siddons's performance qualifies her for the label 'artist', the theatrical metaphor of 'performance' is used to describe Reynolds's form of artistic expression.[21]

The spectacle of female sexuality and the ambiguity of the Muse

The lives of actresses, like those of well-known courtesans, became visible public property within late eighteenth- and early nineteenth-century society. The widespread dissemination of cheap engraved copies of portraits, and popular prints through which their exploits were caricatured, contributed to some of the popular mythologies constructed around their public and private pursuits. Thus any artistic conventions or borrowed identities (for example as Muse) through which such women might be represented, had to operate within a framework of received knowledge, which was often voyeuristic and replete with sexual innuendo, about their personal lives.

Sarah Siddons could qualify for the enhanced metaphorical status which I have suggested because her private life was apparently scandal free. She was the eldest of twelve children born into an acting family. Her mother Sarah was the daughter of a well-known actor John Ward, and her father Roger Kemble was an actor-manager in the provinces. Sarah Kemble spent her childhood travelling with her father's company where she met her future husband, the actor William Siddons. Despite (or, perhaps, because of) this exclusively theatrical background, many contemporary accounts emphasise her respectable, domesticated life. Her biographer Boaden writing in 1827 (four years before her death) is at pains to stress that her early marriage at the age of eighteen was to 'a man of the most honourable and steady character'.[22] She bore seven children of which four girls died in infancy. But in similar vein Boaden writes 'the growing claims of her family seemed to be the only unresisted calls upon her genius'.[23] Although some later accounts reveal a more complex personal life[24] Boaden suggests that her professional abilities are somehow enhanced by her supposedly temperate domesticity. Straub has also identified this emphasis in Boaden's construction of the 'public' character of Siddons when she writes, 'Boaden insists on the domestic as the defining factor in an actress's respectability.'[25] Boaden actually wrote, 'The uniform temperance of female life had its share in the conservation of this fullness of power.'[26] We are reminded here of the reference to 'purer distinctions' in my opening quotation, without which (as I am now suggesting) her portrait might qualify less easily as a paradigmatic 'historical portrait'.

However, such possibilities of meaning are by no means fixed or consistent in writings on visual imagery of actresses from the period. As I suggested earlier, a flick through the pages of The Theatrical Inquisitor from the decade after its first publication in 1812 indicates that heated debates around the status and 'moral conduct' of the stage were flourishing around the turn of the eighteenth and the early nineteenth centuries. While the sexuality of the actress became an important trope for the representation of status and professionalisation, the metaphorical power of written and painted images of Siddons which I have been discussing so far should not overshadow the power of what I will call the trope of 'ambiguity' in representations of the actress. At least two of Siddons's contemporaries, Mary Robinson and Dorothy Jordan, were subject to some more publicly contested images of themselves as actress and Muse. The private lives of both actresses were constantly featured in the pages of the national press, a voyeuristic interest which was fuelled by the fact that both had relationships with royal princes. 'Ambiguity' is a term used somewhat defensively by Boaden in his 1832 biography of Jordan. In describing Mrs Jordan's notorious love-life he writes that there 'was an ambiguity in her situation, always productive of annoyance.'[27] Straub has picked up on this idea of 'ambiguity' of the actress – with its connotations of 'was she or wasn't she a whore?' – suggesting that many written representations seek to resolve the problem with recourse to various strategies, among them class.[28] Thus those actresses who were perceived to be the most actively and dangerously sexual were often seen as deriving from the working or peasant classes.

But how might this notion of 'ambiguity' be mediated through the medium of visual imagery? The private lives of both Robinson and Jordan had become visible public spectacles, at least partly through their respective liaisons with royal princes. And such dangerous liaisons can be implicated or at least suggested not only in popular or graphic imagery, but also in

6 *Florizel and Perdita*, anonymous print published 18 October 1783, showing Mrs Robinson and the Prince of Wales combined as one head

some of the high art paintings of both actresses. References in the popular press were, or course, on a more obvious and deliberately caricatured level, as in an anonymous print called *Florizel and Perdita*, first published in 1783 (figure 6) which represents the then notorious relationship between Mary Robinson and the Prince of Wales (later George IV). According to popular myth, the prince was first attracted to Robinson when he saw her play Perdita in Shakespeare's *The Winter's Tale*, hence the characterisations in this print. In such popular images derogatory sexual connotations were usually uppermost. On the other hand Gainsborough's relatively dignified and elegant portrait of Robinson provides a more discreet clue to the adulterous liaison as she holds a miniature portrait of the Prince of Wales (figure 7).[29] Moreover, this painting, like many other portraits of Robinson was known not simply as *Mrs Robinson* but as *Mrs Robinson – Perdita*.

Throughout her life, and in subsequent accounts, Robinson's public persona was confused with those acting roles for which she had won renown. In his biography of Siddons, Boaden even introduces a dramatic contrast with the personal life of Mary Robinson, who made a more 'unfortunate match' in her marriage at the age of fifteen to an unscrupulous clerk, Thomas Robinson, who was imprisoned for squandering their income. The marriage failed and she turned to the stage as a career. For Boaden this betrayal of honour sowed the seeds of Robinson's subsequent status and acting roles: 'the die was thrown that sealed the condition of the enchanting Maria, and she became in melancholy reality the Perdita'.[30] The medium of high art, with its allegorical conventions, was well suited to represent this easy elision between the public and private roles of actresses. The 'ambiguity' arises when these assumed roles carry with them connotations of adulterous or illicit liaisons, of an undomesticated sexuality.

The extraordinary range of painted and graphic representations of Dorothy Jordan, best known for her comic roles, provides complex material for the analysis of these ambiguities. In the popular press the representation of her acting roles is rarely separated from her mythological private life. The daughter of an actress Grace Philips and a 'gentleman' Francis Bland, she first appeared on stage in Dublin in 1777 and soon became known for her comic roles. After becoming pregnant by an Irish theatre manager Richard Daly, she changed her name to 'Mrs Jordan' and moved to England. In 1784 she was engaged by Sheridan at Drury Lane, and in 1791 she became the mistress of the Duke of Clarence, the third son of George III who later became King William IV. They lived together for twenty years and she bore him ten children before being cast aside in favour of a more politically viable match for a future king.[31] The liaison was appropriated in the satirical press by many political factions, through which the

7 Thomas Gainsborough, *Mrs Robinson – Perdita*, 1781

8 John Hoppner, *Mrs Jordan as the Comic Muse*, 1786

'ambiguity' of Jordan's sexuality is used as a pivot or focus around which
is demonstrated the inept lasciviousness, profligacy and pretensions of the
Duke.

The sexuality of the actress and her symbolic potential is often coded
in rather more complex ways in paintings which declared themselves as
high art, in particular the allegorical portrait. John Hoppner's *Mrs Jordan
as the Comic Muse*, which was first shown at the Royal Academy exhibition
of 1786 (figure 8) could be seen as Hoppner's attempt to place himself as

Reynolds's equal in his use of a large-scale (238 × 136cms) mythological portrait to represent a contemporary theatrical star. While Mrs Siddons was framed by her Aristotelian attendants Pity and Terror, Mrs Jordan is accompanied by mythical characters who reaffirm her status as the *comic* Muse. The roles of these characters are clearly indicated in the full title which Hoppner gave the painting for the 1786 exhibition: 'Mrs Jordan in the character of the Comic Muse, supported by Euphrosyne, who represses the advance of a satyr'.[32]

Hoppner's use of the ugly satyr, with its mythological baggage of lechery, voyeurism and predatory sexuality, infuses this image (unlike Reynolds's *Mrs Siddons*) with many possible levels of sexual innuendo. As the object of the satyr's lecherous gaze, Dorothy Jordan is implicated as an object for sexual consumption. As she engages the viewer's gaze she is thus defined as a spectacle of desirable feminine sexuality. Moreover, Hoppner reaffirms the desirability of the actress in his depiction of her prettified, sweetly smiling face, her muslin dress embroidered with stars, her visible left ankle and golden sandals. She holds the mask of Comedy, asserting her theatrical status and, perhaps reinforcing the popular association of femininity and masquerade, the notion of woman as consummate actress. She is represented as both beguiling and somehow 'masked'.

Not surprisingly, perhaps, many contemporary reviewers saw Hoppner's depiction of Jordan as lacking the appropriate 'dignity' required of high art. Although commentators rarely spelt out directly that this lack was due to the sexual ambiguity of the work, the threat which Jordan's image represented to acceptable allegorical femininity is often implicit in writings on this portrait. Thus the (anonymous) reviewer in *The Morning Herald* wrote, 'the very design has a disadvantage to encounter in the person of Mrs Jordan: her statue does not answer the accepted ideas of Thalia. A dwarfish muse cannot be the presiding genius of *mature* comedy'.[33] Once again the female object of representation becomes a metaphor – or as in this case a metonym – for the artistic value of the whole painting. The reviewer fixates of her stature – her apparently dwarfish character – as indicative of this work's lack of 'genius', and by implication of the lack of decorum in the figure of the actress.

There are, however, other possible allegorical levels of meaning which could be seen to complicate this representation of Jordan both as a spectacle of feminine sexuality and as lacking the 'dignity' of high art. In her biography of Jordan, Claire Tomalin has argued that the leering satyr was probably intended to represent the male theatregoer, who was notorious for viewing the female actress as easy sexual prey.[34] The so-called Jordanmania which greeted Jordan's first London performances was interpreted in these terms by some late eighteenth-century commentators. One theatre critic writing in 1786 in an attempt to salvage her reputation with a more balanced and sensible form of approbation described her work as 'unfriended by the servile adultation of prostituted criticism'.[35] It could be argued, then, that the use of the metaphor of prostitution betrays the same partly veiled narratives of sexuality.

Hoppner and his wife (who often posed as his model for Euphrosyne) were close personal friends of the actress and it is possible that this image was intended both by the artist and the sitter to suggest Jordan's rejection of the sexual innuendo and voyeurism for which her (male) audiences became notorious. As I show in the following section, Jordan's correspondence contains her written responses to some of the scurrilous and sexually offensive attacks on her personal conduct which appeared in the pages of respectable newspapers, including *The Times*. In her responses she consistently pleaded her case, seeking to correct misrepresentations and requests to be judged on her professional skills alone.[36] Although this portrait provides its audience with an image of desirable femininity, both women are shown vehemently rejecting the voyeurism of the satyr, and Jordan turns her body away from him in a dramatic and physically contorted pose.

Of course, without documentation we can only speculate on these issues, but the evidence suggests that Hoppner may have participated with Jordan in the construction of another level of meaning or 'in-joke' in this painting. It is also possible that some of the increasing numbers of women spectators who visited both the theatre and the Royal Academy shows in the late eighteenth century would have sympathised with – or at at least acknowledged – the possible veiled reference in this painting. Attempts to civilise and professionalise the theatre, in particular the London theatres, brought with them an increase in middle-class audiences which included large numbers of 'respectable' women. But the pictorial devices I have described could be double-edged. In-jokes could also contribute to the mock-heroic possibilities of works in which the sitter is depicted in mythological or historical disguise. Feminine portraiture was particularly vulnerable to the mock-heroic in that women (as I have argued) were more easily masked in allegorical roles.[37] On one level portraits of the actress, whose assumed role in a painting was more easily confused with her role in life, were less vulnerable to mocking or pathos. But the very public nature of her life and theatrical roles allowed for many voyeuristic and prurient assumptions to be projected into a portrait image, particularly one with elevated pretensions. The in-joke and the mock-heroic device could thus serve to confuse the level at which the work should be read, and in the process to reinforce what I have called the 'trope of ambiguity'.

Authorship and agency: women as artists and agents of creativity

With the steady growth of claims for the civilising and progressive professionalisation of the theatre and the dramatic arts around the turn of the
eighteenth century, critical terms which were more often reserved for
literary, poetic and visual arts are increasingly to be found in reviews of
the theatre to describe the work of actors or actresses. We have seen that
some of Mrs Siddons's tragic roles won her considerable critical acclaim as
interpreter of dramatic texts and a 'transcendent Artist', albeit an acclaim
which was qualified by public perceptions of her sexuality. This critical
tendency was reinforced in the early nineteenth century with the growth
of the biographical genre purporting to document the lives of famous
actresses (Boaden's biographies of Siddons and Jordan were published in
1827 and 1831 respectively). In his biography of Siddons, Boaden is at
pains to point out that 'the growing Purity of the stage' had brought with
it 'a corresponding delicacy' which allowed 'women of virtue' to flourish
on the stage.[38] Thus Siddons was enabled to display her 'genius', which 'At
length fully kindled, it burst forth with a brilliancy that, in her own sex,
had never been witnessed.'[39]

      This growing tendency to allow actresses (in the appropriate cir-
cumstances) to be perceived as talented 'artists' is paralleled by a growing
body of criticism around the issue of women painters and a desirable
'feminine' art. Within the highly public and codified context of the Royal
Academy of Art, notions of academic or 'Grand Style' art were often
founded on certain gendered assumptions about the nature of, and the
intellectual abilities required for, the production of high art. Although
contemporary perceptions of 'masculine' and 'feminine' forms of artistic
creativity were by no means fixed, many of the critical writings which
helped to establish and consolidate the activities of the Royal Academy
reveal gendered perceptions of artistic styles and genres. For example
Reynolds's writings were full of references to what he called the 'more
manly and dignified manner' suitable for historical and allegorical
works.[40] As is now well documented, only two women were among the
founding members of this academy, Angelica Kauffman (1741–1807) and
Mary Moser (1744–1819), and no women were subsequently admitted to
the full rank of Royal Academician until 1922. Kauffman won renown for
her extensive use of history painting, generally perceived as unusual at the
time for a woman painter who was more often expected to work in the
lesser genres of portraiture and flower painting. Kauffman's appropriation
of the 'more manly' style represented her own claim for painterly erudition,
and helped to generate an ongoing debate in the late eighteenth century

about what kind of artistic (genius) might be suitably applied to women artists. If women were to be seen as creative agents, then the origins of that creativity must be carefully qualified. After Kauffman had exhibited a number of historical works, including a portrait of the actress Mary Robinson as *The British Sappho*, in the Royal Academy show of 1775, a review in *The London Chronicle* had ruminated on her notable abilities, writing, 'For, though a woman, she is possessed of that bold and masculine spirit which aims at the grand and sublime in painting, as well as in poetry.'[41] Kauffman's professional achievements, though recognised, are rationalised as having borrowed from (or being possessed of) a more sublime 'masculine' spirit.

My arguments thus far suggest that a parallel debate was developing in the late eighteenth century about what forms of theatrical 'talent' were appropriate for female performers. I have suggested that perceptions of creative 'genius' in the work of actresses were mediated by contemporary assumptions about the sexuality and class origins of the actress. We have seen that Siddons's artistic 'genius' was at least partly dependent on a public perception of her sexuality as safely and honourably contained.

But the question remains, to what extent did actresses from this period actively seek to contribute to – or challenge – their public images? To what extent should we view them as passive victims of a discriminatory and gendered discourse, or as actual agents of their own creative roles, adopting strategies to help them negotiate and overcome social prejudice? Of course there are no easy answers to such questions, but there is ample evidence that each of the three actresses featured in this study sought (in different ways) to participate in the construction of their public image, that they adopted some complex strategies of self-narration.

Siddons is known to have taken an active interest in visual art and even attempted to make sculpture when she tried modelling in clay in 1789. And she actively and self-consciously contributed to the construction of her own public image through her reported reminiscences. In a biography of Siddons published in 1834, Thomas Campbell includes lengthy quotations from the actress in which she recalls various events in her life. According to these reminiscences, she willingly described the reception her acting received from various eminent contemporary men. She recalled: 'O glorious constellation! Burke, Gibbon, Sheridan, Windham, and, though last, not least, the illustrious Fox ... And these great men would often visit my dressing-room, after the play, to make their bows and honour with their applauses ... O Glorious days! Neither did his Royal Highness the Prince of Wales withhold this testimony of his approbation.'[42] Campbell quotes her giving a similarly dramatic account of her sitting for Reynolds's portrait of her as a Tragic Muse: 'When I attended him for the first sitting, after many more gratifying encomiums than I dare repeat, he took me by the hand, saying, "Ascend your undisputed throne; and graciously bestow upon me some grand idea of the Tragic Muse." I walked up the steps and seated myself instantly in the attitude in which She now appears.'[43] Whatever the veracity of this account, it suggests that Siddons was anxious to represent herself as actively contributing to the 'dignified' image for which Reynolds won so much contemporary acclaim. Moreover, her emphasis in the earlier quotation on the unrestrained admiration which she received from well-known men of intellectual standing evokes a sense of her own admirable intelligence in her dramatic performances. Shearer West has argued that Siddons actively contributed to a public perception of her dignified, queenly persona. Both on and off stage she self-consciously adopted a 'fairy-tale regality' which reinforced the artistic representation in Reynolds's portrait.[44]

However, we have seen that both Mary Robinson and Dorothy Jordan were more vulnerable to negative forms of public imagery which involved literal or metaphorical references to their private lives. Robinson, in particular, increasingly came to see her own concerns as directly implicated in the wider philosophical debates about women's social roles and notions of 'feminine' propriety which were gathering ground around the turn of the eighteenth century. Around this time a growing middle class was nurturing the values of domesticity and respectable femininity, in response to which there was a growth in popular and theoretical writings by women which (despite its anachronistic connotations) has been labelled 'proto-feminism'. The writings of Mary Wollstonecraft and Catherine Macaulay on the 'rights of women' are now well known, but many lesser known women contributed to the discourse. Although Mary Robinson is best known for her acting career, she took up writing seriously after ill-health made her acting difficult to sustain, and wrote novels, poetry, began her own memoirs and produced a pamphlet on the issue of women's rights in the 1790s. This article which appeared in 1799 under the non de plume of Anne Frances Randall was titled *A letter from the Women of England, on the Injustice of Mental Subordination*.[45] She argues vehemently against a cultural, legal and educational system which denies women adequate rights of self-representation and self-defence, drawing in part, one suspects, on some of her own experiences as a once successful actress who subsequently suffered at the hands of social prejudice and fell upon hard times. The text is full of emotive and heartfelt references to woman's impotence in the face of social prejudice:

> Supposing that a WOMAN has experiences every insult, every injury that her vain-boasting, high-bearing associate, man, can inflict: imagine her, driven from society; deserted by her kindred; scoffed at by the world;

exposed to poverty; assailed by malice; and consigned to scorn: with no companion but sorrow, no prospect but disgrace; she has no remedy. She talks of punishing the villain who has destroyed her: he smiles at the menace, and tells her, *she is* a WOMAN.[46]

But Robinson's analysis of a culture which (as she feels) oppresses her for her gender goes beyond her sense of personal injustice and engages with the thorny problem of notions of 'masculine' and 'feminine' forms of expression, which I highlighted in the critical responses to the work of Kauffman. Robinson recognises that if a woman appropriates a 'masculine' language of self-expression, it can be seen as a threat to the very masculinity from which it supposedly borrows:

> Prejudice (or Policy) has endeavoured and indeed too successfully, to cast an odium on what is called a *masculine* woman; or to explain the meaning of the word, a woman of enlightened understanding. Such a being is too formidable in the circle of society to be endured, much less sanctioned. Man is a despot by nature; he can bear no equal, he dreads the power of woman.[47]

The problems of negotiating such fears on the part of male colleagues were confronted in different ways by women who were seeking to identify themselves as 'artists' within the spheres of both the visual and dramatic arts at the turn of the eighteenth century. Actresses such as Robinson and Siddons actually participated in the production of their own life histories and biographies, seeking to play some kind of role in the construction of themselves as public myths and spectacles. And I have argued elsewhere that Kauffman's portrait of Robinson in the role of Sappho was itself a means of giving the actress and writer a 'disguise' which both affirmed her role as creative artist, but also conformed to the conventions of allegorical portraiture.[48] Robinson's assumed role as Sappho both fitted a traditional symbolic system, but also threatened it.

Yet social prejudice and intimations of an actress's unconventional sexuality continued to intervene in assessments of her status as 'artist' in early nineteenth-century discourse on the theatre, as is evidence by the ongoing debates implicated in the pages of theatrical journals and reviews. Shortly after her 21-year relationship with the Duke of Clarence had ended, Jordan returned to the stage for financial reasons, and became easy prey for the more misogynistic and scurrilous of the contemporary theatre critics. After her performance at Covent Garden in Susannah Centlivres's comedy *The Wonder: A Woman keeps on Secret*, she was viciously attacked by a lengthy article in *The Times* which suggested that the large audience had gathered to see her for the wrong reasons (to do with her private life) and that because she had been 'admitted to the secrets of harems and palaces'

she was inappropriate to the role.[49] As on previous occasions when she had
been attacked in the popular press, Jordan sent a letter to a sympathetic
paper, seeking to justify her return to the profession, and defending the
Duke of Clarence against the insinuations in the article. Behind her
characteristically modest defence is an underlying sense of the vulnera-
bilities of her position as a *woman* and an *actress*:

> I am too happy in having every reason to hope and believe that, under
> these circumstances, I shall not offend the public at large, by seeking their
> support and protection: and while I feel that I possess those, I shall
> patiently submit to that species of unmanly persecution, which a female
> so particularly situated must always be subjected to.[50]

The controversy aroused much public interest and in March 1813
The Theatrical Inquisitor entered the fray in a piece titled 'Mrs Jordan and
the Times', which opens with the assertion: 'The comparative state of
estimation in which the theatrical profession is held by the great body of
the people, is always a correct criterion of their intellectual progress.' The
writer goes on to suggest that given the 'eminent talent' which the
profession now displays it might be expected that it would be regarded with
appropriate respect. But, as the writer bemoans, this is not the case as actors
and actresses are still stigmatised by prejudice, as in the 'scurrilous and
unmanly attack on Mrs Jordan' which had appeared in the pages of *The
Times*. What is significant in the context of my arguments above is that
this writer skilfully attacks the tendency of contemporary reviewers to
confuse salacious gossip about Jordan's sexuality with her professional
talents as an actress. As if acknowledging that her gender may determine
the critical language with which her work is assessed, it is argued:

> We cannot admit the privilege of any individual, to convert the theatre,
> into a scene of public inquisition on the morals and domestic character
> of the performers. It is on their professional talents alone; on their power
> to excite the terror, the rapture, or the merriment of the spectators, that
> the public has a right to express its opinion. Neither Mrs Jordan nor Mrs
> Henry Johnstone, solicits the patronage of the audience as a woman of
> virtue, but as an actress; they do not challenge the moral approbation of
> the audience but its critical applause.[51]

Yet such efforts to counter the 'ambiguity' of an actress were often
double edged. In defence of Jordan's powers of interpretation the writer
describes how rewarding it can be for 'the man of feeling and education'
to witness the expression of moral and intellectual virtues (in Jordan's
performance) which 'he has loved and cherished in domestic intercourse'.[52]

Conclusion

Jordan's talents, then, albeit saved from prejudiced criticism, merely serve to illuminate the nature of 'feminine sensibility', a sensibility which can still maintain its separateness from any notion of 'masculine' creativity. Despite this 'separateness', we have seen that in written and visual texts from the period actresses could become potent metaphors for both the professionalisation of the stage, and the 'dignity' of high art. Yet the possibilities of this metaphorical status were mediated by public perceptions of their sexuality. Although notions of intellectual authority or creative expression were rarely applied without reservation to their work, some women devised complex strategies to enable them to participate in, and contribute to, forms of creative expression more often associated with 'a bold masculine spirit'. The Muse has many guises.

Notes

1   *The Theatrical Inquisitor*, 1 July 1814.
2   For biographical information on Sarah Siddons see James Boaden, *Memoirs of Mrs Siddons*, 2 vols London (Henry Colburn, 1827); Thomas Campbell, *Life of Mrs Siddons*, 2 vols (London, Effingham Wilson 1834); Naomi Royde-Smith, *The Private Life of Mrs Siddons* (London, Gollanz, 1933); and Siddons's own recorded comments in William van Lennep (ed.), *The Reminiscences of Sarah Kemble Siddons, 1773–1785* (Cambridge, Mass., Widener Library, 1942).
3   I am using the term 'academic' here to mean belonging to an Academy or Institution concerned to professionalise, codify and thereby raise the status of the practice to that of a 'high' art.
4   This 'struggle' has been convincingly analysed in the written discourse of the eighteenth century in Kristina Straub's book *Sexual Suspects: Eighteenth Century Players and Sexual Ideology* (Princeton, Princeton University Press, 1992).
5   In 1735 the 'Playhouse Bill' was passed which limited the activities of troupes of strolling players, and in 1737 an Act was passed making it illegal for a company to perform without a royal patent. This meant that the only legal London companies at the time of the Act were the Drury Lane and Covent Garden theatres.
6   As Straub has written: 'beginning almost concurrently with women's entrance into theatre, the gradual professionalisation of acting throughout the eighteenth century ended to place players of both sexes within the realm of public representation and regulation': *Sexual Suspects*, p. 89.
7   Much of Dorothy Jordan's correspondence has been collected by A. Aspinall, *Mrs Jordan and her Family, being The Unpublished Letters of Mrs Jordan and the Duke of Clarence, later William IV* (London, 1951). See footnote 45 for details of Robinson's publications.
8   According to classical mythology the Muses were nine sisters, daughters of Zeus and Nemosyne, who presided over learning and the arts, especially music and poetry. They were usually represented as young and beautiful virgins.
9   Roseann Runte, 'Women as Muses', in S. Spencer (ed.), *French Women and the Age of Enlightenment* (Bloomington, Indiana University Press, 1984), p. 143.

10 I have discussed this issue in G. Perry, 'The British Sappho': borrowed identities and the representation of women artists in late eighteenth century British art', *Oxford Art Journal*, 18, 1. (1995), p. 48, and in my essay 'Women in disguise – likeness, the grand style and the conventions of feminine portraiture in the work of Sir Joshua Reynolds', in G. Perry and M. Rossington (eds), *Femininity and Masculinity in Eighteenth Century Art and Culture* (Manchester, Manchester University Press, 1994).

11 I discuss this appropriation of the Sappho myth in Perry 'The British Sappho', p. 49.

12 *The Theatrical Inquisitor*, 17 (August 1815), p. 93.

13 The 1784 version is now in The Henry E. Huntingdon Collection, San Marino, California, and the 1789 version is in Dulwich Picture Gallery, London.

14 R. R. Wark, *Mrs Siddons as the Tragic Muse*, Henry E. Huntingdon Library and Art Gallery (Pasadena, California, The Castle Press, 1965), pp. 324–5.

15 N. Penny (ed.), *Reynolds* (London, Royal Academy of Arts, 1986), p. 325.

16 Apart from Reynolds, Johann Zoffany became renowned for his work in this genre, including his many portraits of David Garrick acting dramatic roles.

17 Perry and Rossington, *Femininity and Masculinity*.

18 Wark, *Mrs Siddons*, p. 3.

19 A. Graves and W. V. Cronin, *A History of the Works of Sir Joshua Reynolds*, PRA, vol. 3 (London, 1899–1901).

20 The reviewer uses the category 'HISTORICAL PAINTINGS' to describe the portrait of Mrs Siddons and another work by Reynolds in the same Royal Academy show of 1784.

21 *The Public Advertiser*, April 29, 1784. Shearer West has also argued that Siddons's performances were increasingly viewed as if they were 'works of art rather than an exhibition of nature': see West, 'The public and private roles of Sarah Siddons', in R. Asleson (ed.), *A Passion for Performance: Sarah Siddons and Her Portraits* (Los Angeles, The Paul Getty Museum, 1999), p. 22.

22 Boaden, *Memoirs of Mrs Siddons*, vol. 1, p. 10.

23 Boaden, *Memoirs of Mrs Siddons*, p. 11.

24 see Royde-Smith, *The Private Life of Mrs Siddons*.

25 Straub, *Sexual Suspects*, p. 95.

26 Straub, *Sexual Suspects*, p. 90.

27 J. Boaden, *The Life of Mrs Jordan*, 2 vols (London, Henry Colburn, 1831), pp. 4–5.

28 Straub, *Sexual Suspects*, p. 90.

29 The portrait originally commissioned by the Prince of Wales in 1781 is now in the Wallace Collection, London.

30 Boaden, *Memoirs of Mrs Siddons*, vol. 1, pp. 78–9.

31 For biographical details of the relationship see Claire Tomalin, *Mrs Jordan's Profession: The Story of a Great Actress and a Future King* (London, Penguin, 1995).

32 Euphrosyne (or Good Cheer), one of the Graces known for her cheerfulness, had already been employed by Reynolds to grace the character of a noble sitter in his portrait *Mrs Hale as Euphrosyne* of 1766: see Perry, *Reynolds*, p. 110.

33 *The Morning Herald*, 17 May 1786.

34 Tomalin, *Mrs Jordan's Profession*, p. 70.

35 *The Morning Herald*, 1 May 1786.

36 See Tomalin, *Mrs Jordan's Profession*, pp. 126 and 267.

37 See Perry and Rossington, *Femininity and Masculinity*.

38 Boaden, *Memoirs of Mrs Siddons*, p. 5.

39 Boaden, *Memoirs of Mrs Siddons*, p. 11.

40 See Perry, 'The British Sappho', p. 52.

41 'Remarks on the paintings in the Exhibition of the Royal Academy (cont)', *The London Chronicle*, 4–6 May 1775.

42 Quoted in Wark, *Mrs Siddons*, p. 7. Wark draws on Siddons's *Reminiscences* (see note 2).

43 Quoted in Penny, *Reynolds*, p. 324. Taken from Campbell, *Life of Mrs Siddons*.

44 See West, 'Public and private roles of Sarah Siddons', pp. 29–35.

45 A key source of information on the life and achievements of Mary Robinson is *Memoirs of the late Mrs Robinson, written by herself*, completed and edited by her daughter Maria and published in 1801 (republished London, Cobden-Sanderson, 1930). Robinson published volumes of poems in 1775, 1791 and 1800. A collection of poems was published posthumously: *Poetical Works* of 1806.

46 See V. Jones (ed.), *Women in the Eighteenth Century, Constructions of Femininity* (London, Routledge, 1990).

47 Jones, *Women in the Eighteenth Century*, p. 238.

48 Jones, *Women in the Eighteenth Century*, p. 238.

49 Jones, *Women in the Eighteenth Century*, p. 239.

50 See Perry, 'The British Sappho'.

51 *The Times*, 11 February 1813.

52 Tomalin, *Mrs Jordan's Profession*, p. 269.

Distant prospects and smaller circles: questions of authority in Maria Edgeworth's Irish writings

Madeline Thompson

Maria Edgeworth's (1767–1849) first novel, *Castle Rackrent: A Hibernian Tale taken from the facts and from the manners of the Irish squires before the year 1782* (1800), takes the form of a historical account of the Rackrents by the family steward Thady Quirk. Incidents considered likely to provoke incredulity in the (English) reader are verified by the authoritative testimony of the fictional 'Editor', who sets the interpretative parameters of the account. For example, to Thady's statement 'I wiped down the window seat with my wig' is added an explanatory footnote:

> Wigs were formerly used instead of brooms in Ireland, for sweeping or dusting tables, stairs, &c. The Editor doubted the fact, till he saw a labourer of the old school sweep down a flight of stairs with his wig; he afterwards put it on his head again with the utmost composure, and said, 'Oh, please your honour, it's never a bit the worse'.[1]

The status of the 'Editor' derives from the fact that, as is evident from the footnote, he is upper class and a speaker of Standard English, factors which create a distance between him and the scene he surveys. The relationship of the *Castle Rackrent* 'Editor' to his subject matter is analogous with that of the scholar to his field: both are able to elicit and communicate the significance of their material. Edgeworth shared the class status of the 'Editor' and, as a member of the Anglo-Irish gentry, had an identity distinct from the Irish who were the subject matter of many of her books. However, the 'Editor' in *Castle Rackrent*, like the archetypal scholar, is male. Edgeworth's assumption of a fictional male identity can be interpreted as a creative response to a significant obstacle to women's participation in scholarly and intellectual pursuits: it enables her to adopt an authoritative stance without transgressing contemporary norms of femininity. Although none of Edgeworth's subsequent novels have such an extensive editorial apparatus as *Castle Rackrent*, she continued to use footnotes to gloss words and phrases and to explain customs. Simultaneously emerging from Edgeworth's work, though, is an equivocal attitude to the relationship between an editor or scholar and his material. More broadly, Edgeworth displays an ambivalence to contemporary evaluations of men's and women's and to 'masculine' and 'feminine' knowledge. Some of this ambivalence may be due to the contradictions of her position as a female member of the Anglo-Irish gentry, to her marginal place in a politically, economically and socially powerful group. Before discussing Edgeworth's status and work in terms of gender, I want to explore the relationship between Edgeworth's membership of a ruling class and her authoritative depictions of the Irish. More specifically, I will demonstrate that this sense of authority derived from the fashioning by Edgeworth and her father Richard Lovell Edgeworth (1744–1817) of an identity as enlightened and conscientious members of this ruling class.[2]

Ruling and representing the Irish: intellectual and moral authority

With her writings on Ireland, a small number of which she co-authored with her father, Maria Edgeworth contributed to a number of important debates of the late eighteenth and early nineteenth centuries. Some of these debates were political and economic, including concerns with the 'state of Ireland', the role of the Anglo-Irish gentry, and the nature of the relationship between England and Ireland following the Act of Union of 1800. Others were cultural and intellectual, such as the issue of how the Irish were and should be represented and the status of non-standard English. As proponents of Ireland's 'improvement' and modernisation, the Edgeworths adopted 'progressive' stances in relation to these issues. They promoted the introduction of the principles of political economy and supported free trade between England and Ireland, investment in education and improvements in the rights of Irish Catholics, including the vote on equal terms with Protestants.[3] They censured the English for their stereotypical views of the Irish, and were passionate defenders of linguistic and cultural differences. Their defence of such differences did not, though, extend to practices and customs perceived as obstacles to economic and social modernisation. In her accounts of the process of turning Edgeworthstown into a 'model' estate, for example, Edgeworth emphasises the importance of inducting tenants into efficient working practices and of encouraging self-sufficiency.[4] In Edgeworth's novels the habits of the unreformed Irish are subjected to humorous, often vicious, derision.[5] Ireland's improvement depended upon raising the 'lower' Irish out of their indolent, improvident and indigent state. For the Edgeworths, these developments could best be achieved through a close alliance between Ireland and England, and through governance by a reformed Protestant Anglo-Irish gentry.[6]

Running through Maria Edgeworth's work is a sustained critique of absentee and inefficient landlord-magistrates. In novels such as *Ennui* (1809) and *The Absentee* (1812), poverty, inertia, waste and a corrupt judicial system are associated with the absence of enlightened management. The protagonists – and the readers – of these novels are educated in the importance of managing the transition from a colonial to a modern system. With these depictions of landlords coming to understand their responsibilities, Edgeworth points to the future economic and moral regeneration of Ireland. The assumption of their responsibilities by the protagonists is presented as a turn from absorption in their private concerns to learning to 'think of the public good'.[7] R. L. Edgeworth associated his return to his Irish estate in 1782 with his 'sincere hope of contributing to the melioration of the country, from which I drew my subsistence'.[8] The sense of Ireland as ready for improvement and modernisation, and the Anglo-Irish gentry as fit for such a task, is reinforced by the designation by Maria Edgeworth of the Irish as a people 'peculiarly subject to the influence and example of a great resident Irish proprietor'.[9]

Such a portrayal of the Anglo-Irish gentry and their relationship with their Irish tenants could be interpreted as a rather blatant attempt to justify the place of the Anglo-Irish in Ireland. However, it could also be seen as part of an attempt to secure a more equal and economically favourable relationship between Ireland and England. It is important to note that the Edgeworths had their work published in England and wrote for a predominantly English audience.[10] An issue which had long been important to elements of the Anglo-Irish was 'whether Ireland should remain the first of Britain's colonies (and thus *de facto* a trading competitor), or incorporate within the heart of what was already termed the Empire, in the expectation of gaining favoured terms of trade'.[11] The Edgeworths argued that barriers to free trade between England and Ireland undermined the significance of the constitutional Union: 'it is a farce to talk of an incorporating union having taken place between two countries, whilst the frontiers of each are guarded by a host of customhouse officers'. Trade barriers were preventing Ireland from becoming 'a flourishing part of the British empire'.[12] In presenting Ireland as undergoing a process of modernisation, the Anglo-Irish gentry as capable of disinterested and efficient rule, and the Irish as improvable, the Edgeworths were making a case for the colonial relationship between England and Ireland to be superseded by a partnership of equals.[13]

These depictions of contemporary Ireland were in conflict with opinions prevalent in England. While early nineteenth-century English commentators disagreed as to the most important causes of the condition, many concurred with Coleridge's designation of the population of Ireland as 'with few exceptions, the least civilised of Christian Europe'.[14] As a participant in both cultures – Edgeworth lived in Ireland but was educated in England and mixed in London social circles – she was well placed to intervene in these debates. She could draw on an extensive knowledge of Ireland, and she shared many of the social, cultural and political assumptions of her English audience. I will return later to the issue of Edgeworth's relationship with this audience, and its significance in understanding the scholarly elements of her work. A desire to counter the image of Ireland as uncivilised motivates all of Edgeworth's Irish works, but is most explicit in *Essay on Irish Bulls* (1802), regarded as the first book-length study of stereotyping.[15] She and her father wrote *Irish Bulls* to challenge the impression of Ireland as a land of fools and barbarians – an impression underpinned by the belief that 'the Irish nation is prone to those (linguistic) blunders, which are usually called bulls'.[16] Through a mixture of anecdotes, cross-cultural comparisons, dialogues and linguistic analysis, the Edgeworths demonstrate: first, that linguistic blunders ostensibly peculiar to the Irish can be found in other cultures ranging from Ancient Greece to contemporary England; second, that examples of speech which the English, in their ignorance, regard as nonsensical usually comply with an alternative but internally coherent set of linguistic rules; third, that the Irish variant of the English language is exceptionally vibrant and expressive. This re-evaluation of Hiberno-English by the Edgeworths follows from their understanding that the language of a people is often regarded as 'a just criterion of their progress in civilisation'.[17] By elevating the status of Hiberno-English, they hope to elevate the status of the Irish. More broadly, their efforts to overcome the ignorance of the English are in keeping with the Enlightenment faith in rationality: they assume that prejudice precedes inequality and can thus be corrected through education. The distinction I made earlier between political and economic debates and cultural and intellectual debates can, therefore, not be maintained: the issue of how the Irish were and should be represented is fundamental to the issue of the nature of the relationship between England and Ireland. And for the Edgeworths, enlightened and efficient rule by the Anglo-Irish gentry and their ability to know and accurately represent the Irish are mutually dependent, each one functioning to validate the other. To understand

Maria Edgeworth's claims to authority on the subject of Ireland, it is necessary to understand her conviction that the management of the Edgeworthstown estate by her family was beneficial to all.[18]

Such attitudes are now difficult to comprehend because we view the situation through layers of subsequent historical developments and debates. It is important to remember that the Catholic nationalist movement which dominates the history of nineteenth-century Ireland was only just forming when Edgeworth began to write. It was not until much later in her life that Edgeworth witnessed, with the successes of Daniel O'Connell's Repeal Movement in the 1830s, a powerful and coherent challenge to rule by the Protestant gentry. And the image of the Anglo-Irish as too removed from and lacking in sympathy with the real or 'hidden' Ireland for their representations of it to have any validity did not crystallise until decades after her death in the cultural contests of the late nineteenth and early twentieth centuries.[19] This essay is not concerned with these developments and debates, but with the *mentalité* of late eighteenth and early nineteenth century 'progressive' Anglo-Irish such as the Edgeworths, who prided themselves on what they regarded as enlightened loyalty to Ireland.[20] This loyalty enjoined on them the responsibility not only of beneficent rule, but of 'diffusing a more just and enlarged idea of the Irish than has been generally entertained' in order to challenge the cultural superiority the English felt towards the Irish.[21]

The Edgeworths presented their version of the Irish as a corrective of accounts both from within Ireland and by the English. They were dismissive of work by Catholic historians such as Sylvester O'Halloran, and censured the concern of 'rusty antiquarians' with the Gaelic past as a distraction from the 'fate of the present race of (Ireland's) inhabitants'.[22] (As settlers in Ireland, the Anglo-Irish had reason to discredit attempts to locate Irishness in the distant past and establish ethnicity as the key to Irish identity.[23]) The Edgeworths were more concerned, though, to contest the authority of contemporary English reports of Ireland. In their caustic review of John Carr's *The Stranger in Ireland* they contend that while those:

> who make a tour through a country see objects in a new, and often in a more entertaining point of view, than persons whose long residence in the country have rendered most objects familiar ... on certain points, we can hope to obtain accurate information from those only who have lived in the country, and who, in their political and economical observations, have taken time into the account.[24]

This review was published anonymously but, in its claim that analytical insight results from observations made over an extended period of time, it enhances the Edgeworths' credentials as authorities on Ireland.[25] Residence in Ireland is a prerequisite of expertise on the state of the nation.

Residence, though, is not in itself sufficient to acquire understanding of Ireland and the Irish. For the Edgeworths, such knowledge results from and is the mark of beneficent rule. It is, therefore, suggestive of moral as well as intellectual authority. The Edgeworths make the case for beneficent rule in their non-fictional publications, but the argument is also given powerful expression in the comic renditions in Maria Edgeworth's novels of the chaos resulting from the mismanagement of Irish estates. The construct of the model landlord-magistrate is developed in opposition not only to absentee landlords but to several other figures. Edgeworth's work features landlords who are variously tyrannous, negligent and ignorant of the principles of political economy. The emergence of popular nationalism and the 1798 Uprising, which Edgeworth witnessed, made impossible faith in the blanket loyalty of the Irish. Consequently, displays of allegiance could be seen as suspect. Deference might be tongue-in-cheek, grudgingly given, or a cover for the seditious activities of the dispossessed. The Edgeworths argued that tyrannous rule engenders servility rather than loyalty, and that circumstances can generate tendencies to mendacity: 'the people are, from poverty and *subordinate* situation, continually tempted to deceive'.[26] In contrast, they imply, the tenants of 'model' landlord- magistrates have no inducements to servility, no motives to deceive. Consequently, loyalty to benevolent and equitable landlords can be taken as authentic.[27] In this model, over-indulgent and negligent rule also provides motives to deceive. The protagonist of *Ennui* states that he 'wished to make all my dependants happy, provided I could accomplish it without much trouble'. He contravenes one of the central rules of political economy by giving 'indiscriminate donations' without waiting 'to inquire, much less examine into the merits of the claimants'. He is soon surrounded by 'crowds of eloquent beggars' who 'left their labour for the easier trade of imposing upon my credulity'.[28] In contrast, Edgeworth is able to proclaim that her father (like her fictional 'model' landlord-magistrates) 'became individually acquainted with his tenantry – saw, heard, talked to them, and obtained full knowledge of their circumstances and characters'.[29] The linkage of moral and intellectual authority is further suggested by the coincidence of Maria Edgeworth's decision to stop writing about the Irish and developments in the 1830s which rendered the claim of beneficent rule much less tenable. Edgeworth's frequently quoted statement from 1834 on the impossibility of representing Ireland 'as she now is' is indicative of the Anglo-Irish loss of a sense of place and purpose in Ireland following the growth in popularity and power of the Catholic nationalists. Particularly upsetting for Edgeworth was that even some of the Edgeworthstown tenants voted in opposition to the wishes of the landlord – in Edgeworth's opinion a betrayal of the contract between landlord and tenant.[30]

Gender and scholarship

For the Edgeworths, fitness to govern and knowledge of one's tenants are interlinked. Representations of Ireland and the Irish, based on such knowledge, derive their authority in part from the status of the enlightened landlord-magistrate. As a benevolent and conscientious overseer of the estate, his observations have moral as well as empirical authority. Maria Edgeworth had a complicated relationship to this source of authority. As a woman she occupied a marginal position within the Anglo-Irish gentry. The figure of the landlord-magistrate was male. In practice, though, Edgeworth took on many of the responsibilities and accrued many of the privileges attendant on this role. In the absence of a son of a suitable age, R. L. Edgeworth took her as his assistant when he surveyed his estate. After her father's death, in the face of serious mismanagement by her brother Lovell, she assumed increasing responsibility for the estate and, to prevent land going out of the hands of the family, bought up sections of the land Lovell auctioned to meet his debts. Edgeworth recorded these events in an unpublished Appendix to her grandfather's Black Book of Edgeworthstown, a combination of family history and records of the dealings of the estate. From this account it is evident that she was conscious of limits to her authority in this role. She states that 'Less is expected from a woman as to the exercise of power or free will and independent judgement' and goes on to list some of the duties which could only be undertaken by a man, including the settling of disputes, decisions about improvements, public meetings and magistracy.[31] Her account reveals frustration at the lack of a suitable member of the family to undertake these duties, along with a mixture of discomfort and pleasure, doubt and pride, from the experience of fulfilling traditionally male responsibilities. Edgeworth's continuance of the Black Book is of interest in itself: her grandfather's assumption that it would descend through the male line of the family is implicit in the Preface he attached to the manuscript.[32] Although she assumed responsibility for recording the dealings of the estate and producing a family history, she gave her work the title 'Appendix or Humble companion to my grandfather's Black Book'.[33] Edgeworth's life illustrates the privileges and difficulties for a woman resulting from close alignment with, and emulation of, patriarchal authority. These experiences may account for some of the ambivalence which, I will argue, marks her work.[34]

Another source of ambivalence is the conflicts and contradictions of Edgeworth's position as a female intellectual in the early nineteenth century. A scholarly education was generally considered unsuitable for women, even of Edgeworth's class. Until she was fourteen, Edgeworth attended schools where accomplishments such as embroidery, handwriting and French dominated the syllabus. Subsequently, having joined her family at the Edgeworthstown estate in Ireland, her education was supervised by her father. A description by Edgeworth illustrates the dramatic change in subject matter and intellectual demands thus occasioned. Having been asked by her father to write 'an enquiry into the causes of poverty in Ireland' she becomes 'immersed in Politics, among old newspapers, older pamphlets, Blackstone's *Commentaries*, Burgh's *Political Disquisitions*, De Lolme on *The Constitution of England*, &c, &c, &c.'.[35] Despite familiarity with such weighty material, Edgeworth recognised that she was not in command of other forms of privileged knowledge. Discussing the joint authorship with her father of *Irish Bulls*, she draws attention to the fact that she has not had a classical education: 'All passages, in which there are Latin quotations or classical allusions, must be his exclusively, because I am entirely ignorant of the learned languages'.[36]

This recognition may have motivated her attempts to carve out and validate alternative forms of knowledge. Edgeworth collected information about everyday life – a sort of ethnology of the Irish. In a literal sense, Edgeworth has no connection with the field of ethnology emerging at the beginning of the nineteenth century: ethnology involved the study of non-European peoples. However, her work is analogous to this discipline in two respects. George Stocking states that, from the early ethnology through to anthropology in the present, the dichotomy between the 'civilised observer and the culturally distant (and objectified) "other" has always been central to the … tradition'.[37] While the sense of difference between the European and non-European was often of a higher order, the use of the Irish as a barbarous, uncivilised 'other' against which the English and Anglo-Irish could define themselves as civilised had a long history.[38] As the quotation from Coleridge illustrates, at the turn of the century the Irish were often regarded as barely European. One of the sources of fascination of Edgeworth's work is that even as she critiques such opinions, she litters her texts with descriptions of the 'antics of the crazy natives'.[39] Edgeworth's authority on the subject of Ireland appears to depend upon her emphasis of the strangeness of the country and people, a point I will elaborate later. There are also certain methodological similarities between ethnology and the publications of Edgeworth and Mary Leadbeater (1758–1826), whose work will be discussed below. Their use of people as the 'raw material' for their studies fits the ethnological tradition which 'has been defined primarily by its human subject matter'.[40] The use of people as subject matter circumvents obstacles encountered by women such as lack of access to libraries, archives and scholarly works. Although access to books and documents was not a problem for Edgeworth, she combined her scholarly knowledge with information acquired by less formal means.

Material was gathered by requests to friends and relatives for relevant examples, and by social interaction. In addition, Edgeworth's responsibilities as an assistant to her father involved keeping records of communications between him and his tenants.[41] From such encounters, Edgeworth amassed examples of social customs, events, and monologues and dialogues, especially as they exemplified linguistic peculiarities. Some of these were of a technical nature, others took the form of usually humorous narratives. Drawing on these examples when writing her fictional and non-fictional works enabled her to imbue them with the status of the authentic. These social methods of accumulating evidence could be accommodated within the daily routines of upper-class women. (Similarly, some of the material for Edgeworth's other field of expertise – the education of children – was generated by her involvement in the education of younger members of the family.)

Edgeworth and Leadbeater may have benefited from working in a field which had yet to undergo the processes of institutionalisation which, Joan Thirsk has argued, tend to exclude women.[42] Participation was not dependent on qualifications, membership of institutions, or adherence to a set of principles and practices. This type of information gathering may also have attracted women because it corresponded with the contemporaneous assumption that the skills required – observational skills, attention to detail and understanding of the local and the domestic – were typically female. For example, Hannah More (1745–1833) argues of women that:

> Both in composition and action they excel in details; but they do not so much generalise their ideas as men, nor do their minds seize a great subject with so large a grasp. They are acute observers, and accurate judges of life and manners, as far as their own sphere of observation extends; but they describe a smaller circle. A woman sees the world, as it were, from a little elevation in her own garden, where she makes an exact survey of home scenes, but takes not in that wider range of distant prospects which he who stands on a loftier eminence commands.[43]

More metaphorically figures the difference between men's and women's knowledge as a matter of location: she suggests that what you know depends upon where you stand, which for her is determined by sex. While Edgeworth's material from local sources falls into More's category of female knowledge, Edgeworth combines this with knowledge traditionally understood as masculine. In *Castle Rackrent*, over a fifth of the text is given to a glossary which, in addition to the Preface and substantial footnotes, constitutes the contribution of the 'Editor'. The tale recounted by the family steward Thady Quirk is, therefore, framed by the apparatus of scholarship. While this apparatus should be read as a comic literary device, it is also a vehicle for the display of an impressive familiarity with scholarly sources, such as: the transactions of the Royal Irish Academy; an extract from 'a MS. of Lord Totness's in the Lambeth library' given to the Editor by 'a learned friend'; the work of the linguist John Horne Tooke.[44] A similar array of sources is cited or quoted in other fictional and non-fictional works by Edgeworth. These sources extend her range beyond the limits of her own experience and lend authority and prestige to her work. However, Edgeworth also employs the apparatus of scholarship to enhance the value of her 'feminine' knowledge: the local and particular, anecdotes and gossip. In footnotes and glossary entries, Edgeworth repeatedly makes epistemological truth claims such as: 'This was actually done at an election in Ireland'; 'Verbatim'; 'the following extract from an examination lately taken by an Hibernian magistrate'.[45] These function not only as verifications of authenticity, but to indicate that the material is worthy of interest. In turn, this establishes the 'Editor'/Edgeworth as sufficiently educated and cosmopolitan to recognise the strangeness of this culture and language to 'his'/her audience.[46]

The editorial apparatus of *Castle Rackrent* and, to a lesser extent, of her subsequent Irish books create a space in which Edgeworth's scholarly and local knowledge can exist alongside one another. A decade after her first fictional performance as an editor, Edgeworth provided an editorial commentary for Mary Leadbeater's *Cottage Dialogues Among the Irish Peasantry* (1811). Inspired by Hannah More's *Cheap Repository Tracts* (1795–98), Leadbeater wrote *Cottage Dialogues* to encourage cleanliness, thrift and sobriety among the Irish lower classes.[47] Like Edgeworth, Leadbeater drew on her knowledge of local customs, manners and dialect. In the Preface and Glossary – which were added only to the English editions – Edgeworth repeated the combination of scholarly and local knowledge found in the editorial of *Castle Rackrent*. Marilyn Butler identifies a dialogic pattern in the Glossary to *Castle Rackrent*. For example, in a Glossary entry on the Ullaloo, or Irish funeral wail, the 'Editor' 'quotes at length from a sympathetic article in *Transactions of the Royal Irish Academy* on ancient Irish funeral rites, and goes on to deflate it with an amused piece of rapportage on the customs of the present day'.[48] In a Glossary entry to *Cottage Dialogues*, Edgeworth makes a more overt challenge to scholarly knowledge by taking on the 'most authoritative and intrepid of our grammarians, including Harris, Lowth, and Johnson'. Considering the Hiberno-English phrase 'I will thank you', she states: 'The pure English grammarian would here, perhaps, substitute *shall* for *will*. But this is a nice point of grammar, which depends on a yet nicer point of metaphysics' (emphasis in original). Having given a parodic explication of the theories of Lowth and Johnson on the correct usage of will and shall, Edgeworth demonstrates that these theories are inadequate to a full understanding of

Hibernian-English. She concludes her argument: 'But if the English *shall* be the most accurate and grammatical, the Hibernian *will* is the most affectionate and eloquent ... the Irish generally find the most eloquent expressions of their feelings'.[49] Although both these entries are written for comic effect, they also pose a serious question about scholarship. Might not, they implicitly ask, commonsensical forms of knowledge sometimes be more appropriate than scholarship? Might not the rational, abstract perspective of scholars blind them to the subtleties of experience? In the second example, scholarship is dismissed as reductive: assessing grammatical issues in isolation from emotional eloquence results in failure to address the complexity of language. By suggesting that other skills and approaches are required – capable of encompassing such complexities – Edgeworth validates her own field of expertise. These examples might be seen as attempts to bring into question the prestige of sanctioned knowledge and to promote the feminisation of scholarship.

Edgeworth illustrates how commonsensical knowledge can complement or even challenge traditional scholarship: less theoretical approaches can engender new, often more subtle and creative, interpretations. However, in the absence of claims to theoretical principles or methodological standards, much of the authority of commonsensical knowledge derives from the status of the person who articulates it. In *Castle Rackrent*, Edgeworth stages an encounter between a voice invested with authority and a voice which lacks it. The 'Editor's' command of scholarly material and 'his' recognition of the need to explain Irish practices denote an educated and cosmopolitan perspective. This is in stark contrast to the parochial perspective of the narrator, Thady Quirk. Much of the humour of the novel derives from the fact that, in the words of the 'Editor', Thady 'tells the history of the Rackrent family in the full confidence that Sir Patrick, Sir Murtagh, Sir Kit, and Sir Condy Rackrent's affairs will be as interesting to all the world as they were to himself'.[50] Thady cannot conceive of an audience with different interests and knowledge to himself. In the Preface, the 'Editor' argues that Thady's 'plain unvarnished tale' has value, but only as a sort of unwitting testimony. 'He' writes of Thady as one of those who 'without enlargement of mind to draw any conclusions from the facts they relate, simply pour forth anecdotes, and retail conversations, with all the minute prolixity of a gossip in a country town'.[51] The significance of this is not just that the figure of the gossip is stereotypically female but that the excessive attention to details and trivial matters, which denotes an inability to discern what is of genuine importance, is simply a comic and more overtly deprecatory version of More's account of female attributes. And yet Thady is a man, and the low status of his testimony is due to his position as a family servant and to his Irishness. Garrulity and such lack of discernment were also thought characteristic of the lower classes and the Irish. In *Castle Rackrent* the male perspective is not monolithically privileged but differentiated as it intersects with ethnicity and class. Thady, like women, is able only to describe a small, local sphere. The full meaning of Thady's testimony can only be elicited by someone with a masculine and cosmopolitan perspective such as the 'Editor' who, with a 'wider range of distant prospects', is able to abstract from particulars and draw broad lessons from the account. In contradistinction to More's division of perspectives according to men's and women's ways of seeing, perspectives in *Castle Rackrent* are divided along the lines of 'masculine' and 'feminine'. These gendered ways of seeing are mapped on to the Anglo-Irish and Irish, the upper and lower classes. Does, then, Edgeworth unsettle More's categories of male and female knowledge only to rank 'masculine' over 'feminine' knowledge?

When thinking about this question, it is important to remember that the 'Editor' is a fictional character and that it is not possible to be sure of the extent to which Edgeworth endorses 'his' evaluation of Thady's account. Recent readings of *Castle Rackrent* have tended to present Thady as more knowing than the 'Editor' allows. Much of the interest of the novel lies in the question of the extent to which Thady is artless, knowing, or both. For Tom Dunne, Thady is 'a Caliban in the guise of a quaint stage-Irish Ariel'. Thady's assertions that he is giving the account out of loyalty are a cover for his own part in the downfall of the family.[52] Terry Eagleton argues that Thady's loquacity is 'a kind of artlessness', but can also be read as 'the rhetorical strategy of the "lower Irish", disarming authority by its rumbustious spontaneity and wrapping unpalatable truths in its endless parataxis'.[53] The doubleness of Thady is usually read as an articulation of the ambivalent attitudes of progressive Anglo-Irish to the lower Irish. Convincing as these interpretations are, by focusing on Edgeworth's status as a member of the Anglo-Irish gentry, and largely disregarding her subordination as a woman, they neglect other possible readings. It is conceivable that Edgeworth was less dismissive than her 'Editor' of Thady's narrative because it represents the perspective of the subordinate. Thady's intimacy with and dependency on his subject matter, the Rackrent family, is incompatible with having an overview of the situation. But his enmeshment also gives rise to insights not available to more dispassionate observers. Eagleton likens Thady's knowledge to a wife's knowledge of her husband.[54] Interestingly, in an early satirical piece 'An essay on the noble science of self-justification' (1795), Edgeworth examined the uses to which wives can put their knowledge of their husbands in the battle of the sexes. The self-serving insider knowledge of wives and servants is the antithesis of scholarship, but Edgeworth's writing suggests that there may be a kind of wisdom in utterances usually dismissed as trivial, deceitful, unconstrained and inconsequential.

Scholarship and audience

Thady's account does not, though, override the contribution of the 'Editor'. *Castle Rackrent* is a dialogic text, and insights are provided by the two narratives and by their juxtaposition. The Glossary of *Castle Rackrent* is itself dialogic. The result is a layering of different perspectives: the 'raw material' of Thady's account, the commentary based on everyday knowledge and the scholarly commentary. The accommodation of competing perspectives may be seen as an expression of Edgeworth's ambivalence about the value of types of knowledge and the validity of different standpoints, but it is a very creative ambivalence.

While the freedoms of fiction enable Edgeworth to avoid assigning final authority to any of the perspectives in *Castle Rackrent*, it remains that some voices have more weight than others. Edgeworth's adoption of a voice invested with intellectual authority enables her to present more lowly material as of interest to an educated English audience. Her familiarity with the English and her understanding of them as in need of enlightenment about the Irish provided her with a clearly defined audience for her material. This facilitated Edgeworth's assumption of an editorial and scholarly role not only in relation to her own work but to Leadbeater's: the role of interpreter of a culture depends upon a relationship with the receiving society. Edgeworth received a request from a friend, Mrs O'Beirne, to write a Preface for a book by her protégée Mary Leadbeater. Edgeworth not only agreed to write a Preface, but offered to supply notes as well. She produced a 70-page 'Glossary and notes for the use of the English reader' and, with her father, found an English publisher for *Cottage Dialogues*. Edgeworth's recognition that the dialogues could be of interest to an audience beyond that originally intended – the 'lower' Irish – was not shared by Leadbeater. In a letter to a friend, Edgeworth wrote that Leadbeater's dialogues 'give such an excellent picture of the lower Irish, that I am in hopes that they will interest in England. Of this she, poor modest simple creature, had not the least hope or idea till we suggested it'.[55] Leadbeater was immensely grateful to Edgeworth for securing an English publication of her work, but the publication also conferred prestige on Edgeworth. A reviewer stated: 'we are grateful to Miss Edgeworth for presenting them [*Cottage Dialogues*] to a wider and more exalted circle; we thank her for attaching her Preface and Notes, like the wings of Daedalus, to a body that would otherwise have been confined to its native soil'.[56] Due to the humble character of its original intended audience, and its heavy didacticism, *Cottage Dialogues* had low cultural status. By representing Leadbeater's material within a scholarly framework, Edgeworth transforms it into a product of interest to a 'more exalted' audience. This enables Edgeworth to display her intellectual credentials, but also to affirm the value of lowly, feminine and regional perspectives. Edgeworth's work both emulates scholarly authority and questions some of the assumptions and values embedded within it.

Notes

1   M. Edgeworth, *Castle Rackrent and Ennui*, ed. M. Butler (London, Penguin, 1992 [1800 and 1809]) p. 104.

2   Clearly there are problems with presenting Edgeworth's and her father's views as coterminous. However, there was a large degree of overlap. For a thorough discussion of their views, including points of difference, see M. Butler, *Maria Edgeworth: A Literary Biography* (Oxford, Clarendon Press, 1972). I refer to Maria Edgeworth both by her full and by just her surname, and to her father always as R. L. Edgeworth.

3   M. Edgeworth and R. L. Edgeworth, Review article (anon) (1807) of John Carr's *The Stranger in Ireland*, reproduced in Edgeworth, *Castle Rackrent and Ennui*, pp. 342 and 341.

4   R. L. Edgeworth and M. Edgeworth, *Memoirs of Richard Lovell Edgeworth, Esq. Begun by Himself and concluded by his daughter Maria Edgeworth*, 2 vols (London, R. Hunter, 1820), vol. II, pp. 17–31 and 366–9.

5   For example, see the discussion of the Irish propensity to procrastinate in the first entry in the Glossary to Castle Rackrent: Edgeworth, *Castle Rackrent and Ennui*, p. 123.

6   Edgeworth and Edgeworth, *Memoirs of Richard Lovell Edgeworth*; Butler, *Maria Edgeworth*.

7   M. Edgeworth, *The Absentee*, ed. W. J. McCormack and Kim Walker (Oxford, Oxford University Press, 1988 [1812]) p. 129.

8   Quoted in Butler, *Maria Edgeworth*, p. 77.

9   Edgeworth, *The Absentee*, p. 261.

10   On the ethnic composition of the audience for Irish writers of this period see J. C. Beckett, 'The Irish writer and his public in the nineteenth century', *The Yearbook of English Studies*, II (1981) p. 115.

11   M. Butler, Introduction to Edgeworth, *Castle Rackrent and Ennui*, pp. 34–5.

12   Edgeworth and Edgeworth, Review article of John Carr's *The Stranger in Ireland*, p. 342.

13   *Castle Rackrent* does not fit easily with this aim because it looks back to the eighteenth century and takes to comic extremes the failings of the unreformed gentry. Much of the editorial matter deals with contemporary Ireland.

14   S. Deane, *Civilians and Barbarians* (Derry, Field Day, 1983), pp. 6–7.

15   M. J. Croghan, 'Swift, Thomas Sheridan, Maria Edgeworth and the evolution of Hiberno-English', *Irish University Review*, 20: 1 (1990), pp. 19 and 29.

16   M. Edgeworth and R. L. Edgeworth, *Essay on Irish Bulls* (London, J. Johnson, 1802), p. 5.

17   Edgeworth and Edgeworth, *Essay on Irish Bulls*, p. 52.

18   Edgeworth and Edgeworth, *Memoirs of Richard Lovell Edgeworth*, vol. II, pp. 14–42
      and 366–71; National Archives of Ireland (NAI) MS M2320, M. Edgeworth,
      'Appendix or Humble companion to my grandfather's Black Book'.

19   For an interesting discussion of these cultural contests see D. Cairns and S. Richards,
      Writing Ireland: Colonialism, Nationalism and Culture (Manchester, Manchester
      University Press, 1988), ch. 4.

20   Edgeworth and Edgeworth, *Essay on Irish Bulls*, pp. 313–14.

21   Edgeworth and Edgeworth, *Essay on Irish Bulls*, p. 315.

22   Edgeworth and Edgeworth, *Essay on Irish Bulls*, pp. 312–15.

23   Edgeworth, *Castle Rackrent and Ennui*, p. 344, n. 29.

24   Edgeworth and Edgeworth, Review article of John Carr's *The Stranger in Ireland*,
      p. 379.

25   The claim is developed, in fictional form, in Edgeworth, *The Absentee*, pp. 81–3.

26   Edgeworth and Edgeworth, Review article of John Carr's *The Stranger in Ireland*,
      p. 337 (emphasis in original). Tom Dunne explores this aspect of Edgeworth's
      belief-system in 'Maria Edgeworth and the colonial mind', O'Donnell Lecture, Cork,
      1984, pp. 18–21.

27   Confidence in the loyalty of their own tenants might have been strengthened by
      the fact that the 'Edgeworthstown tenants remained attached to their landlord's
      family throughout the next half century of class and sectarian strife, until the
      political ferment of the 1830s imposed strains that proved too strong for individual
      or family ties': Butler, *Maria Edgeworth*, p. 87. From this we can conclude nothing
      about <u>why</u> the tenants remained attached to the Edgeworth family; it tells us
      nothing about the motives of the tenants.

28   Edgeworth, *Castle Rackrent and Ennui*, pp. 189–90.

29   Edgeworth and Edgeworth, *Memoirs of Richard Lovell Edgeworth*, vol. II, p. 17.

30   These events are discussed in M. Hurst, *Maria Edgeworth and the Public Scene*
      (London, Macmillan, 1969), ch. 2; Butler, *Maria Edgeworth*, pp. 452–4.

31   NAI MS M2320, M. Edgeworth 'Appendix or Humble companion to my grand-
      father's Black Book', ff. 57 and 59.

32   The Preface is reproduced in H. J. Butler and H. E. Butler, *The Black Book of
      Edgeworthstown and Other Edgeworth Memories* (London, Faber and Gwyer, 1927),
      pp. 4–6.

33   NAI 'Appendix' M 2320, title page.

34   For a lengthy discussion of this conflict and its impact on Edgeworth's publications
      see E. Kowaleski-Wallace, *Their Fathers' Daughters: Hannah More, Maria Edgeworth
      and Patriarchal Complicity* (New York and Oxford, Oxford University Press, 1991).

35   Quoted in Butler, *Maria Edgeworth*, p. 90.

36   Edgeworth and Edgeworth, *Memoirs of Richard Lovell Edgeworth*, vol. II, p. 337.

37   G. W. Stocking, *Victorian Anthropology* (New York, The Free Press, 1987), p. 47.

38   N. Canny, 'Identity formation in Ireland: the emergence of the Anglo-Irish', in
      N. Canny and A. Pagden (eds), *Colonial Identity in the Atlantic World, 1500–1800*
      (Princeton, Princeton University Press, 1987).

39   The phrase is Declan Kiberd's: D. Kiberd, Review of S. Deane's *Strange Country*, in
      Times Literary Supplement, 30 May 1997, p. 14.

40   Stocking, *Victorian Anthropology*, p. 47.

41   Butler, *Maria Edgeworth*, pp. 245–7 and 87–8.

42   J. Thirsk, 'The history women', in M. O'Dowd and S. Wichert (eds), *Chattel, Servant*

or Citizen: Women's Status in Church, State and Society (Belfast, Institute of Irish Studies, The Queen's University of Belfast, 1993), pp. 1–2.

43   H. More, *Strictures on the Modern System of Female Education*, 2 vols (London, T. Cadell & W. Davies, 1799), vol. II, p. 25.

44   Edgeworth, *Castle Rackrent and Ennui*, pp. 124, 131, 137 and 123.

45   Edgeworth, *Castle Rackrent and Ennui*, pp. 96 and 171; M. Leadbeater, *Cottage Dialogues Among the Irish Peasantry*, with Preface and a Glossary by M. Edgeworth (London, J. Johnson, 1811), p. 300.

46   In contrast to her Irish novels, Edgeworth's English novels only very occasionally contain footnotes to document the authenticity of a phrase, anecdote or incident. For example, in *Belinda* (1801), a lengthy novel, there are only three or four such footnotes.

47   See the unpublished correspondence between Leadbeater and Edgeworth, National Library of Ireland microfilming, Ballitore Papers, Bundle E, 1–40. Some of these letters are reproduced in M. Leadbeater, *The Leadbeater Papers*, ed. R. D. Webb, 2 vols (London, Dublin, 1862).

48   Butler, Introduction to Edgeworth, *Castle Rackrent and Ennui*, p. 17.

49   Leadbeater, *Cottage Dialogues*, pp. 325–8.

50   Edgeworth, *Castle Rackrent and Ennui*, p. 62.

51   Edgeworth, *Castle Rackrent and Ennui*, p. 62.

52   Dunne, 'Maria Edgeworth and the colonial mind', p. 8.

53   T. Eagleton, *Heathcliff and the Great Hunger: Studies in Irish Culture* (London, Verso, 1995), p. 162.

54   Eagleton, *Heathcliff and the Great Hunger*, p. 167.

55   Letter from Edgeworth to Anna Letitia Barbauld, 1 August 1810, in A. L. Le Breton, *Memoir of Mrs Barbauld* (London, George Bell & Sons, 1874), p. 150.

56   Anonymous review, *The British Review*, I (1811), p. 403.

Scholarship and sensibility: Anna Jameson and Sydney Morgan in siren land

Chloe Chard

Anna Jameson (1794–1860) wrote her *Diary of an Ennuyée* (an account of travels through France and Italy, published anonymously in 1826) early in her career; she later became a well-known literary figure, acquiring a scholarly reputation from works such as *Memoirs of the Early Italian Painters, and of the Progress of Painting in Italy* (1845) and *Sacred and Legendary Art* (1848). In the *Diary of an Ennuyée*, however, scholarly aspirations are strongly masked by the literary device that serves to order Jameson's travels as a fictionalised narrative: as in Mary Wollstonecraft's *Letters Written during a Short Residence in Sweden, Norway, and Denmark* (1796), the traveller presents herself as unhappily in love, and, in detailing her efforts to overcome her unhappiness in foreign places, draws the reader into the emotional drama in which her travels play a part. The book, in other words, sets up a structure of *mise-en-abyme*, encouraging an absorption in the sorrows of a woman who is so utterly absorbed in them herself. This structure is established at the very beginning of the *Diary* by a note, written as though the book has been prepared for publication by a male editor who feels driven to express his fascination with the author: 'As a real picture of natural and feminine feeling, the Editor hopes that it may interest others as much as it had interested him.'[1]

Like Wollstonecraft, Jameson places great emphasis on the power of suffering to accentuate the traveller's responsiveness to the places visited. At the beginning of her *Diary of an Ennuyée*, Jameson, hinting at the reasons for her unhappiness, speculates on whether travel through France and Italy can soothe her 'torn and upset' mind: 'Who knows but this dark cloud may pass away. Continual motion, continual activity, continual novelty, the absolute necessity for self-command may do something for me.' The traveller then minutely and elaborately assesses every place that she visits for its therapeutic or destructive effect. In Venice, 'pleasure and wonder are tinged with a melancholy interest; and while the imagination is excited, the spirits are depressed.' Travelling southwards, she remarks: 'I will say nothing of Bologna; — for the few days I have spent here have been to me days of acute suffering.' On reaching Florence, and reading 'those admirable and affecting passages' in Germaine de Stael's novel *Corinne; ou, l'Italie* (1807) that relate to the city, she exclaims in despair: 'I can suffer enough, feel enough, think enough, without this.' In Santa Croce, she experiences some respite: 'All memory, all feeling, all grief, all pain were swallowed up in the sublime tranquillity which was within me and around me.' Once Jameson sets out for Naples, her responses become more complex, and the reader is almost encouraged to feel that she might recover: ' – my senses and my imagination have been so enchanted, my heart so very heavy – where shall I begin?' When climbing Vesuvius, her exhaustion proves merely physical, since she continues, 'with recruited spirits' after consuming 'a glass of *Lachryma Christi* and the leg of a chicken'. At Autun, however, on the return journey, an editorial note informs the reader – mendaciously – that the writer has died 'in her 26th year'.[2]

Feminised responsiveness

Such intense self-involvement might seem to threaten the traveller's claim to one of the forms of authority that assumes a central role in the discourses of travel from the early eighteenth century onwards: the authority of the eyewitness, who has scrutinised the objects of commentary on the spot. On arriving at Padua, Jameson describes herself as 'unable to see or even to wish to see any thing'. A secondary form of authority, however, which often reinforces the claim to eyewitness experience of the foreign in the late eighteenth and early nineteenth centuries, is the claim to have responded emotionally to the objects described. Intense emotions, it is assumed, testify to the on-the-spot immediacy of the traveller's encounter with the foreign. Hyperbolic responsiveness, moreover, allows the traveller uttering the commentary to claim additional authority, by demonstrating his or her ability to appropriate the foreign as a source of dramatic difference: the figure of hyperbole necessarily registers a departure from the mundanely familiar. Anna Jameson's strategy of testing out the power of the topography of foreignness to distract her from her own sorrows allows her to generate quite exceptionally hyperbolic demonstrations of a power to respond. At Gaeta, she at first claims that her senses are 'blinded and dulled by dejection, lassitude, and sickness', and asks: 'shall I own even to myself the mixture of anguish and terror, with which I shrunk back, conscious of the waste within me?' The next morning, however, her account of her own imperviousness to natural beauty only accentuates all the more sharply the receptivity that can survive such dejection and lassitude:

> I wished to convince myself whether the beauty on which I had lately looked with such admiration and delight, had indeed lost all power to touch my heart. The impression made upon my mind at that instant I can only compare to the rolling away of a palpable and suffocating cloud: every thing on which I looked had the freshness and brightness of novelty: a glory beyond its own was again diffused over the enchanting scene from the stores of my own imagination.[3]

In travel literature of the late eighteenth and early nineteenth centuries, as in many other cultural contexts, responsiveness is assumed to be a feminised attribute. In Laurence Sterne's *Sentimental Journey through France and Italy* (1768), the traveller-narrator Yorick, at Calais, proclaiming his susceptibility to feeling in a reference to his later visit to the grave of Father Lorenzo (a monk whom he treats first rudely and then apologetically), declares that various features of the scene 'all struck together so forcibly upon my affections, that I burst into a flood of tears', and adds: '*but I am as weak as a woman*; and I beg the world not to smile, but pity me' (emphasis added).[4] Sydney, Lady Morgan, embarking on her account of Milan in her travel book *Italy* (1821), lays claim to a heightened emotional involvement with the objects of commentary that she specifically defines as feminine:

> The very name of this city, as I write it, awakens feelings which the impartiality of veracious narrative should distrust. From pages like the present, the bias of affections and the influence of sentiment should be excluded. I trust, however, that in a woman's work, sex may plead its privilege; and that if the heart will occasionally make itself a party in the *concern*, its intrusions may be pardoned, as long as the facts detailed are backed, beyond the possibility of dispute, by the authority of contemporary testimonies.[5]

Curiously, then, one of the primary sources of authority claimed by traveller-narrators, both male and female, within a discourse that previously allows little alternative to a definition of the Grand Tour as a confirmation of masculinity, is the ability of the traveller to align himself or herself with the feminine. At the same time, travel writings insist that feminised responsiveness is readily compatible with appeals to forms of authority that are explicitly identified with the masculine. This insistence is especially striking in commentaries in which the traveller-narrator writes as a woman self-consciously defining her approach to the foreign as that of a man. Mary Wollstonecraft, in Sweden, proclaims her powers of enquiry by remarking: 'At supper my host told me bluntly that I was a woman of observation, for I asked him *men's questions.*'⁶ Anna Jameson voices her hyperbolic delight in the warm south by specifically aligning herself with a masculine experience of pleasure: 'One leaves Naples as a man parts with an enchanting mistress, and Rome as we would bid adieu to an old and dear-loved friend.'⁷

Art and affectation

Among the rules that regulate the ways in which travel writings of this period appeal to different concepts of gender is the principle that, in order to claim any form of masculine authority, the subject of feminised responsiveness needs to demonstrate several closely related qualities that are marked as manly: simplicity, sincerity and restraint. Travellers proclaim their own manly simplicity, it is assumed, by an avoidance of affectation. One particular variety of affectation is defined especially frequently as a threat to the subject's authority to describe and comment: the effusiveness that oversteps the bounds observed by sincere, manly emanations of emotion.

Whereas the subject of sincere responsiveness is feminised yet manly, then, the subject of effusiveness is feminised in a way that renders him or her incapable of manliness. The distinction between the two positions is explicitly established in an attack on 'silly affectations' in responses to art, in James Barry's *Inquiry into the Real and Imaginary Obstructions to the Acquisition of the Arts in England* (1775). In expressing his contempt for those who 'affect such nice feelings and so much sensibility, as not to be able to bear the sight of pictures where the action turns upon any circumstance of distress', Barry explicitly links this 'piece of ridiculous nicety' to a failure in manly restraint, sincerity and directness. He comments on such affectations: 'they are beneath men who have either head or heart; they are unworthy of women, who have either education or simplicity of manners; they would disgrace even waiting-maids and sentimental milliners'.⁸

The first two of these three categories include spectators of works of art who are capable both of manliness and of feminised responsiveness; heart as well as head, Barry indicates, will rescue men from absurd affectation, and both 'education' and 'simplicity of manners' will render women capable of manly sincerity. The painter makes it clear that it is not responsiveness itself that compromises the spectator's authority: on the contrary, those devoid of 'silly affectations' will feel 'an extreme pleasure' at works such as 'the expiring Laocoon and his children, the plague of Poussin, the death of

Ananias by Rafaelle, the possessed boy by Domenichino, the Conversion
of S. Bruno by Le Sueur, or even the S. Cecilia by Maderna'.[9]

Barry's sequence of three categories of spectator nonetheless implies
that women may be especially vulnerable to suspicions of feminised
mawkishness: the brief outline of his second category carefully specifies
that women require the redeeming influence of education and simplicity
in order to command respect as critics of art, and his category of spectators
of whom little can be expected ('waiting-maids and sentimental milliners')
is identified as female as well as plebeian. Travel writers who define their
own identity as female register a similar awareness that writing as a woman
may invite suspicions of insincere effusiveness. Jameson, on the very first
page of her travel book, anxiously attempts to distance herself from the
'thread-bare raptures' and 'poetical effusions' to be expected from a 'young
lady, travelling for the first time on the continent'.[10]

Within commentary on art, travellers who deploy a rhetoric of
responsiveness often present this rhetoric as compatible with sincerity by
rejecting a second variety of affectation, distinct from the affectation of
effusiveness (though sometimes elided with it, and often invested with
some form of rhetorical immoderation): the affectation of those who claim
to speak with specialised expertise.[11] Hester Lynch Piozzi, in her *Observations and Reflections Made in the Course of a Journey through France, Italy,
and Germany* (1789), concludes her account of Leandro Bassano's *Raising
of Lazarus*, which she views in Naples, by a remark that affirms both her
own warmth of response and her innocence of any affectation: 'How can
one coldly sit to hear the connoisseurs *admire the folds of the drapery?*'[12]

Anna Jameson, however, adopts another strategy in order to dis-
claim affectation. Her plot of travelling in the hope of reviving her
downcast spirits allows her to establish at an early point in her narrative
that her comments on works of art are the product not of an inclination
for 'thread-bare raptures' but of commendable restraint and even fortitude.
Meditating on her own enchantment, in Paris, on viewing 'the Pont des
Arts, on a fine moonlight night', she muses: 'it appears to me that those
who from feeling too strongly, have learnt to consider too deeply, become
less sensible to the works of art, and more alive to nature.' Reflecting 'Are
there not times when we turn with indifference from the finest picture or
statue?', she concludes: 'never are we so inclined to claim kindred with
nature, as when sorrow has lent us her mournful experience.' This distinction between nature and art allows her to claim a sensibility born of
restraint and not of impulse when she turns her attention to painting and
sculpture: her observations, she implies, are the product both of feminised
responsiveness and of manly self-control. In the church of San Severo in
Naples, for example, she displays her proclivity for 'feeling too strongly',

yet, through this very reminder of her emotional vulnerability, hints to the reader that she must have made a commendable effort to subdue her emotions in order to engage in sightseeing at all: 'The Dead Christ covered with a veil, by Corradini ... is most painful to look upon; and affected me so strongly, that I was obliged to leave the church, and go into the air.'[13] In her commentaries on art, then, Anna Jameson deploys autobiographical fictionalising in order to draw the paintings and sculptures of Italy into a drama that, through the very audacity of the claim to sympathy that it establishes, boldly disavows any fear of affectation. When she focuses on expression, she is, in fact, able delicately to suggest that she might possess an added insight into the passions portrayed, by virtue of her own sufferings: in her account of Guido Reni's famous *Magdalene*, in Rome, she remarks: 'the countenance is heavenly; though full of extatic and devout contemplation, there is in it a touch of melancholy, "all sorrow's softness charmed from its despair," which is quite exquisite'.[14]

Antiquity: the traps of pedantry and affected rapture

In her commentaries on ancient sites, however, Jameson is less ready to claim that her responsiveness invests her with an added authority. When emphasising her own ability to 'find ample matter to excite feeling and reflection' at such sites, in Rome, she suggests, defensively, that this penchant for feeling and reflection leaves her especially vulnerable to accusations of affectation:

> I have met persons who think they display a great deal of common sense, and very uncommon strength of mind, in rising superior to all prejudices of education and illusions of romance – to whom enthusiasm is only another name for affectation – who, where the cultivated and the contemplative mind finds ample matter to excite feeling and reflection, give themselves airs of fashionable *nonchalance*, or flippant scorn – to whom the crumbling ruin is so much brick and mortar, no more – to whom the tomb of the Horatii and Curatii is a *stack of chimneys*, the Pantheon *an old oven*, and the Fountain of Egeria a *pig stye*. Are such persons aware that in all this, there is an affectation a thousand times more gross and contemptible, than that affectation (too frequent perhaps) which they deign to ridicule?[15]

Like many other travellers of the period, Jameson uses scornful reference to the pedantry and pomposity of a previous travel book in order to affirm her own freedom from the affectation located in a display of classical 'shew-knowledge', as Shelley terms it.[16] Like other travellers, too, she selects as the target of this dismissal John Chetwode Eustace's *Tour Through Italy* (1813): expressing her pleasure in recognising 'the passage which formed the communication between the Coliseum and the Palace of the Caesars', she declares loftily, 'If I had time I might moralize here, and make an eloquent tirade *à la Eustace* about imperial monsters and so forth' (figure 9).[17]

A more oblique method of disclaiming pedantry that Jameson adopts is to emphasise the general ignorance that overshadows the ruins of Rome, and assert her own ability to derive particular pleasure from the mystery with which these ruins are invested:

> I have heard the remains of Rome coarsely ridiculed, because after the researches of centuries, so little is comparatively known, because of the endless disputes of antiquarians, and the night and ignorance in which all is involved. But to the imagination, there is something singularly striking in this mysterious veil which hangs like a cloud upon the objects around us.[18]

In noting the fascination that ruins acquire by virtue of their mysteriousness and remoteness, Jameson invokes the aesthetics of association, as outlined in such works as Archibald Alison's *Essays on the Nature and Principles of Taste* (1790). Alison defines the power of cultural memory to heighten the aesthetic impact of ruins (and other sites to which associations are attached) as dependent not only upon our knowledge of the ancient past but also upon the remoteness of that past. For 'the antiquarian, in his cabinet', Alison argues, 'the gallantry, the heroism, the patriotism of antiquity rise

Inter.ᵃ dell' Anfiteatro Flavio, detto il Colos:ᵒᵒ. Interieur de l'Amphithéâtre Flavien dit le Col:

9 *The Interior of the Coliseum*, engraving in Carlo Fea, *Descrizione di Roma e de' contorni ... abbellite delle più interessanti vedute*, 1822

again before his view, softened by the obscurity in which they are involved, and rendered more seducing to the imagination by that obscurity itself'.[19] In emphasising the charms of mystery rather than those of familiarity, Jameson is able to affirm her own ability to derive aesthetic pleasure from the topography without embroiling herself in the rhetorical dangers of 'shew-knowledge'. As the Marquis of Normanby points out, in one of the narratives that he includes in *The English in Italy* (1825), the principle that lack of knowledge of the past may actually heighten its fascination ensures that the traces of the ancient past can be enjoyed even by ignorant females. In the short story 'L'Amoroso', an Englishman accompanies an Englishwoman around a site in southern Italy:

> Lord Spottiswood was familiar with all the springs of association connected with the scene; – without pedantry, he explained them to Matilda, who felt not the less delighted for being ignorant of the names and times that rendered this scene so glorious. The obscure and even unidentified relic of antiquity is as much revered, and perhaps more, than when the Cicerone has exerted his antiquarian skill thereon, and baptized it with some classic name. Who that looks from the Capitoline hill down upon the Forum, feels his delight a jot enhanced by having point out to him the Curtian lake, or the very spot where the famed fig-tree grew.[20]

Jameson, however, registers a conspicuous reluctance to limit her own responses to a fascination with 'this mysterious veil'. Her reference to 'the endless disputes of antiquarians' obliquely draws the reader's attention to the proliferation of information about ancient sites to which any traveller to Italy, male or female, had access, through the mediation of other travel books, guidebooks, and the on-the-spot pronouncements of *ciceroni*. Like most other travel writers, she frequently offers snippets of such information to the reader: in carefully throwaway style, she observes: 'We arrived after a short and most delightful journey ... at Velletri, the birth place of that wretch Octavius.' In more truculent mood, Jameson declares: 'During our examination of Trajan's Forum today, I learnt nothing new, except that Trajan levelled part of the Quirinal to make room for it' (figure 10). Even her dismissal of Eustace is elaborated into a revelation that she too is given to summoning up the narratives of ancient history, when suitably inspired by the associations of the spot: 'but in fact I *did* think while I stood in the damp and gloomy corridor, that it was a fitting death for Commodus to die by the giddy playfulness of a child, and the machinations of an abandoned woman'.[21]

A similar desire to make some sort of gesture of appropriation towards the ancient world is registered in another work in which the traveller writes as a woman: Sydney Morgan's *Italy*. This travel book explicitly defines antiquity as accessible to women as well as men, as a

avanzi del Foro, e Colonna Trajana; Restes du Forum et Colonne Trajane

10 *The Trajan Forum*, engraving in Carlo Fea, *Descrizione di Roma e de' contorni ... abbellite delle più interessanti vedute*, 1822

result of the mediatory role of the classical knowledge gained from early education. Morgan carefully refers to aspects of education which can be assumed to be common to males and females. In an attack on Mariano Vasi's *Itinerario istruttivo di Roma* (1763), and on those who are happy to accept its pronouncements, she declares:

> Yet even the most Gothic traveller, with a mind steeped deepest in Romanticism, and a judgment least imbued with 'the vulgar prejudices of the learned,' comes to Rome influenced by associations imbibed with early lore, incorporated with youthful prepossession, and connected with child-hood's first dream of something which existed beyond its own sunny sphere and span of being. Remembrances of fancied virtue and imaginary heroism, with all the false impressions to which they gave rise, will recur to the least classic taste; and names early learned by rote, and conned in pages never forgotten, will recur to the memory, in spite of the 'prejudices against prejudices,' which render Rome a subject of suspicion to all who dread the infection of pedantry, the epidemia of pretension. Mutius Scævola, and his burning hand; Quintus Curtius, and his headlong leap; Clœlia, and her aquatic venture, Virginius, and his ferocious independence; Brutus, and his patriot steel; – rise on the imagination, together with the Scipios, and the Catos, Pompey, Antony, Cæsar, and Cicero, and hover over the dreams of antiquarian anticipation.[22]

Footnotes to four of the references in the last sentence lead Morgan into further historical reflections. A few pages later, she emphasises yet more explicitly that the ancient world may become entangled with childhood memories for women as well as for men (and, at the same time, implies that travel itself – on-the-spot experience of ancient sites – may, for the 'school-girl', provide a substitute for erudition): 'The Capitol, from Virgil to the last learned school-boy, or travelled school-girl, who has visited it, has been a theme of description, of wonder, and reminiscence.' [23]

This gesture of appropriation towards antiquity is, however, protected and disguised by an elaborate rhetorical smokescreen. At Reggio ('or, in the language of the antiquarian, REGIUM LEPIDI, FORUM LEPIDI'), Lady Morgan mocks classicising tours of Italy by arguing (with reference to her own Anglo-Irish background) that two obscure Irish towns – 'Much-injured *Maughirow!*' and 'Neglected *Magherafelt!*' – might be considered equally deserving of interest, were it not for 'the fatality of a geographical position':

> Did your ruins now strew, and your mire now defile, an *Italian* Dukedom, instead of an Irish district, the learned would pause over your hovels, and your very pigs would be objects of classic interest; you would be considered as an historic feature in the land; and escaping from the mute inglorious destiny that now awaits you, your glories would be reiterated by the Addisons and Eustaces of future ages, and your fame would be given to the deathless echoes of imitative tourists.[24]

At Bologna, Lady Morgan embarks on a more wide-ranging attack on scholarship. Commenting on the learned women of that city, she makes it clear that she has little admiration for erudition in men, and robustly denies that such a quality should be applauded in women:

> Profound and recondite learning has not been frequently united with that wondrous, that mysterious gift of Nature, called *Genius!* – and though a BYRON may speak Greek, and a MOORE write it, it is doubtful if either of these eminent individuals would have qualified for a *professorship* at Bologna ... But if genius, in man, so soon starts from the cumbrous association of book-worm erudition, – in woman, whose talent is only another word for developed sensibility, and who but learns by what she feels – in woman, genius and abstruse learning never yet went together: and it is gracious to believe that works, calculated to extend the sphere of fancy and of feeling, to open the springs of human sympathy, to correct the selfishness of human egotism, and to increase the sum of literary enjoyment, may flow from a woman's pen, without requiring the sacrifice of that time and attention, which belong, by the finest law of nature, to her better duties of wife and mother! [25]

Morgan's reference to 'developed sensibility' suggests that she intends to claim this quality for herself, and so take up the rhetoric of responsiveness in a full-blooded manner. When she does emphasise her own sincerity of response, however, in describing her feelings on entering Rome, she sets such sincerity in opposition not to 'book-worm erudition' alone, but to a show of learning that she presents as continuous with affected emotion: 'The heart of the classic traveller throbs high with raptures – the heart of humanity throbs too, but with a far different emotion.' Embarking on her account of the Eternal City, she singles out as one of her targets a female commentator on ancient ruins: the heroine of Germaine de Stael's novel *Corinne; ou, l'Italie*: Mariano Vasi, she declares, settles the date when Rome was founded 'at a word', in defiance of the scholarly debate surrounding the event, and does so 'to the consolation of the very many modern Anacharses and Corinnas, who trade upon his book, "fancy raptures which they never knew," and affect to revive recollections which they never cherished.' When the Tarpeian Rock provides her with an occasion for deploring public executions, later in the chapter, she once again elides effusiveness with pedantry, placing *Corinne* in the same category of works redolent of affectation as the topographical writings of Carlo Fea and Antonio Nibby. She herself, she notes, is taken to see the Rock by 'a dirty stable-boy':

> It were vain, under such unfavourable circumstances, to conjure up one classical association, to affect one of those *thrills* which vibrate in the hearts of all true Corinnas, when the very sound of the *Tarpeian Rock* meets their ear; but even had it been seen under the consecrated authority of those arch-mystagogues of all classic lore, *Signori Fea* and *Nebbi*, to the heart of an unlearned woman it could bring no throb of pleasure; nor could its view increase the sum of interest or respect which the Capitoline heroes still awaken in the minds of the most erudite.[26]

This last sentence exemplifies the rhetorical device that characterises Morgan's treatment of classical antiquity in general: the device of distracting the reader's attention from confident pronouncements on matters that entail an appeal to classical scholarship, simply by claiming to speak as 'an unlearned woman', rejecting scholarship in general, classical travellers, travellers who effuse over ancient Rome, and (in many cases) the ruins themselves. Like Jameson, then, Morgan designates the ruins of Rome as objects of commentary that pose rhetorical problems, and implies – much more explicitly than Jameson – that these problems may have something to do with her stance as a traveller writing as a woman.

Antiquity and femininity

In rejecting *Corinne*, Morgan rejects a work which, by ingenious manipulation of some of the conventions of travel writing, manages to avoid the effect of unease in writing about antiquity as a woman that is produced in her own travel book, and in the *Diary of an Ennuyée*. The novel makes use of Corinne as a figure who, unlike the traveller-narrator, who is implicitly defined as a female foreigner who has visited Italy, is able to mediate between Italy and northern Europe. (Corinne appears to be Italian, but reveals, late in the novel, that her father is English, and that she has spent much of her adolescence in England.) The heroine is, moreover, also able to mediate between antiquity and contemporary life. As she makes her initial appearance on the Capitol, in Rome, where she is to be crowned with laurel in recognition of her talents as an *improvvisatrice*, the narrator notes that 'elle donnoit á la fois l'idée d'une prêtresse d'Apollon, qui s'avançoit vers le temple du Soleil, et d'une femme parfaitement simple dans les rapports habituels de la vie'.[27]

De Staël uses Corinne to accomplish a task that travel writing constantly sets itself from around the middle of the eighteenth century onwards: the task of transmuting historical time into personal time. Writings of this period often select as objects of commentary ancient sites that bear the trace of an antique female presence, and implicitly invoke an established elision between a version of the feminine and a domain of intimate, personal emotion. The feminine, in such commentaries, can also serve as a metaphor for the combination of mystery and imaginative accessibility that the theory of association locates within ancient sites. In Canto IV of Byron's *Childe Harold's Pilgrimage* (1818), for example, the narrator, contemplating the Tomb of Cecilia Metella, explains at enormous length how little we know about the woman whom it commemorates: 'Was she as those who love their lords, or they / Who love the lords of others?', he asks – was she 'Profuse of joy – or 'gainst it did she war, / Inveterate in virtue?' After two further stanzas of speculations, he eventually decides that he has forged a rather closer, more satisfactory relationship both with the women whom the tomb commemorates and with the ancient past:

> I know not why – but standing thus by thee
> It seems as if I had thine inmate known,
> Thou tomb! and other days come back on me
> With recollected music [28]

In *Corinne*, the use of the heroine as a mediatory figure allows the narrator, in identifying with her, to claim especially direct intuitive access to the spectral female characters of antiquity who haunt the topography of the Grand Tour. At the Tomb of Cecilia Metella, Corinne's eyes fill with tears as she compares her own destiny with that of the woman commemorated by the monument. Corinne's role as a woman of inspiration allows her to identify with the sibyls of Tivoli (where she shows Lord Nelvil around her 'maison de campagne') and of Cuma (she invokes this latter sibyl in an improvisation at the Promontory of Miseno; just after she has described the Sibyl of Cuma as 'agitée par une puissance cruelle', Corinne concludes her performance by fainting, as though to demonstrates that she too is moved by a cruel power.[29]

Anna Jameson invokes both *Childe Harold's Pilgrimage* and *Corinne* in the course of her tour of Italy; while she applauds the role of both texts in enriching the accumulation of associations around particular spots, she does not present either of them as facilitating her imaginative access to the ancient past. At the Tomb of Cecilia Metella, she observes: 'What this massy fabric wanted in classical fame Lord Byron has lately supplied in poetical interest.' At Terracina, she endorses yet more strongly the strategy of adopting ancient places as starting points for further fictionalising:

> The Promontory (once poetically the *island*) of Circe is still the Monte Circello: here was the region of the Lestrygons, and the scene of part of the Eneid and Odyssey: and Corinne has superadded romantic and charming associations quite as delightful, and quite as *true*.[30]

Jameson does, however, make use of the strategy of selecting female figures from the ancient past, and using them to accomplish shifts between the historical and the personal. She observes: 'Naples wears on her brow the voluptuous beauty of a syren — Rome sits desolate on her seven-hilled throne, "*the Niobe of Nations*".' In the 'Song of the Syren Parthenope', inserted in her travel narrative, the siren, addressing 'Ye who have wander'd hither from far climes', notes that these northerners have come to her shores 'To breathe my bland luxurious airs'.[31]

The sirens, in travel writing of the period, are often presented as allegorical personifications of the effeminatory effects of a warm climate – a relaxation of the bodily fibres, a disinclination to exertion and a receptiveness to pleasure. Henry Swinburne, for example, in his *Travels in the Two Sicilies* (1783–85), suggests that the Sirens, 'divested of their fabulous and poetical disguise', may refer back to an ancient female sovereign, presiding over 'piratical subjects':

> Thus they may have rendered themselves formidable to mankind by violence and martial exploits; but is is more natural to vest the power of the Sirens in the arts and corruptions of peace, and more consonant to the idea generally entertained of them. The sweet retreats that abound in the Surrentine peninsula; the enchanting prospects; the plenty of all the necessaries, and even luxuries of life, and the soft temperature of the climate could not fail of attracting strangers: there they must insensibly have acquired a relish for pleasure and indolence that enervated both their bodies and minds, and rendered every other country odious to them.[32]

Jameson, in Naples and its environs, presents herself as undergoing just such an effect of enervation, and as enraptured by it:

> I know not whether it be incipient illness, or the enervating effects of this soft climate, but I feel unusually weak, and the least exertion or excitement is not only disagreeable but painful. While the rest were at Capo di Monte, I stood upon my balcony looking out upon the lovely scene before me, with a kind of pensive dreamy rapture, which if not quite pleasure, had at least a power to banish pain: and thus hours passed away insensibly –
>
> > 'As if the moving time had been
> > A thing as stedfast as the scene,
> > On which we gazed ourselves away.'
>
> All my activity of mind, all my faculties of thought and feeling, and suffering, seemed lost and swallowed up in an indolent delicious reverie, a sort of vague and languid enjoyment, the true '*dolce far niente*' of this enchanting climate. I stood so long leaning on my elbow without moving, that my arm has been stiff all day in consequence.[33]

The traveller, in other words, shifts to a gendered position rather different from that of the feminised yet manly subject of responsiveness: she now presents herself as a northern European effeminated by the warm South. In Keats's sonnet 'Happy is England!', the speaker, voicing his 'languishment / For skies Italian', concludes by invoking an aquatic southern domain of siren-like females, possessed of a power to divert the traveller's purposeful progression into gratifyingly aimless floating:

> Happy is England, sweet her artless daughters:
> > Enough their simple loveliness for me,
> > > Enough their whitest arms in silence clinging:
> > Yet do I often warmly burn to see
> > > Beauties of deeper glance, and hear their singing,
> And float with them about the summer waters.[34]

Jameson, it has already been noted, declares on her return northwards that 'one leaves Naples as a man parts with an enchanting mistress'. Her account of effemination in the warm South plays with the possibility of identifying with a man overcome by topographically specific female enchantments, and so gaining access to the domain of classical mythology and history through an effort of intuitive imagination.

It is only when she reaches Naples that Jameson embarks on this fiction of identification, enchantment and enervation. Her invocation of the sirens depends on a major difference between the established classifications of the two cities. The South, within the established narrative of the Grand Tour, forms a sequel to the visit to Rome: the site of self-confirmatory pleasure and cultural consolidation, the site of an encounter with authority (the authority of the ancients, for example, and the authority represented by the great works of art in the city) and, at the same time, the major geographical goal that the Tour sets up.[35] The traveller to Naples, then, moves beyond the duty to combine pleasure with cultural benefit, and progresses to a domain of happy irresponsibility, a region visited as an indulgence rather than as an obligatory element within the itinerary of the Tour. Matilda's reactions to Naples, in the Marquis of Normanby's 'L'Amoroso', are mapped out in a way that emphasises the status of the more southern city as one in which the traveller is freed from the weight of constraining cultural expectations:

> After imperial Rome ... the traveller is in fancy apt to underrate the magnificence of Naples; and he pursues his journey Southward, more to enjoy the climate, the view of Vesuvius, perhaps, and of the Bay, than for the sake of visiting the loveliest and most regal city of modern Italy. To Matilda this pleasing disappointment, that generally strikes the traveller on the sight of Naples, was even stronger, from her having, very justly indeed as an unlearned female, thought Rome a hideous place.[36]

Jameson's fiction of herself as a traveller under the sway of the sirens, then, exploits this classification of Naples as a domain of freedom and unpredictability, after the duty to confront the authority of the ancients that the Tour imposes in Rome. Even Lady Morgan, despite her suspicions of classical scholarship in any guise, relents slightly when she moves beyond the Eternal City, and discovers a female figure who, for a moment, raises the possibility of intuitive access to the ancients. At Terracina, the pavement, 'though filthy, was strewed with myrtles, in honour of some festa'. These branches invest a young local woman with the power to summon up antiquity to the imagination:

> As we proceeded with difficulty ... to the convent of St. Francis ... a lovely creature, that looked on the verge of girlhood and of the tomb, sprang from a group of rickety imps – her eyes of fire, her white teeth, and her dark complexion deeply tinted with the hues of the mal-aria, formed a frightful contrast. She touched my arm playfully with a myrtle branch, and begged, with the smile of a young Sibyl, to accompany us, being, she said, a good '*cicerone per gli antiquità*'.[37]

Morgan's reservations about claiming such intuitive access to the past are already apparent in her indication that the vision is one of illness as well as of the antique. She swiftly banishes any suggestion that the ancient past might be about to resurge within the contemporary topography: 'but alas! we had already our *cicerone*, a poor lame, distorted creature, hobbling with difficulty, and telling us, "the *mal-aria* (in his own words) *had done his business*".[38]

Both Sydney Morgan, in dismissing this fiction, and Anna Jameson, in fictionalising more freely, draw attention to the difficulties of writing as a woman. Morgan registers a determination not to be tempted into the affected raptures into which, she implies, in Rome, female travellers may be especially inclined to throw themselves. Jameson obliquely indicates that experiencing the pleasures of antiquity in the warm South is most easily imagined as an experience available to men – to the man who can be enchanted by topographically specific mistresses and then leave them. She is not the only female traveller to show an interest in the ways in which men and their mistresses may become metaphorically entangled with the encounter with the foreign: at the very end of Hester Piozzi's *Observations and Reflections*, in an account of the effects of travel on different personalities, the traveller takes up this same metaphor. For Piozzi, the man is far from enchanted, and she has no hesitation in dismissing him as one of the varieties of traveller who fails to benefit from his opportunity to see the world:

> Others there are, who, being accustomed to live a considerable time in places where they have not the smallest intention to fix for ever, but on the contrary firmly resolve to leave *sometime*, learn to treat the world as a man treats his mistress, whom he likes well enough, but has no design to marry, and of course never provides for.[39]

Jameson, however, defining travel as an adventure of the self, rather than a form of consolidation of cultural identity, and constantly referring to her own attempts to free herself from a distressing romantic attachment, suggests that the man who can be enchanted by his mistress and then leave her (however reluctantly) might provide an enviable and even commendable model for the traveller who wishes to establish that she is responsive but not effusive.

Notes

1   A. Jameson, *Diary of an Ennuyée* (London, Henry Colburn, 1826), p. 1. For a wide-ranging and extremely useful account of Jameson's work, see Judith Johnston, *Anna Jameson: Victorian, Feminist, Woman of Letters* (Aldershot, Scolar Press, 1997).

2   Jameson, *Diary*, pp. 4, 5, 65, 84, 110, 114, 208, 237, 354.

3   Jameson, *Diary*, pp. 65, 265, 266.

4   L. Sterne, 'A Sentimental Journey' with 'The Journal to Eliza' and 'A Political Romance', ed. Ian Jack (Oxford, Oxford University Press, 1984), p. 21; emphasis added.

5   [Sydney] Lady Morgan, *Italy*, 2 vols (London, Henry Colburn & Co., 1821), vol. 1, p. 71.

6   *Letters Written during a Short Residence in Sweden, Norway, and Denmark* (1796), in Mary Wollstonecraft and William Godwin, *A Short Residence in Sweden and Memoirs*

         of the Author of 'The Rights of Woman', ed. Richard Holmes (London, Penguin,
         1987), p. 68.

7   Jameson, *Diary*, p. 308.

8   J. Barry, *Inquiry into the Real and Imaginary Obstructions to the Acquisition of the Arts
         in England* (London, T. Becket, 1775), pp. 156, 158.

9   Barry, *Inquiry*, p. 157.

10   Jameson, *Diary*, p. 3.

11   For a satirical account of affectation of this kind, see, for example, John Moore, *A
         View of Society and Manners in Italy*, 2nd edn, 2 vols (London, W. Strahan and
         T. Cadell, 1781), vol 1, p. 65 (see also pp. 62–3).

12   H. L. Piozzi, *Observations and Reflections Made in the Course of a Journey through
         France, Italy and Germany*, 2 vols (London, A. Strahan and T. Cadell, 1789), vol
         II, p. 80.

13   Jameson, *Diary*, pp. 29, 29–30, 254.

14   Jameson, *Diary*, p. 154.

15   Jameson, *Diary*, pp. 207–8.

16   In a letter to Thomas Love Peacock, Shelley describes Rome as an 'inexhaustible
         mine of thought & feeling' for the traveller, and declares: 'Hobhouse, Eustace, &
         Forsyth will tell all the shew-knowledge about it – "the common stuff of the earth"':
         Percy Bysshe Shelley, *Letters*, ed. F. L. Jones, 2 vols (Oxford, Oxford University
         Press, 1964), vol. II, p. 89; letter of 23 March 1819.

17   Jameson, *Diary*, p. 186.

18   Jameson, *Diary*, p. 181.

19   A. Alison, *Essays on the Nature and Principles of Taste*, 6th edn, 2 vols (Edinburgh,
         'Printed for the heirs of D. Willison for A. Constable'; London, Longman, Hurst,
         Rees, Orme, Brown and Green, 1825), vol. I, pp. 39–40.

20   [Constantine Henry Phipps]; Marquis of Normanby, *The English in Italy*, 3 vols
         (London, Saunders and Otley, 1825), vol. I, pp. 132.

21   Jameson, *Diary*, pp. 206, 161, 186.

22   Morgan, *Italy*, vol. II, pp. 173–4.

23   Morgan, *Italy*, vol. II, p. 176.

24   Morgan, *Italy*, vol. I, p. 274.

25   Morgan, *Italy*, vol. I, pp. 292–3.

26   Morgan, *Italy*, vol. II, pp. 171, 172–3, 179.

27   Germaine de Staël (Anne Louise Germaine de Staël-Holstein), *Corinne; ou, l'Italie*,
         ed. Claudine Herrmann, 2 vols (Paris, Éditions des femmes, 1979), vol. I, p. 46.

28   Byron (George Gordon Noel Byron, Baron), *The Complete Poetical Works*, ed. Jerome
         J. McGann, 7 vols (Oxford, Oxford University Press, 1980–92), vol. II, p. 159: stanza
         104, lines 1–4. For a much more detailed exploration of the relation between the
         feminine and the antique in travel writing of this period, see my *Pleasure and Guilt
         on the Grand Tour: Travel Writing and Imaginative Geography 1600–1830* (Manchester
         and New York, Manchester University Press, 1999), pp. 126–56.

29   De Staël, *Corinne*, vol. II, pp. 76, 77. The possibility that a female traveller may
         gain access to the ancient world through some structure of identification with a
         woman of antiquity is taken up in Mary Shelley's 'Author's Introduction' to her
         novel *The Last Man* (1826), in which the female author claims to be transcribing
         a tale told on 'Sibylline leaves' discovered in the Sibyl's cave, near Cuma (*The
         Last Man*, ed. Hugh J. Luke Jr, with an introduction by Anne K. Mellor (Lincoln
         and London, University of Nebraska Press, 1993), p. 3).

30   Jameson, *Diary*, pp. 187, 209.

31   Jameson, *Diary*, pp. 286 and 224; in her description of Rome as '*the Niobe of Nations*',
      Jameson quotes Byron, *Childe Harold's Pilgrimage*, Canto IV, stanza 79, line 1;
      Complete Poetical Works, vol. II, p. 150.

32   H. Swinburne, *Travels in the Two Sicilies in the Years 1777, 1778, 1779, and 1780*,
      2 vols (London, P. Elmsley, 1783–85). II, 163–4.

33   Jameson, *Diary*, pp. 261–2. The quotation, identified by Jameson simply as 'Word-
      sworth', is from the poet's 'Peter Bell. A Tale' (lines 268–70, slightly altered;
      Wordsworth, [William], *Poetical Works*, ed. Thomas Hutchinson and rev. Ernest de
      Selincourt (Oxford, Oxford University Press, 1981), p. 190).

34   'Happy is England! I could be content', lines 12–14: John Keats, *Complete Poems*,
      ed. John Barnard (Harmondsworth, Penguin, 1977), p. 96.

35   For a detailed exploration of travellers' experience of Rome at this period, as the
      site of an encounter with authority, see Richard Wrigley, 'Infectious enthusiasms:
      influence, contagion and the experience of Rome', in Chloe Chard and Helen
      Langdon (eds), *Transports: Travel, Pleasure, and Imaginative Geography, 1600–1830*
      (New Haven and London, Yale University Press, 1996), pp. 75–116.

36   Phipps, *The English in Italy*, vol. I, pp. 30–1.

37   Morgan, *Italy*, vol. II, pp. 325–6, 326.

38   Morgan, *Italy*, vol. II, p. 326.

39   Piozzi, *Observations and Reflections*, vol. II, p. 387.

11 Richard Rothwell, *Portrait of Mary Wollstonecraft Shelley*, 1840

Mary Shelley as editor of the poems of Percy Shelley

Richard Allen

When Percy Bysshe Shelley (1792–1822) died suddenly just short of his thirtieth birthday, his poetic remains comprised some hardly noticed printed work and chaotic manuscripts. Through her editing work Mary Shelley (1797–1851) (figure 11) turned that awkward mass into something that laid the foundation for Shelley's status as a cornerstone of English Romantic poetry. Her work could be described as scholarship in the modern sense in that she took the poems, studied their origins, reviewed variants and produced what were in her view accurate and definitive texts; all subsequent editors have had to acknowledge her work and for most of the century after his death they simply built on it. But there is another dimension to her work which takes discussion beyond academic literary studies, since this establishment of Shelley's reputation came at the beginning of a time when ideas about the place of education and English Literature were changing. The latter part of the nineteenth century saw a major crisis in religious belief and in the connection between religious belief and morality; literature in turn moved from the private study to play a much larger role in the life of a nation which was redefining itself as a world power. Tracking Mary Shelley's editing of Shelley's work gives us valuable insights into the sources of this process.

Editing and authorship

At the beginning of *A Defence of Poetry* written a year or so before his death but not published until Mary Shelley's edition of the prose of 1840, Shelley sets out his idea of the poet as first of all 'like an instrument over which a series of external and internal impressions are driven, like the alternations of an ever-changing wind over an Aeolian lyre', with the result as an 'ever changing melody'. But more than this, the poet is not simply a servant of these impressions but works on them to produce 'not melody alone, but harmony'. This can be immediately translated into an image of Mary Shelley and her editing work; through her efforts the 'melody' in the mass of Shelley's unpublished work can sing out in 'harmony', 'prolonging in its voice and motions the duration of the effect'. For Shelley 'to be a poet is to apprehend the true and the beautiful';[1] should we not see Mary Shelley's aim as to catch the truth and beauty of the poet himself?

Yet her own work should prompt us to think of these matters in a more complicated way, catching the full force of the Romantic idea of creation. From this point of view Shelley's aim 'to apprehend the true and the beautiful' must be seen as an unrealisable desire rather than a matter of fact. *Frankenstein* (1818), for example, contains a much darker story of creation. That story tells of individuals like Shelley's poet over whom 'external and internal impressions are driven', but the lesson here is that the poet, like the rest of us, must apprehend nightmare alongside truth and beauty.[2] The possibility that the poet can create harmony must be put beside other darker visions of the creator, of a Frankenstein who loses control and ownership of that which he creates and comes even to despise her/his own creation.

Mary Shelley's editing of Percy Shelley's poetry cannot be understood without reference to her relationship with Percy Shelley the man and *Frankenstein* offers useful metaphors in the stormy closeness of Frankenstein and his creature and the tragic fate of Frankenstein and his beloved Elizabeth. In August 1821 Mary Shelley wrote, 'Need I say that the union between my husband and myself has ever been undisturbed'.[3] The now muted echoes of the events of the preceding three years show this was not a claim that could be made easily. In them we hear of a child born during the winter of 1818/19; the baptism record gives Percy and Mary as the parents but it is clear from Mary's letters and journals that she is not the mother. More certainly Percy is the father of the child, perhaps after an affair with their servant girl. But the rumour is also that the mother was Claire Clairmont, the half-sister of Mary who had travelled with Shelley and Mary pretty constantly since their original elopement.[4] (The child died in June 1820.) Signs of tensions can be seen elsewhere. In July and August of 1820 Shelley works on his poem *The Witch of Atlas*. Mary copies the poem for him but without much liking for it. Shelley then adds a prefatory poem 'To Mary' describing her 'objecting to [it] ... upon the score of its containing no human interest' (p. 274), but he uses the poem to reassert his own opinion, describing her criticism as a hand reaching out to 'crush the silken-wingèd fly' of his poem. In *Frankenstein* the struggles between Victor and his creature reach a kind of fulfilment; the suddenness of Shelley's death allowed no such conclusion in Mary Shelley's life.

Understanding Mary Shelley's achievement as an editor is not, then, just a matter of understanding choices about words and the language of the poems; it is to do with things that remained from her life with Shelley, questions of authorship and ownership, memories, and finally her obsessive concern for Percy Florence Shelley, the only child who survived from the five pregnancies of her relationship with Shelley.[5]

Shelley's drowning stunned Mary, but after a period of grief she set to work, copying for Byron and sifting and painstakingly transcribing the often almost illegible manuscripts left by Shelley.[6] The result – *Posthumous Poems* of 1824 – could have been a lasting literary memorial to the man who had had no proper grave and no proper funeral (the hygiene laws in Italy required that his body be burnt where it was brought ashore on the beach near Viareggio). At the risk of over-interpreting, Mary Shelley's title – *Posthumous Poems* – is suggestive of the whole process. It certainly contains the idea that the poetry lives on after the poet's death, and in this respect what is important is the poet's rather than the editor's work. But it also contains the idea that the poems can only live on through the efforts of someone other than the dead poet. Thus Mary Shelley is very much to the fore, the book attesting to her authority and to the fact that *her* relationship with Shelley was the central one. Claire Clairmont, in particular, was at last marginalised.

Mary's satisfaction in her achievement was brief, however, because *Posthumous Poems* immediately brought her into conflict with Shelley's father, Sir Timothy Shelley. The details here are tortuous but they are important because they show both how dependent Mary Shelley was on Sir Timothy after 1822 and how she was prevented from enjoying any of the 'property' that belonged to her after Shelley's death, be it her son, or money, or the poetry that could be a sign of her relationship with Shelley. Shelley came from a wealthy landed family. As was still common at the time, the substantial part of the Shelley inheritance – especially the land and the right to the income from it – passed through the male line, from Sir Timothy to Percy and then to Charles Shelley (Percy's son from his first marriage). Percy Shelley did leave Mary everything he could outside that which was tied up in this way, but his will could only be executed after Sir Timothy's death. Sir Timothy Shelley had been hostile to his son's life and work and Percy's death provided an opportunity to remove a stain from the family's honour. Mary Shelley was to be shut out of the Shelley family. Shelley's writings and his reputation as a poet were to be suppressed. Percy Florence was to be acknowledged as part of that family but entrusted to some respectable clergyman. Mary Shelley rejected this proposal and in the end Sir Timothy agreed that she could keep Percy Florence and receive an allowance for his needs, but he then used that allowance ruthlessly to get his way. When Mary published the *Posthumous Poems* he immediately threatened to stop the allowance, demanding that she withdraw the book. Mary was sanguine; she wrote 'there is no great harm in this, since he is above 70, & from choice I should not think of writing memoirs *now*'.[7] Sir Timothy was made of stronger stuff and lived until 1844, so for almost twenty years Mary Shelley had to keep the most important part of her self and her achievement private. Two entries from her journal from 1833 indicate the stress this imposed:

> 14 Nov. Thursday
>
> I know not what to say, or write, – I know not what to think! – I ought to be content; – in peace, my child – well; – I cannot forget <u>here</u> – Yet reason brings many topics of self congratulation – and hoping no more – wherefore fear I? – my whole Future centred in my boy, why is my heart for ever struggling with Memories
>
> Nov. 23
>
> I am copying Shelley's letters. Great God! What a thing is life! In one of them, he says 'The curse of this life is that what we have once known, we cannot cease to know' – and thus is Harrow like the shirt of Nessus to Hercules, to my wounded aching thoughts.
>
>   I am going to begin the lives of the Italians – God grant I find lessons during that study to teach & tranquillise my disturbed & sorrowing mind. Ah better than all to find the single drop of thirsted for liquid which may bring Lethe to my soul. Why do I ask what is to be – What better than the past? – & that past – it is torture to think upon.[8]

Here intertwined are the four main strands of the story of Mary's life in the time before she began her major work editing Shelley's poems: the story of knowing and yet being silenced (in Shelley's words, 'what we have once known, we cannot cease to know'); the story of the mother's love for her only surviving son;[9] the story of Mary Shelley's struggle for the intellectual and material property vested in her Shelley; and finally the story of her struggle to earn money through her own writing.

Shelley's reputation and the public interest in his life and work did not diminish and for twenty years Mary Shelley was trapped between the fact that she was forbidden to publish anything on Shelley herself while the value of her property was always at risk from unauthorised publication.[10] Sir Timothy's final agreement in 1839 to her editing a volume of Shelley's poems (which was specifically not to include a memoir of his life) came from just the threat of an uncontrollable pirate edition. A letter to her publisher shows how Mary went about managing what she plainly saw as financial as well as emotional assets, insisting on her authority over Shelley's work and her achievement in creating a coherent collection:

It gives me great pleasure to publish Shelley's poems with you ... I am content with your offer of £200 for the edition of 2,000 – but I should be glad to dispose of my entire interest & for that I think I ought to have £500. I feel sure among other things that the copyright of the Posthumous Poems must be entirely mine. The M. S. from which it was printed consisted of fragments of paper which in the hands of an indifferent person would never have been decyphered – the labour of putting it together was immense – the papers were in my possession & in no other person's (for the most part) the volume might be all in my writing (except that I could not write it) in short it stands to reason, & I think that it is law that a posthumous publication must belong entirely to the editor, if the editor had a legal right to make use of the Ms. - ... think that £500 is not too much to ask for the entire copy rights which I will take pains to render as valuable as I can. I hope you will agree to this additional sum in which case we might at once conclude [an agreement].[11]

Biography and interpretation

Why after all these years did Mary Shelley propose the sale of her 'entire copyrights' outright? Maybe after the years of being so relentlessly short of money, the promise of £500 was just too tempting? But perhaps, in more ways than one, selling the copyright outright did not reduce Mary Shelley's rights? After all, she still retained Shelley's actual papers and the memories that they brought with them. But more importantly through the edition she created and retained a different and more enduring 'copyright' on Shelley. Sir Timothy had stipulated that there be no memoir of his son; Mary complied in form but circumvented his instruction in practice through the extended and largely biographical notes she wrote for the edition. Biography foregrounds the poet – the man who is 'like an instrument over which a series of external and internal impressions are driven' – and becomes in turn the reader's principal means of understanding the poems. (The effect is heightened in the original four-volume edition where volumes 3 and 4 are arranged in a series of, as it were, chapters – 'Poems written in 1816', 'Poems written in 1817', etc.) But Mary Shelley's involvement in the story alongside Shelley also foregrounds her own self, showing her equally able to produce 'not melody alone, but harmony' (see p. 78 above). The poet Shelley has become Mary Shelley's creation.

How might one characterise Mary Shelley's work as an editor of her Shelley? Sometimes she draws on material in her possession, making the text of the poem conform to what she knew directly was Shelley's own intention. But at other times the difficult circumstances of her life meant that she did not have this direct evidence and then she used her instincts to conjecture a best reading. Overall, she seems to have had a particular concern for punctuation, editing the poems to conform to her view of proper style. Examples drawn from *Adonais* and from *Alastor* can illustrate each of these ways of working in turn.

Adonais (the poem Shelley wrote as a memorial for Keats) was written in Italy in 1821 and Shelley himself supervised the production of a printed edition that year in Pisa. He sent this printed version to Charles Ollier hoping the poem would be published in London, but nothing came of this. In the Pisa edition the latter part of stanza 8 reads as follows

> The eternal Hunger sits, but pity and awe
> Soothe her pale rage, nor dares she to deface
> So fair a prey, till darkness, and the law
> Of mortal change, shall fill the grave which is her maw.

In the 1839 edition the last line is different: 'Of change, shall o'er his sleep the mortal curtain draw'. The change here is 'authorised' because Mary Shelley had it direct from Shelley during his lifetime and had indeed secretly supplied it to the pirated *Poetical Works of Coleridge, Shelley and Keats* published by Galignani in Paris in 1829;[12] the provenance of the correction is further reinforced by the existence of letters from Shelley to Charles Ollier in 1821 and 1822 to which Mary also had access.

Alastor provides an illustration of Mary Shelley making the best of the material to hand. As we now accept it, lines 484 to 488 contain the evocative

> But undulating woods, and silent well,
> And leaping rivulet, and evening gloom
> Now deepening the dark shades, for speech assuming,
> Held commune with him, as if he and it
> Were all that was;

Shelley himself had this poem printed along with a few others in a slim volume in 1816 in the hope of interesting a publisher in his work. When Mary Shelley included it in her immediately posthumous edition of Shelley's work in 1824, 'leaping' in line 485 by accident emerged as 'reaping'. When she came to re-edit the poem for the 1839 *Poetical Works of Shelley* she plainly saw that 'reaping' was incorrect but amended it not to 'leaping' but to 'rippling'. Perhaps she thought this was returning the poem to what Shelley preferred but it is as likely that she just did not have a copy of the 1816 printing – there had only ever been 250 copies – and simply changed it to something she thought made poetic sense; 'rippling' certainly parallels 'undulating' in the previous line, and with 'rivulet' creates an alliterative effect appropriate to tumbling water.[13]

Adonais again provides an example of Mary Shelley editing to implement her own preferences for punctuation; something any editor or even compositor of the time would feel they had every right to do. In the prose preface we see her adding commas usually to mark off clauses more rigidly. Where Shelley has 'a heart made callous by many blows, or one, like Keats's composed of more penetrable stuff', Mary Shelley's edition adds a comma after 'Keats's'. Where Shelley has 'almost risked his own life, and sacrificed every prospect to unwearied attendance upon his dying friend', Mary Shelley adds a comma after 'prospect'. The same thing happens in the poem itself where she adds commas particularly it seems to prompt the reader to notice the end of the line. In effect she is telling us how to read. Modern editions usually discard these additional commas but the effect can be seen in the following examples where her added commas are in square brackets.

> God dawned on Chaos; in its steam immersed[,]
> The lamps of Heaven flash with a softer light
>
> The leprous corpse[,] touched by this spirit tender[,]
> Exhales itself in flowers of gentle breath;
> Like incarnations of the stars, when splendour
> Is changed to fragrance, they illumine death[,]
> And mock the merry worm that wakes beneath;
> (Stanzas xix and xx, ll. 167–8 and 172–6)

Understanding the importance of punctuation in texts of this time is extremely difficult. Some would argue that punctuation in printed books of this time is so haphazard that it is impossible to draw firm conclusions about the author's or the editor's intentions. Punctuation was regularly just left to the compositor. Perhaps Mary Shelley just took them over from the pirated Galignani edition of 1829 where they also occur? To my mind there remain grounds for thinking that the 'comma-ed' text is Mary Shelley's. She had, after all, secretly supplied material for the Galignani edition and this comma-ed style corresponds directly with her own prose style.[14] Moreover the effect – the controlling of the reader – is directly in line with her overall aim in her Shelley edition.

On the face of it the biographical notes that Mary Shelley added to the poems in 1839 embody a different order of work from that involved in establishing correct texts for the poems themselves, but the two different kinds of work can be brought together. Until 1839 most of the poems existed only in private, so Mary Shelley's editing brought them into a public existence. Surely, too, the notes bring Shelley himself from his private world into the public domain, shaped and authenticated by her own testimony. And as she edited the poems in accord with her poetic sense, so too through her notes she 'edited' Shelley the man into a form that made sense to her. Sometimes she provides factual information about

Shelley which she can helpfully pass on to the reader. Following the section 'Poems of 1816' in volume 3 Mary Shelley writes, 'He spent the summer on the shores of the Lake of Geneva. The "Hymn to Intellectual Beauty" was conceived during his voyage round the lake with Lord Byron. He occupied himself during this voyage, by reading *La Nouvelle Heloïse* for the first time'.[15] Later in the same volume the note to 'Poems written in 1818' tells the reader that '*Rosalind and Helen* was begun at Marlow, and thrown aside until I found it; and at my request it was completed ...'.[16] Something more is going on here, however, for now Mary Shelley herself is claiming a sort of stake in the actual production of the poem. Overall, the notes regularly move beyond the supply of facts to – as it were – interpret Shelley himself and in so doing they foreground the interpreter, Mary Shelley herself, as the author of this coherent narrative of his character. The note to *Alastor*, for example, uses the poem as a springboard for a more general interpretation and defence of the man and work:

> This is neither the time nor place to speak of the misfortunes that chequered his life. It will be sufficient to say that, in all he did, he, at the time of doing it, believed himself justified in his own conscience; while the various ills of poverty and loss of friends brought home to him the sad realities of life. Physical suffering had also considerable influence in causing him to turn his eyes inward.
>
>   The poem ought rather to be considered didactic than narrative: it was the outpouring of his own emotions, embodied in the purest form he could conceive, painted in the ideal lines which his brilliant imagination inspired.[17]

Here Mary Shelley engaged in some delicate balancing. She and the now 20-year-old Percy Florence were still dependent on Sir Timothy and all her work was carried out under his ever-hostile eye. She can be seen adjusting things so as not to give offence and risk another proscription.[18] Her note to the poem 'A Summer Evening Churchyard' refers to its being written 'during his [sic] voyage up the Thames, in the autumn of 1815'.[19] Sufficient in the circumstances, one might say, and understandable that Mary Shelley passes over the fact that Harriet Westbrook, still Percy's wife, was not with him while Mary herself was – along with her sister Claire Clairmont and Thomas Love Peacock. In the note on *The Revolt of Islam* Mary writes that, 'He was very fond of travelling ... In 1816 he again visited Switzerland, and rented a house on the banks of the Lake of Geneva'.[20] The note is true, so far as it goes, but is also silent about a good deal. Shelley – still married to Harriet Westbrook – was again travelling with Mary, and with them was Claire Clairmont. The three of them met up with Byron and John Polidori at Lake Geneva, not least because they needed to talk to Byron about the fact that Claire was expecting his child

(Allegra Byron was born the following year). We pass over, too, the fact that at Lake Geneva the Shelley/Byron group became themselves a spectacle for other tourists.[21] It was there too, of course, that Mary Shelley herself began *Frankenstein*. Perhaps these omissions are just a matter of tact, a desire to remain in the background, but such a conclusion hardly squares with the way elsewhere Mary expresses her feelings very directly.

In the 1839 edition longer pieces, in effect those published in Shelley's lifetime and which he himself probably most valued such as *Queen Mab, Alastor, The Revolt of Islam, Prometheus Unbound, The Cenci,* etc., come first. As mentioned above, the other poems then become a kind of narrative first of Shelley's life but increasingly also of Mary Shelley's. Towards the end the notes rise to a climax of emotional intensity; in the note on the poems written in 1821, she writes, 'My task becomes inexpressibly painful as the year draws near that which sealed our earthly fate; and each poem and each event it records has a real or mysterious connection with the fatal catastrophe'.[22] After the 1822 poems she wrote:

> [I have] a burning desire to impart to the world, in worthy language, the sense I have of the virtues and genius of the Beloved and the Lost ... Recurrence to the past – full of its own deep and unforgotten joys and sorrows, contrasting with the succeeding years of painful and solitary struggle – has shaken my health. I dislike speaking of myself, but cannot help apologising to the dead, and to the public, for not having executed in the manner I desired the history I engaged to give of Shelley's writings.[23]

A romantic framework

Across the years, surely, we can still feel the power of these words. They carry an authority that springs from direct knowledge and direct feeling. They are 'romantic' in testifying to Mary Shelley's love for Shelley in life and in death. They are also Romantic in the overwhelming emphasis on an 'I' who is creator, and who is tortured by creation (just as Frankenstein is tortured by thoughts of his creation, see p. 78 above).

Not surprisingly, perhaps, Mary Shelley's Shelley has had an enduring power. The Oxford Standard Authors *Shelley,* edited by Thomas Hutchinson, for example, is still in print and very commonly available in shops and libraries. This dates substantially from 1904 and was in turn largely based on the edition produced by H. Buxton Forman in 1876–77. In some respects Forman's edition is genuinely different from Mary Shelley's 1839 edition; he followed early printed editions whereas she would always return to the manuscript where that was possible; it did not include her notes. But the arrangement of poems, including the year by year grouping of the shorter poems is preserved there and throughout later editions.

Indeed when Buxton Forman came to produce a new edition of his text in 1882 he reintroduced Mary Shelley's notes to be picked up in turn by Hutchinson and to remain in most editions to this day.

Within this broad continuity, one particular set of changes in editions of Shelley particularly throws the nature of Mary Shelley's project into relief. Her edition begins with a section of 'Early Poems' drawing together his work before 1816. When she and Shelley met he was twenty-two with an Oxford degree, a marriage to Harriet Westbrook, two children, a novel and a body of poetry already behind him. Moreover, barely two years after he and Harriet separated – and probably a good deal because of this – she committed suicide. Needless to say the Westbrook family were as hostile to Shelley and Mary as was Shelley's own father. None of this made it easy for Mary Shelley to feel her collection of Shelley's early work was complete; but her acknowledgement of the problem in the notes is interestingly mixed with an assertion of her own competence and authority:

> The loss of nearly all letters and papers which refer to his early life, renders the execution more imperfect than it would otherwise have been. I have [however] the liveliest recollection of all that was done and said during the period of my knowing him. Every impression is as clear as if stamped yesterday, and I have no apprehension of any mistake in my statements as far as they go.[24]

In fact, Harriet's family had a notebook which Shelley had used up to 1814.[25] Poems from this manuscript began to appear after William Michael Rossetti somehow had access to it, but significantly almost all later editors since Rossetti have been so plainly awed by Mary Shelley's edition that they have simply accommodated newly discovered poems into her narrative-like structure.

The Romantic framework within which the work surely exists should, however, prompt us to look more widely in understanding the importance of Mary Shelley's *Shelley*. A *Defence of Poetry* provides a prompt. It is shot through both with a desire to exalt the imagination, and with a sense of a social mission for poets and poetry, culminating in the famous words of the last paragraph:

> The most unfailing herald, companion, or follower of the awakening of a great people to work a beneficial change in opinion or institution, is poetry ... Poets are the unacknowledged legislators of the world.[26]

Putting this beside the following passage from Mary Shelley's note on *The Witch of Atlas* suggests how much this kind of idea was in her mind but also how she judged Shelley's actual achievement:

> Shelley did not expect sympathy and approbation from the public; but

the want of it took away a portion of the ardour that ought to have
sustained him while writing ... I believed that all this morbid feeling
would vanish if the chord of sympathy between him and his countrymen
were touched. But my persuasions were vain, the mind could not be bent
from its natural inclination ... he loved to shelter himself rather in the
airiest flights of fancy forgetting love and hate, and regret and lost hope,
in such imaginations as borrowed their hues from sunrise and sunset).[27]

With hindsight what is important here is not so much the diagnosis of
Shelley's failure as the way of thinking which links poetry seamlessly on
the one hand to the imagination and the personality of the poet and on
the other to, in effect, the good of the nation – be it conceptualised in the
almost Miltonic terms in 'the awakening of a great people' or in 'the chord
of sympathy between him and his countrymen'.

In a project aiming to restore women to their proper place in the
canon of nineteenth-century thinking and writing, it might be tempting
to claim Mary Shelley as originating some new way of thinking and feeling,
but the parallel between her thinking and that of Shelley himself makes
this hazardous. Better to remember that she was responsible for the first
publication of A Defence of Poetry in 1840 and was an important agent in
the dissemination later in the century of the notion that literature born of
emotion and imagination was as valuable in the forming of nation and
empire as rational or mechanical thinking or politics.

Literature, in particular, was able to have this effect through the
education system and it is therefore apt to note how education was a key
element in Mary Shelley's life. As a child she lived in a household where
her father and her stepmother wrote and published educational books. She
herself wrote at least two moral dramas for children and her non-fictional
writing always had a strongly didactic and improving tone. Moreover Mary
Shelley was for some years an everyday spectator of the English public
school system; straitened resources meant she could only afford for Percy
Florence to be a day boy at Harrow and she lived there with him from
1833 to 1836. At this time English Literature had a smaller part to play
in formal education than Classical Literature, but ideas were changing in
a way that was very much in step with the thinking about poetry embodied
in Mary Shelley's Shelley.[28] In brief, classical education and scholarship
changed from something heavily dependent on philology and the private
study of details of the text to something much more to do with the moral
education which was increasingly central to the British public school
system. This shift is neatly demonstrated in the words of a schoolmaster at
Eton around 1840; bemoaning the poor work of his pupil, he wrote that if
he could not himself produce passable imitations of Greek poetry then he
would not become a good man: 'if you do not write good longs and shorts,

how can you ever be a man of taste? If you are not a man of taste, how can you ever be of use in the world?'.[29] The increasing sense of Britain as a colonial power around this time suggests that we should interpret the last phrase here – 'in the world' – quite widely. The schoolmaster was, after all, speaking five years after Thomas Macaulay's *Minute on Indian Education* had put English Literature and education at the heart of British rule there (a shelf of the kind of books taught in English schools, he said, was worth all of Hindu literature).[30] If one puts the schoolmaster's comment alongside Mary Shelley's note on *The Witch of Atlas* (see p. 86 above) one can hardly avoid feeling that in the longer term the 'chord of sympathy' of which she speaks is a more valuable and durable quality than his adherence to 'taste'.

But this positive conclusion about the values put forward by Mary Shelley sits alongside certain contradictions. Her Shelley is a man of feeling, intellect and imagination and as the years passed he moved closer to the centre of the canon of English poetry. Yet we must also see his life as ultimately one of tragic failure. In his 'Stanzas from the Grande Chartreuse' of 1855, for example, Matthew Arnold (1822–88), one of the most im-portant prophets of culture of the time, presents an image of Shelley which perpetuates Mary Shelley's idea of a Shelley who 'loved to shelter in the aeriest flights of fancy' (see p. 87 above) – someone whose work lacks any persisting force to change the world or even to relieve those whose hearts are 'restless' at the problems of the day:

> What boots it, Shelley! that the breeze
> Carried thy lovely wail away,
> Musical through Italian trees
> Which fringe thy soft blue Spezzian bay?
> Inheritors of thy distress
> Have restless hearts one throb the less?[31]

Throughout the nineteenth century Mary Shelley's tragically inef-fective Shelley seems to have become the norm of what it meant to be a poet. But exactly at the same time writers from the past – Shakespeare, Milton, Virgil – came closer to the centre of moral values, their work seen as the key to the creation of harmony in a chaotic world and to a greater moral good. To understand this paradox is to understand that what one might describe as political ineffectiveness does not diminish the poet. Arnold perpetuated the Romantic notions of the function of the poet and poetry in *Culture and Anarchy* and elsewhere; when eventually he identified touchstones of value in great literature that gave meaning to life, his examples dwelt on death and loss, on pain, and on the transience of glory and happiness. These are inward turning values, less concerned with the emotions of the triumphant imperial nation and much more like the emotions of the widow. If Arnold can stand as an emblem of the moral force that carried forward the British Empire, then Mary Shelley and her Shelley can stand as emblem of the combination of burning desires, ideas of purest form and brilliant imagination which gave that moral force its power.

Notes

1 See D. Wu, *Romanticism: An Anthology* (Oxford, Blackwell, 1994), pp. 956–7.

2 I am thinking here particularly of the episode in Book 2 when the creature is educated by his secretly observing the De Lacey family: M. W. Shelley, *Frankenstein*, ed. J. Rieger (Chicago, Chicago University Press, 1982 [1818]), p. 97ff.

3 M. W. Shelley, *Letters*, ed. B. T. Bennett, 3 vols (Baltimore, Johns Hopkins University Press, 1980–88), vol. I, p. 207.

4 Shelley plainly found Claire attractive. We know also that Mary for her part could sometimes scarcely bear to refer to Claire by name in her Journal, and that 'Heigh-ho the Clare, & the Ma Find something to fight about every day –: Shelley, *Letters*, vol. I, p. 158.

5 Presenting Mary Shelley's career as an editor in isolation, as I do here, risks confining her within this role. It is important to remember the many other books and stories she published after Shelley's death, not least because they gave her some independent income. After 1824 she was almost relentlessly busy. Her book-length works include *The Last Man* (1826) *Matilda*, 1819 (but unpublished in her lifetime), *Valperga* (1823), *Perkin Warbeck* (1830), *Lodore* (1835), *Faulkner* (1837), *Lives of the most Eminent Literary and Scientific Men of Italy, Spain and Portugal*, vols 1–2 (1835), *Lives of the most Eminent Literary and Scientific Men of France*, vols 1–2 (1838–9), *Rambles in Germany and Italy* (1844). In addition she produced many short stories, particularly for *The Keepsake* annual.

6 'After all I spend a great deal of time in solitude. I have been hitherto fully occupied in preparing Shelley's MSS – it is now complete & the poetry alone will make a large Volume': Shelley, *Letters*, vol. I, p. 404, 27 November 1823.

7 Shelley, *Letters*, vol. I, p. 444.

8 The second entry refers to the possibility of the publication of an edition of Shelley's letters. That there was talk of Mary receiving £600 for such an edition is a sign of the extent to which publication of his work could by this time have given her an independent income: M. W. Shelley, *Journals 1814–1844*, ed. P. R. Feldman and D. Scott-Kilvert, 2 vols (Oxford, Clarendon Press, 1987), vol. II, pp. 531–3.

9 This story acquired a new twist when Percy Florence's step-brother Charles Shelley died in 1826, leaving Percy no longer the poor relation but the heir.

10 At least twice after 1824 Mary's allowance was stopped on suspicion of her having colluded with a publisher in a book about Shelley.

11 Shelley, *Letters*, vol. II, p. 300.

12 P. B. Shelley, *Shelley's 'Adonais': A Critical Edition*, ed. A. D. Knerr (New York, Columbia University Press, 1984), p. 22.

13 P. B. Shelley, *Complete Poetical Works of Percy Bysshe Shelley*, ed. N. Rogers, 2 vols (Oxford, Clarendon Press, 1975), vol. 2, p. 337.

14 See, for example, M. W. Shelley, *The Last Man* (Lincoln, University of Nebraska Press, 1993; 1st pub. 1826).

15 P. B. Shelley, *Collected Poems*, ed. M. Wollstonecraft Shelley, 4 vols (London, Edward Moxon, 1839), vol. 3, p. 35.

16 Shelley, *Collected Poems*, vol. 3, p. 159.

17 Shelley, *Collected Poems*, vol. 1, pp. 139–40 and 141–2.

18 The poems are also censored but usually in a more public way. In *Queen Mab*, words that could only refer to Sir Timothy were replaced with an ellipsis mark (…) and a similar tactic was used to conceal Shelley's association with Mary Shelley's dangerously radical father William Godwin.

19 Shelley, *Collected Poems*, vol. 3, p. 16.

20 Shelley, *Collected Poems*, vol. 1, p. 375.

21 'We passed the house in which lord Byron lives in a sullen and disgraceful seclusion … Besides his servants, his only companions are two wicked women' wrote one (quoted in W. St Clair, *The Godwins and the Shelleys: The Biography of a Family* (London, Faber, 1990), p. 405).

22 Shelley, *Collected Poems*, vol. 4, p. 149.

23 Shelley, *Collected Poems*, vol. 4, p. 26.

24 Shelley, *Collected Poems*, vol I, p. xvi; see also *ibid.*, vol. 3, p. 6.

25 This manuscript, known as the Esdaile notebook, did not come fully into the public domain until 1962.

26 Wu, *Romanticism*, p. 69.

27 Shelley, *Collected Poems*, vol. 4, pp. 51 and 53.

28 Mary Shelley and Percy Bysshe Shelley shared a love for classical literature – Mary learnt Greek from Percy in the early years of their relationship and throughout their lives turned to Greek and Latin literature for inspiration and consolation.

29 C. O. Brink, *English Classical Scholarship* (Cambridge, James Clarke, 1985), pp. 148–9.

30 See, here, for example, H. Trivedi, *Colonial Transactions: English Literature and India* (Delhi, Papyrus, 1993), p. 73ff.

31 M. Arnold, *Matthew Arnold: Poetry and Selected Prose*, ed. M. Allott and R. Super (Oxford, Oxford University Press, 1986), p. 303.

Women and education in nineteenth-century England

Rosemary O'Day

For much of the nineteenth century there was no academic discipline of education. Teaching was the poor relation of a career in the Church and, in general, male teachers in the public and private schools had no interest in furthering it as a profession with its own special expertise, remuneration and high social standing. Teachers in schools for lower middle-class and working-class children were barely better educated than their pupils and the emphasis was upon passing on practical skills of pedagogy (as in the pupil-teacher system).

Women such as the educationalist sisters Emily and Maria Shirreff played a large part in creating such a discipline and in marking out a path to be trodden by male as well as female educationalists and teachers in the future. Their major influence was upon the development of female education, but their work also had a more generalised import. The history of the pioneers of women's education has now been widely researched and encouraged by the activities of the women's movement. This essay is concerned with the contribution of women to education as a discipline in both its practice and its theory. Women scholars operated on both a highly individualistic and a collective level. A biographical approach is as helpful as a view that emphasises 'networking' and collaboration in the service of a common cause. Using both approaches, this essay examines the major contribution that women made to the development of education as a serious subject during the nineteenth century.

Such a study brings into focus a whole range of issues: the extent to which the need for pedagogical knowledge and the development of theories of education were relevant and important to women because they saw their own nature as determined by their roles as mothers and carers; the pressures placed upon middle-class women by the need to earn a living in a market saturated with untrained teachers and governesses; the extent to which women's own thinking about education was itself marked by class consciousness; the need for access to the world of the professions via improved 'formal' education, and admission to the universities; the desire for a system of qualification and licensing and acceptance as 'specialists'; and the whole debate about the nature of the curriculum specifically designed for women.

This essay is concerned with the contribution of women in four areas: what education was and what it was for; the institutionalisation of education and the desirability of teacher training; the form of education to be offered young children; and the distinctive contribution of female theorists and practitioners to the educational curriculum. Interpretation, application and the integration of theory and practice are equally important in understanding women's contribution to the advancement of learning.

Women and education: their experience of the issues

One of the problems that women faced during the period was that their activities were gender-determined and their vocations thought to be dictated by their domestic relationships. The ability to realise and fulfil their callings was thought to be relatively easy to acquire. Some women were content to develop their views on education within this traditional framework, but during the nineteenth century, and especially towards its end, there was a determined effort on the part of others to free the concept of female education from the bonds of familial relationships.[1] Such attempts took many different forms and the theories which were developed to justify them belonged to several philosophical traditions. Because women were struggling against established positions they made a distinctive and important contribution to educational theory itself.

A further preoccupation grew out of debates about the 'proper' roles of both men and women – this concerned the respective occupations thought to be appropriate and available to men and women and the qualifications required for them, access to the places of learning where such qualifications were acquired, and freedom to obtain the licensing and certification to pursue the chosen career. Women were unable to enter the learned professions because they were excluded from the institutions that conferred the qualifications that gave access to those professions. Women sought empowerment and access to places of formal education as a necessary preliminary, distinct from a desire for education for its own sake. The pursuit of qualifications was not always accompanied by a wish to influence the curriculum or syllabus, or by a thirst for knowledge.

Much, but by no means all, of the work of historians of women educationalists has been slanted towards the issue of women's empowerment.

A study of women's involvement in the history of the teaching profession at all levels (primary, secondary and tertiary sectors) becomes doubly interesting therefore. Women's concern for empowerment had profound repercussions for the development of the teaching professions.

The haphazard education received by women educators had its own impact. Formal education, denied on a regular basis to so many, became a thing highly prized both for themselves and for their pupils. For the generation born in the 1820s and 1830s there was little formal educational opportunity beyond the private or village school or the governess. These girls, if they were so inclined, educated themselves, and those who succeeded often did so because of unusual family backgrounds and circumstances. The Shirreff sisters (Emily, Maria and Caroline) were the daughters of a well-connected naval captain and his equally well-connected spouse. The premature death of the sons meant that the daughters were drawn much more into the intellectual and political life as well as the social life of the family. Their intellectual proclivities were thus encouraged and enhanced. In contrast (Sarah) Emily (1830–1921) and Jane Davies, the daughters of an evangelical clergyman, found that their three brothers received a conventional and systematic schooling while they were forced to pick up the crumbs and 'make do', even being denied access to novels and light literature.[2] Such education as women could acquire was through two main channels, governesses and family support. Even early women tutors at Oxford, Cambridge and London had frequently been educated by parents and governesses. Such tutors included Clara Pater (who taught Latin at Somerville), Katherine Tristram (who taught mathematics at Westfield) and Winifred Mercier (who taught at Girton).[3] As late as 1914, 21 per cent of female academics at Oxford and 8 per cent of female students at Oxford had been educated at home.[4] The paucity of provision of formal secondary and higher education for girls made it inevitable that young women had to make extraordinary efforts to acquire a regular formal education. The pioneers in women's education were the ones who made that effort and succeeded. They were the ones who did not participate in the traditional forms of schooling for middle-class girls described in the textbooks.[5] They sought access for girls and women to formal academic education and they developed their own ideas about appropriate pedagogy and curriculum.

Usually women concentrated upon issues concerning early childhood education or female education. They built upon their own experience and were able to appeal to it as a source of their own authority. These were the two areas where there was some acknowledgement of their right to be involved; some opportunity for them to make an input and some motivation on their part to act. Nonetheless, women approached the issues surrounding education from a variety of standpoints and there were considerable differences of opinion. Some consciously complied with existing conventions and adjusted their arguments to chime in with them – others were more aware of a wider challenge. Some urged that, in order to be good wives and mothers, sisters and aunts, women needed a broad and non-trivial education. Emily Shirreff wrote in 1858:

> What society wants from women is not labour, but refinement, elevation of mind, knowledge, making its power felt through moral influence and sound opinions. It wants civilizers of men, and educators of young. And society will suffer in proportion as women are either driven from necessity or tempted by seeming advantages to leave this their natural vocation, and to join the noisy throng in the busy markets of the world.[6]

In 1871 Maria Grey (née Shirreff) urged that the current educational provision for girls prepared them to catch husbands but not to *be* wives and mothers.[7] Some extended this 'womanly' calling to include work within the community as settlement workers, nurses and midwives. Many other women, including Constance Maynard (Westfield College), Dorothea Beale (Cheltenham Ladies' College) and Alice Otley (Worcester High School), viewed their educational work as a form of service to God.[8] This was extended to service in the community by the Women's University Settlement.[9] Still others advocated an education for those women who had to be economically independent and who wished to become governesses or businesswomen.[10] The Langham Place group founded a journal (1858) and an employment society (1859) specifically to open new jobs to women. The move was echoed in Leeds, Sheffield and elsewhere.[11] Others sought for women a much wider role in society – urging that women, like men, had to identify an individual vocation and pursue it, to look for personal fulfilment and reach out for it.[12] Some argued from the intellectual abilities of women that women could and should benefit from the same educational opportunities as men and stand side-by-side with them in the college and the market place. It would be a mistake, therefore, to assume that all women shared the same views just because they were women. Equally, though, it would be erroneous to believe that particular women held the same views on educational subjects throughout their lives. These differences are the commonplaces of early modern and modern debates about the roles of women.

A biographical approach to women's views on education

Women who became involved in formal educational provision during the century tended to place themselves on one side or the other of the debate about why women needed to be educated, but the stimulus towards involvement was often much more personal. Positions in the debate were wide-ranging and complex. While the study of women in groups, movements and institutions is valid, I would argue the need for a biographical 'case study' approach to identify the contributions of individual women and to determine the place of scholarship in their own lives.[13]

For example, this might lead us to reconsider the manner in which we view Maria Grey. With hindsight she could be viewed as a pioneer of women's formal education and training, a woman who set out from the start to open up the world of secondary education as a career to middle-class girls, a key figure in the empowerment of women through education. But from a biographical perspective the stimulus for her involvement appears much less certain and more paradoxical. Both Maria Grey and her sister Emily Shirreff began their lives as home-educated daughters of a progressive family. They shared in the intellectual life of their father's circle, but they saw their vocation in terms of their private domestic role as wives, daughters, sisters, nieces and friends. They argued for an improvement in the education of women rather than for an alteration in their role. It was only gradually that the Shirreff sisters shifted their position to emphasise the preparation of women for life in a more public arena. An understanding of the lives of these women enhances our appreciation of their intellectual development which clearly interacted subtly with changes in the wider economic and social position of women and the shifting reactions of men. However, these processes were not part of the inevitable march of progress towards equality for women, and some involved resisted arguments about equality, believing that women were not the same as men and did not require the same education.

A detailed biographical approach has another virtue: it allows us to see the public writings and activities of these women in the context of their personal lives. It reveals their sense of familial responsibility and their own involvement in various occupations. For example, we can see Maria and Emily Shirreff acting as carers within their circle of family and close friends and their advocacy of education for women as entirely consistent with this sense of responsibility and love. Or we can see Clara Collet's absorption with the occupational opportunities that women might have as rooted in her own profound dissatisfaction with teaching as a career and in the work she was set in her capacity of civil servant. Or we can see Martha Loane's espousal of a syllabus of domestic subjects in relation to her experiences as a district nurse in Portsmouth.

At this time tremendous persistence was required for a woman to obtain an academic education. Women educationalists were independent, creative rebels, the products to a great extent of self-education. It was this that made them what they were – highly motivated young women with a cause. The rich inheritance of their unorthodox route to self-knowledge and to knowledge of the world has been too little acknowledged – in part because of the gendered perspective upon what is educationally acceptable that led women to mimic male educational forms and lament their own deprivation. In many cases they recommended for their successors a 'system' which was impoverished, lauded uniformity and held their own qualities in disdain. Nonetheless, they appreciated the fact that a girl's access to a sound education was then dependent upon chance, upon her personal circumstances and upon fashion. In yet other cases, women were in the vanguard of progressive educational ideas that challenged the approach of both state and public boys' schools. Such women set their hearts upon developing a new curriculum suited to the needs of young women having to find their way in the world. In some instances they thought it necessary to rethink the entire educational 'system' and so contributed to the development of pedagogy and scholarship.

Another issue with which to engage is the way in which the Victorians regarded education as a universal panacea. On whatever political or philosophical platform one stood, education was promoted – from Samuel Smiles to John Stuart Mill, from Thomas Arnold to Thomas Burt – and some women were at the forefront in developing it. Education was widely viewed as the route to citizenship; men without much or any real property and, therefore, an interest or stake in society could nevertheless strive for and achieve this through intellectual property. Women moved on both fronts – seeking propertied independence at the same time as they sought access to both knowledge and entry to the learned professions. If women were interested in education in terms of self-interest they also saw educational reform as important for social reasons. It was envisaged that proper education and training would enable young women to support themselves financially and would make good mothers out of the 'inadequate' women of the working classes and would ensure the proper development (physical, spiritual and intellectual) of the young of all classes.

Women and early childhood education: the kindergarten movement

Some theorists thought that the woman, as mother, was particularly qualified to specialise in the education of young children.[14] In Britain the work of women theorists in this area is well illustrated in the development of the Froebel movement, in which Emily Shirreff was a key mover. This is one section of educational thought and practice where British developments were part of a wider European movement and where women's accomplishments in modern European languages (especially in German and French) helped considerably. Froebelian and Pestalozzian ideas of education have become so much the stock-in-trade of twentieth-century British education that it is easy to forget that Froebel was little known in Britain until the 1890s. Although the dissemination of Froebel's ideas has frequently been attributed to Edmond Holmes's *What Is and What Might Be* (1911), the success of the Froebel movement owed a great deal to the work of the Froebel Society. Its prime movers were a group of self-educated middle-class women of both British and émigrée backgrounds.

Friederich Froebel (1798–1852) believed that children have a natural pattern of development that adults should nurture in the same way that a gardener tends his plants. The analogy was built into the very name he gave to his early childhood centres – kindergartens. Play, handicrafts and exercise encourage the child's natural growth in spirit, body and intellect. He first directed his ideas at men but, when they were greeted by more rapturous applause from German women, he redirected them at women. His kindergarten movement 'developed rapidly along with the political and religious movements (of 1848). That only girls and women should lead the kindergarten, that Froebel wished to entrust early-childhood education only to women, seemed to me a delightful idea', wrote the revolutionary Malwida von Meysenburg. Both Christian and Jewish women from liberal and middle-class backgrounds were attracted to theories that provided intellectual and educational justification for female emancipation from the narrow domestic sphere.[15] In fact the development of kindergarten theory in the 1860s and 1870s was in the hands of women such as Baroness Berthe von Marenholtz-Bülow. She guided Froebelian theory in directions of which their originator would have disapproved.[16] The social classes were divided into different kindergarten.[17] Volkskindergarten would help compensate for the disadvantages of social origin; children would be trained for work.[18] The education of the children in these volkskindergarten would be entrusted to upper- and middle-class educated women until such time as working-class mothers became better educated themselves. Marenholz-Bülow saw the kindergarten movement as giving women a vital social role: women would regenerate society through their position as educators both of the family and of the young child. In order to fulfil this function properly women needed a different kind of education based upon a broad and enlightened curriculum.[19]

Women were at the forefront of the establishment of Froebelian education in Britain. The first kindergarten in England was founded at 32 Tavistock Place, London, in 1851 by one of Froebel's pupils, known as Madame Ronge. It catered, significantly, for the children of well-to-do French, German and Italian families taking refuge in London after the 1848

Revolutions. The principles and method were customarily disseminated by an informal personal apprenticeship system which meant that trained recruits were few. In London, Miss Doreck, the émigrée head teacher of Kildare Gardens, discovered when she opened a kindergarten department in the early 1870s that there were no available trained kindergarten teachers. The appearance in the *Education Journal* of a number of articles by Emily Shirreff on the subject of the kindergarten prepared the way for her to remedy this situation, and in 1874 Doreck gathered together a number of like-minded people to found the Froebel Society. Prominent among the assembly were Maria Shirreff Grey, Emily Shirreff, Miss Manning and Mary Gurney.

The Society attempted to publicise Froebelian principles (through exhibitions, conferences and lectures) and provide examinable courses designed to train people to educate and care for infants. Such courses were intended to develop practice and pedagogic theory and scholarship, emphasising the principle of 'wholeness' and unity in education. Doreck lectured on the 'Kindergarten in connection with the school', demonstrating how different school subjects had their origins in the kindergarten; Madame de Portugall spoke on the need to see the education of children of all ages as part of a unified system of natural development; Madame Michaelis showed in her 'Kindergarten games and music' how Froebel's games were not only designed to improve a child's physical prowess but also his or her imaginative and intellectual growth.[20]

Few of Froebel's writings had been translated into English, so knowledge of his work was largely conveyed to the British public by these women who paraphrased, interpreted or expanded upon his ideas and writings.[21] De Portugall's lectures were a key source for the Society, as were the works of members such as Miss Heerwart, who read German. Drawing directly on Froebel's insistence that learning should bring joy and also on a belief that children were being taught to read before they were 'ready', Heerwart went on to discuss phonic and look-and-say methods and the 'right time' to begin teaching this skill.[22] The work of these women had a profound effect upon other women such as Barbara Bodichon (1827–91) who founded her own school and incorporated in its philosophy Pestalozzian and Froebelian ideas.

Emily and Maria Shirreff and early childhood education

There was in the Society an uncomfortable awareness that while they were preaching to the converted, elsewhere infants were in the care of the unenlightened. Male teachers were generally opposed to the professionalisation of teaching and often stood in the way of attempts to raise the status of women teachers. The few colleges that there were provided a higher general education for their students by means of lectures and gave little or no attention to improving teaching methods or discussing educational theory. In 1861 one college alone (the College of the Home and Colonial Society) trained infant school teachers.[23] In 1875, in an important, pioneering initiative, the Society introduced a short course for the training of kindergarten nurses.[24] The Committee for the Examination of Kindergarten Teachers was established and laid down prerequisites for trainees (these included evidence of basic literacy, English grammar, numeracy, history and geography) The curriculum also included history and theory of education, physical education, Froebel's writings, zoology, botany, geology, hygiene, physiology, kindergarten activities and practical teaching, culminating in an examination leading to a Certificate of the Froebel Society. Ten students took the first examination in 1878 (alongside some students prepared by Heerwart at Stockwell).

The sisters Emily Shirreff (President, 1875–97) and Maria Grey (Vice-President) steered the Society through the programme of the next three years – one designed to establish a training college, an inspectorate for kindergartens and a proper examining board for the Froebel Certificates. Funding was the chief stumbling block when it came to founding the Kindergarten Teacher Training College. Fund-raising was based upon appealing to middle-class women: one meeting attracted seventy such women to an exhibition of kindergarten work and an explanation of the virtues of the system. The college was opened at 31 Tavistock Place on 3 May 1879. The inspectorate and registration procedure were also introduced successfully. The audience for the Society's courses and its evening training lectures for teachers dwindled in the early 1880s as the importance of bringing Froebel's ideas into state education became more widely appreciated. Probably Emily Shirreff's greatest contribution lay in her commitment to making Froebel's ideas accessible to those involved in English education – she grasped the importance of a theory of education through practice over a system dominated by rote learning.[25] Her popular *The Kindergarten at Home* strove to familiarise middle-class mothers with Froebel's principles and practice and to encourage them to introduce these into their own homes, so that his teaching would not be restricted to the formal kindergartens. Her commitment to the family, and specifically to the mother's role within it, was unwavering. In this work she insisted that mothers must master 'the fundamental principles on which' Froebel's ideas rested:

> I dwell upon Froebel's system, and set forth, to a certain extent, his practical method, but mainly in order to illustrate those principles which I entreat young mothers to lay to heart and make the law of their daily life with their children.[26]

Knowledge of Shirreff's life history could help us to understand her
spirited espousal of this educational theory. Perhaps Froebel's ideas seemed
all the more enticing because they tallied with the experience she and
Maria had had of self-education, in which rote learning had no part. Apart
from a short and wholly unsatisfactory spell at a boarding school, Maria
and Emily Shirreff had received their education from a French-speaking
governess and from their family life in lower Normandy, southern Spain
and Gibraltar. The Shirreff sisters' education had been guided by their
cousin, William Grey, who encouraged them to read widely, advising the
study of both Locke and Bacon, whose impact on English educational ideas
was very important. They were also taken under the wing of their father's
cousin, Lord Gage, who gave them the run of his library. Their background
and contacts heightened their awareness of and susceptibility to liberal
ideas from the continent of Europe at the time of the Revolutions of 1848.
In that year they again collaborated to produce *Thoughts on Self-Culture
Addressed to Women*, which was published in 1850. Emily followed this in
1858 with her *Intellectual Education and Its Influence on the Character and
Happiness of Women*. In their writings Emily and Maria did not challenge
patriarchy. They argued that within a Christian family setting women
would be accepted as the civilisers of society and educators of the young
and would educate themselves to fulfil this vocation. Such an education
would not be by rote learning but would be systematic as was demonstrated
by Emily herself who devoted eight hours a day to self-education, requiring
self-discipline and energetic commitment.[27]

Emily's close relationship with Henry Thomas Buckle (1821–62)
accentuated her interest in self-education and her practical devotion to the
learning of foreign languages.[28] Her language skills enabled her to spread
and interpret the views of foreign educationalists such as Froebel and
Pestalozzi (1746–1827). Not only did Emily explain Froebel's principles in
her writings but she also used her influence to draw them to the attention
of people in high places, building networks that would prove very useful
in the struggle to reform early childhood education. In the event, their
authority was transferred to the Froebelian pedagogy she helped develop.
Her relationship to the Greys and her sister Maria's marriage to William
Grey gave them access to Liberal politicians with an interest in the reform
of state education.

Women and the professionalisation of teaching

Maria Shirreff (later Grey) shared many of her older sister's preoccupations,
but is best remembered for her leadership of the movement to establish
career training for women teachers. Her work in this area furthered the

professionalisation of teaching in general and the acceptance of education as an academic discipline. Although this could seem like a contradiction of her earlier belief that women needed an education in order to become better wives and mothers, it was in fact a natural development arising out of her personal experience, on the one hand, and her awareness of social change, on the other. The 1860s were a decade of family illness and death. Maria became preoccupied with the conflict between women's family responsibilities and their need for individual fulfilment. Both Emily and Maria had spent a large part of their adult lives caring for various relatives and friends. In 1868 Maria published a novel, Love's Sacrifice, which allowed her to explore in some detail the caring relationships that engaged most women. By spring 1871 Maria was moving into a period of intense involvement with women's formal education. She delivered a lecture on the subject at Chelsea Vestry Hall; in April she put forward specific proposals for female education to the Society of Arts and in May spoke on the issue. She was determined also to make a practical input and in autumn 1871 stood for election to the Chelsea School Board. She was a moving spirit behind the creation of the Women's Education Union in 1871.[29] The Union brought together many groups and individuals who had already been engaged in work towards women's education and representatives from major educational agencies such as the National Association for the Promotion of Social Science (NAPSS) (sometimes called the Social Science Association). The Union proposed to provide low cost day and boarding schools for girls offering education above the elementary level and to attach classes of student teachers to these schools. These were to provide appropriate training for teachers, to aid programmes for the higher and further education of women of all classes and to make the nation aware of the national importance of the education of women. Its offshoots were the Girls' Public Day School Trust (June 1872) and the Journal of the Women's Education Union (1873) and, eventually, the Maria Grey Training College.[30]

The period 1840–1914 saw much progress in the provision of teacher training for both men and women. Until 1839 there were a very few London-based colleges – Borough Road, the Central Schools of the National Society, the Home and Colonial Training Colleges – and some diocesan central day schools that offered a brief training in monitorial methods for teachers in elementary schools. Between 1840 and 1846 the diocesan day centres were replaced by over twenty small residential colleges. In the 1840s a number of elementary training colleges were opened with government financing and students, largely from working-class backgrounds, were recruited directly from among the ranks of pupil-teachers.[31] In both the diocesan and the state colleges students could afford to train only briefly. This problem was alleviated somewhat after 1846, when the government funded four-fifths of the cost of college places, and students who had passed the Queen's Scholarship were required to pay only £3 a year. The system, however, identified elementary teaching as a working-class occupation, unattractive and inaccessible to girls from a middle-class background.[32] The narrow and domestic curriculum was partly to blame.

A number of women became involved in a movement to raise teaching into an occupation for middle-class women. When the activist Angela Burdett-Coutts (1814–1906) launched her campaign to lure middle-class girls into the training colleges and into teaching, her arguments rested upon the economic and occupational suitability and congeniality of school teaching for girls from classes above the manual working class. Her concern was not primarily for the education of the girls themselves, although she was aware that the poor provision for their education made it difficult for middle-class girls to qualify for teacher-training places.[33] Louisa Hubbard began from a similar standpoint – in 1871 she wrote a series of letters to *John Bull* magazine proposing a training college to prepare 'ladies' for elementary teaching.[34] Hubbard's Bishop Otter Training College, Chichester, founded in 1873, was, however, a milestone because it provided an environment designed for 'ladies' rather than for working-class recruits. Because these middle-class girls had been poorly educated at home, this specialist college had to provide for their formal education as well as for their preparation as classroom teachers.[35]

Maria Grey emphasised the need to provide a good education for all women and especially for female teachers. Accepting that teaching offered a career to women who worked through economic necessity, Grey was also convinced that there were strong arguments for careers for women in terms of their personal satisfaction. Her work, and that of the college she founded, grew out of a particular philosophy of education, in contrast to the earlier view of training colleges and schools as places where pedagogic skills were passed on rather than educational philosophy studied. She defined education as preparation for life and not for a special position in society. Her views are best summed up in her own words: 'It is intellectual, moral and physical development, the development of a sound mind in a sound body, the training of reason to form just judgements, the disciplining of the will and affections to obey the supreme law of duty, the kindling and strengthening of the love of knowledge, of beauty, of goodness, till they become the governing motives of action'.[36] The influence of Froebelian ideas was very evident. In 1876 Maria Grey formed the Teachers' Training and Registration Society. Its guiding principles were, however, novel and were expressed in a paper prepared by Emily Shirreff, 'On the Training of Teachers', and delivered by Grey to the Liverpool meeting of the NAPSS's Social Science Congress to publicise their intentions.

Emily Shirreff, who had for a time been Mistress of Hitchin (later Girton) College, Cambridge, was as concerned as her sister to introduce a proper educational programme for women teachers. She was much influenced by methods employed in Europe. The programme that she promoted was based on the ideas of a lengthy period of study after graduation from school to form character and gain additional knowledge; of acquired familiarity with the principles of education as a science and its methods as an art, together with practice teaching; and of the testing of candidates by competent examiners who issued certificates as a guarantee of efficiency. The proposed college would combine a general education and instruction in the science of education. It would offer training, assessment and licensing. The Skinner Street Training College was launched in 1876 to realise this programme – it was a day college that admitted women over the age of 17 (on production of a school certificate) into one of three levels of education. The first two principals, Agnes Ward (1876–92) and Alice Woods espoused progressive educational views; Woods proposed parent/ school co-operation and the introduction of co-education. Numbers were small (18 students in 1881; 32 students in 1891) but growing and in 1885 the college moved to Fitzroy Square, assumed the name Maria Grey Training College, and placed itself under university inspection, thus guaranteeing its reputation and its academic standards. The introduction at Cambridge of the Teacher Training Syndicate in 1879 (which began an examination in the history, theory and practice of education) confirmed the status of 'education' as a discipline and as worthy of academic study, but the work of Maria Grey and her associates was instrumental in developing this subject by rethinking the curriculum.

The curriculum debate and curriculum studies

Women educators joined in the 1870s to reject the idea that education put too much strain on women's health and reproductive capacity.[37] All were in a position, therefore, to prescribe a rigorous intellectual education for women. Yet Maria Grey and her associates were more radical in their thinking about the curriculum for higher education than were Emily Davies and her friends. Dorothea Beale (1831–1906), for example, promoted the serious study of modern languages and history.[38] Her contribution to the journal The Nineteenth Century justified and outlined this curriculum. History was included not to make girls 'ornaments' but to see that pupils become 'better, wiser, abler'; modern languages were not to allow conversation but to enlarge the sympathies with a new literature. A woman's role as educator would be enhanced by a broad curriculum and diminished by mimicking the impoverished and narrow curriculum offered boys. In the long run, both sexes 'should move on together to a higher ideal not as yet realised by either; and perhaps it may be even given to the girls, "the weak things of the earth", to improve the boys'. Davies was criticised by both male and female educators for tying the curriculum at Girton to the outmoded Cambridge model and standards, and for eschewing study of history, modern languages and literature and natural sciences. Davies's arguments against separateness stemmed from her concerns for the em-powerment of women in a man's world.[39] She feared that a reformed curriculum might be impoverished and inferior. At Girton women were made to pursue exactly the same course as men within the same time, even though they were relatively ill-prepared by their former education. Davies believed that, until men reformed the curriculum, women should follow the old syllabus. The 'uncompromising party' established Girton College, Cambridge and Somerville College, Oxford. Those in favour of an inno-vative curriculum for women founded Newnham College, Cambridge and Lady Margaret Hall, Oxford. The debate spilled over into the school and training college curriculum, especially as one of the problems with Davies's policy was that girls were poorly prepared to take examinations in the classics.[40] Near the close of the century the Bryce Commission discovered that in some counties of England and Wales there was virtually no secondary educational provision for girls. In these more rural counties small private boarding schools, which were little more than extended families in their structure and curriculum, were ubiquitous.[41] The provision of schools and the curriculum to be taught in them were major issues.[42]

   Davies's chief contribution (outside of her work in the universities) probably lay in her conviction that the quality of schools and of their women teachers could be raised through association. Interestingly, she modelled this upon the example of the clergy – a profession to which female access was denied. On 19 February 1866 she wrote to Barbara Bodichon that:

> We are about to organize a Schoolmistresses' meeting, a thing analagous to a clerical meeting, which I expect will be useful, partly as a propagandist institution, the more intelligent gradually enlightening the dark and ig-norant, and partly as a body (if it ever grows strong enough) which can speak and act with some authority.

Twenty-five women attended the inaugural meeting on 9 March 1866. The list of members sounds like a roll-call of women with progressive ideas about the education of girls and young women – Buss, Hill, Manning, Clough. This initiative formed the backbone of late nineteenth-century reform and revitalisation of women's education and provides further evi-dence of the power and authority to which women successfully laid claim when they acted in unison.

Ideas about the curriculum suited for girls and young women hinged to a great extent upon thinking about the occupational and professional opportunities available for them once their education was complete. The entanglement of the debates about female education and about the accessibility of the ancient professions to women was extreme.[43] Women, although they were frequently denied the right to deliver their own papers in public, nevertheless ensured that the issues were discussed and their own views taken into account. They presented papers to many learned societies and published essays in leading contemporary journals and newspapers, making the discussion of women's education and training a key part of the Woman Question and their own ideas its currency. Right from the start the National Association for the Promotion of Social Science provided a platform for such dialogue. For example, in 1862 Emily Davies wrote a paper entitled 'Medicine as a Profession for Women'.[44] This was read on her behalf by Mr Russell Gurney – it was regarded as inappropriate for women to speak in public.

The activist Clara Collet investigated the position of women in the labour market and was a prominent member of Charles Booth's team of social investigators in the late 1880s and early 1890s. She published items in *The Nineteenth Century*, *The Economic Journal*, *The Contemporary Review* and *The Charity Organization Review*. She attended meetings at and delivered papers to the Junior Economic Club, The South Place Ethical Society and Toynbee Hall. Her position within the Labour Department of the Board of Trade ensured that the statistics of women's education and employment were collected and given serious consideration alongside those pertaining to men. A former (and disillusioned) teacher herself, she was keen to alert women to the alternative career opportunities.[45] Collet's very positive views concerned the 'difference' between men and women and the need to recognise this difference and 'build hope of women's success in the future'. 'Girls inherit, to some extent, their intellectual capacities from their fathers, just as boys do from their mothers.' Girls, like boys, should have the opportunity to develop these natural gifts and be pointed in the direction of business, design, manufacture and farming where appropriate. The curriculum for such girls would have to be tailored accordingly.[46]

Conversely, many women argued that they were peculiarly qualified to pronounce on certain educational areas. Nursing, health visiting, midwifery, social work and domestic subjects were cases in point. The professionalisation of such occupations owed much to the difficulties women found in entering the ancient professions of law, medicine and the church.

The societies or associations established during the second half of the nineteenth century have been regarded as vehicles for the emancipation movement. They also provided a forum for women to debate

amongst themselves their expanding horizons in employment and education, the meaning and purpose of education for girls, and the nature of the
curriculum at school, training college and university.

Conclusion

Women's contributions to the discipline of education arose from their
perception of the relative educational deprivation of women. They were
enabled to make that contribution by the formal and informal associations
that they formed.[47] Through their work for the Froebel Society from
mid-century onwards, a number of women established a niche for themselves within the discipline of the philosophy of education and curriculum
studies as theorists and expositors as well as practitioners. The success of
the identification of education with 'natural development' in both the state
and private sectors owed much to their scholarship and their emerging
theories of pedagogy.

These interests were paralleled at the turn of the century by women's
study of and dedication to Montessori methods.[48] Women were often
practical scholars, using the schoolroom as their laboratory, rather than
simply communicating instructional skills. They were fascinated by child
studies and philosophies of education. They were willing to learn from
European and North American educationalists and to adapt their theories
and methods to British circumstances. Certain women, through their
espousal of specialist teacher training, became involved in debates about
the appropriate content to a teacher's own education and they drew upon
this reservoir of information on the nature of education and the individual
personality. Their ideas, their writings and their actions were to have a
profound impact upon the philosophy and curriculum of the teacher
training colleges until well after the Second World War. While their
thinking about this issue was often somewhat limited by their desire to be
recognised within a man's world, nonetheless they brought distinctive
scholarly contributions to the debate. Often these were closely related to
their world-views and their personal experiences of education: they were
prone to extrapolate from their own lives. Women also contributed extensively to the discussion of the appropriate content of the curriculum at all
levels, especially but by no means exclusively when applied to girls. Their
ideas, and their experiments, had a considerable effect on the design of the
secondary school curriculum for both boys and girls within the state system.
Practice was as important as philosophising and the scholarly activity of
the women concerned was as liable to be found within the schools and
colleges they founded or the forum of professional teachers' associations as
in the pages of books and learned journals or the proceedings of learned

societies. Yet they diverted English educational studies away from an obsession with pedagogy and into a concentration upon the meaning and purpose of education and into the development of the individual's physique, intellect, spirit and personality.

Notes

1   Joan N. Burstyn, *Victorian Education and the Ideal of Womanhood* (London, Croom Helm, 1980), pp. 131–40, on mixed views about separate spheres.

2   June Purvis, *A History of Women's Education in England* (Milton Keynes, Open University Press, 1991), p. 66.

3   Fernanda Perrone, 'Women academics in England, 1870–1930', *History of Universities*, 12 (1993), p. 350.

4   Perrone, 'Women academics', p. 348.

5   For good descriptions see Purvis, *Women's Education*, pp. 65–73, and Carol Dyhouse, *Girls Growing up in Late Victorian and Edwardian England* (London, Routledge and Kegan Paul, 1981).

6   Emily Shirreff, *Intellectual Education and Its Influence on the Character and Happiness of Women* (London, John Parker, 1858), pp. 147–8.

7   Maria Grey, *On the Education of Women*, Society of Arts, 31 May 1871.

8   Dyhouse, *Girls Growing Up*, pp. 74–6.

9   Eileen Janes Yeo, *The Contest for Social Science: Relations and Representations of Gender and Class* (London, Rivers Oram Press, 1996).

10 Kathryn Hughes, *The Victorian Governess* (London, Hambledon Press, 1993), pp. 189–92, provides an insight into the role of the governess and an excellent discussion of the 'Ladies of Langham Place'.

11 Emily Faithfull, *Shall My Daughter Learn a Business?* (London, Victoria Press, 1863); J. Butler, *Women's Work and Women's Culture* (London, Macmillan, 1869).

12 Emily Davies (1867–68) before Schools Inquiry Commission, Parliamentary Papers, *Schools Inquiry Commission, Minutes of Evidence*, 1867–68, 28, part 4, p. 239; Clara Collet, *Educated Working Women. Essays on the Economic Position of Women Workers in the Middle Classes* (London, P. S. King, 1902).

13 For such an approach see Martha Vicinus, *Independent Women* (London, Virago, 1985).

14 The influence of Rousseau's thought on the concept of separate spheres has been discussed in Barbara Corrado Pope, 'The influence of Rousseau's ideology of domesticity' in Marilyn J. Boxer & Jean H. Quataert (eds), *Connecting Spheres* (New York and Oxford, Oxford University Press, 1987), and Helen Evans Misenheimer, *Rousseau on the Education of Women* (Washington, DC, University Press of America, 1981).

15 For example, Johanna Goldschmidt, Henriette Goldschmidt, Henriette Breyman.

16 Anne Taylor Allen, 'Spiritual motherhood: German feminists and the kindergarten movement, 1848–1911', *History of Education Quarterly*, 22:3 (1982), pp. 326–7.

17 Froebel had envisaged that admission to a specific kindergarten would be regardless of class.

18 This was a Pestalozzian idea.

19 For a good introduction to the Froebel movement in England, see P. Woodham

Smith, 'History of the Froebel movement in England', in Evelyn Lawrence (ed.), *Friederich Froebel and English Education* (London, Routledge and Kegan Paul, 1969), pp. 34–94.

20   See, for a more detailed account of the curriculum of these years, Joachim Liebschner, *Foundations of Progressive Education: The History of the National Froebel Society* (Cambridge, The Lutterworth Press, 1991) pp. 28–9.

21   For example, Johann and Bertha Ronge, *A Practical Guide to The English Kindergarten* (London, Hodson, 1855).

22   Liebschner, *Foundations of Progressive Education*, p. 29.

23   Liebschner, *Foundations of Progressive Education*, p. 31.

24   Froebel Society Minutes, 1875.

25   Emily Shirreff *The Kinder-Garten: Principles of Froebel's System* (London, 1876); idem, *A Sketch of the Life of Friedrich Froebel* (London, 1877); idem, *The Kindergarten at Home* (London, 1882; 3rd edn W. H. Allen & Co. Ltd, 1894); idem, *Moral Training* (London, Philip & Son, 1892).

26   Shirreff, *The Kindergarten at Home*, p. ix.

27   Edward W. Ellsworth, *Liberators of the Female Mind: The Shirreff Sisters, Educational Reform and the Women's Movement* (Westport, Connecticut and London, Greenwood Press, 1979).

28   Buckle was a largely self-educated historian. He mastered eighteen foreign languages and was a great book collector. He was working between 1857 and 1861 towards a *History of Civilization in England*, but published only two volumes.

29   National Union for the Improvement of the Education of Women of All Classes (WEU).

30   The commitment of Maria Grey, Emily Shirreff and other women in their circle to a unified system of education is illustrated by the fact that schools of the Girls' Public Day School Company generally had their own kindergartens; in 1883 the work of training kindergarten teachers was taken over by the Skinner Street Training College which was later renamed the Maria Grey Training College: Woodham Smith, 'History of the Froebel movement in England', pp. 51, 54.

31   R. W. Rich, *The Training of Teachers in England and Wales During the Nineteenth Century* (Bath, Cedric Chivers, 1972 [1933]).

32   Frances Widdowson, *Going up into the Next Class: Women and Elementary Teacher Training, 1840–1914* (London, Women's Research and Resources Centre, 1980), pp. 15–16.

33   Angela Burdett-Coutts, 'Project for young ladies as schoolmistresses. A circular', *The Educational Guardian*, April 1858: see D. Orton, *Made of Gold: A Biography of Angela Burdett Coutts* (London, H. Hamilton, 1980).

34   E. A. Pratt, *A Woman's Work for Women* (London, Newnes, 1898); these letters were republished as *Work for Ladies in Elementary Schools* (London, Longman, 1872).

35   Dyhouse, *Girls Growing Up*, p. 41.

36   *Journal of the Women's Educational Union*, 2 (1874), pp. 132–3.

37   Dyhouse, *Girls Growing Up*, pp. 139–175.

38   D. Beale, 'Girls' schools past and present', *The Nineteenth Century* (1888), 23, pp. 541–53.

39   Burstyn, *Victorian Education*, pp. 151–3.

40   Such debates occurred at a key moment, for the Schools' Inquiry Commission of 1867–68 reported that home education of girls was still typical in wealthy middle-class homes: *Report of the Schools' Inquiry Commission, PP 1867–68*, vol. xxviii,

ch. vi, p. 558. This pattern was thought to entend down through the merchant and professional classes also: see Dyhouse, *Girls Growing Up*, p. 41.

41   Dyhouse, *Girls Growing Up*, pp. 50–1: Winifred Peck, *A Little Learning or, A Victorian Childhood* (London, Faber, 1952), pp. 59ff.

42   A useful coment on the debate can be found in the later *Report of the Consultative Committee on Differentiation of the Curriculum for Boys and Girls Respectively in Secondary Schools, 1923*. The evidence of Buss, Beale and Davies was called and summarised by the committee.

43   For a brief introduction, see Sara Delamont, 'The contradiction in ladies' education' in Sara Delamont and Lorna Duffin (eds), *The Nineteenth Century Woman: The Cultural and Physical World* (London, Croom Helm, 1978), pp. 153–60.

44   Barbara Stephen, *Emily Davies and Girton College* (London, Constable, 1927), p. 74.

45   Collet, *Educated Working Women*.

46   Collet, *Educated Working Women*, pp. 16, 18.

47   See Vicinus, *Independent Women*, for the way in which women used a particular form of association – collegial living and working – to develop a distinctive form of scholarly endeavour which combined a period for self-development with preparation for future life.

48   For this see, for example, the introduction of Montessori methods at Dunhurst Preparatory School, Bedales by Mrs Fish and Amy Clarke: see Roy Wake and Pennie Denton, *Bedales School, The First Hundred Years* (London, Haggerston Press, 1993), pp. 212–15.

Mary Cowden Clarke's labours of love

Cicely Palser Havely

Now that machines can do so much laborious computation, it is hard to imagine the scale of Mary Cowden Clarke's undertaking in compiling the first systematic concordance to the dramatic works of Shakespeare. In fact, it was the first concordance to *any* body of secular literature in English. Every word in every play had to be arranged alphabetically with the line in which it occurs and the scene reference. When *The Complete Concordance to Shakspere* (sic) was published in 1844 it contained approximately 309,600 entries. It had taken sixteen years to compile. The labour it saved its many users can only be guessed at. Half-remembered quotations could be speedily identified; exhaustive surveys of innumerable themes in the plays became feasible, and the foundations were laid for systematic studies of the linguistic characteristics of Shakespeare's works. Victorian productivity in literary studies was as prodigious as in other kinds of manufacture, and Mary Cowden Clarke had built a machine which stimulated output in the favoured critical practices of her day.

Much of her copious publication after the *Concordance* exploited the minute knowledge of Shakespeare's plays which she had amassed during its compilation. It can be roughly divided into two categories, on the one hand what would now be recognised as scholarly work, and on the other, the popular. In the first category belong both her editions of the complete plays (1858 and 1864–68) and the compendious work (shared with her husband Charles) on Shakespeare's stagecraft, the *Shakespeare Key* (1872); and in the second her best-seller, *The Girlhood of Shakespeare's Heroines* (1850). But it is doubtful that she would have recognised any division between the popular and the scholarly, and, as I shall show, that was as much to do with the special place of Shakespeare in Victorian culture, as it was with Mary Cowden Clark's eclectic approach to her work, though in many respects her broad range was typical of the Victorian 'woman of letters'. While Shakespeare was her main subject, she also found time to write children's stories, a novel and quantities of decorative verse, as well as a low-life pastiche of *Hiawatha*.

Educating a 'woman of letters'

Her family background combined a respect for diligence, expertise and attention to detail with insatiable enthusiasm for genteel amusements. Her father, the musicologist Vincent Novello, was Mendelssohn's sponsor in London, and his publishing firm's canny acquisition of the rights to Mendelssohn's work suggests how well attuned they were to middle-class taste. Clara, Mary's sister, trained intensively from an early age to become the finest soprano of her day. Their mother combined charm with iron determination and 'regarded child-rearing as one of the fine arts'.[1] All the children, boys and girls, were educated by their parents at home, and by expert tutors when they reached an appropriate standard. Mary seems to have grown up taking it for granted that she would work, not so much from financial necessity (the family was never poor) but because it was normal in her circle to find worthwhile employment of some kind. Nevertheless, she was proud of her earnings.[2] *My Long Life*, the autobiographical sketch she wrote in 1897, records how she became a governess for a brief period after a year spent in France to learn the language when she was fifteen, and she later used her linguistic skills to translate from both French and Italian in order to contribute to a family enterprise, *Novello's Library for the Diffusion of Musical Knowledge*.

Her spell as a governess was not traumatic, but although she enjoyed 'amiable consideration'[3] from her employer, she left happily enough to marry a family intimate of long standing. Charles Cowden Clarke is now best known as Keats's early mentor. His father had supported the radical journalist Leigh Hunt, who was imprisoned for his unflattering reflections on the Prince Regent, and so the Cowden Clarkes became part of a circle which included Keats, Byron, the Lambs, Haydon, Edgeworth, Bentham, James Mill, the Shelleys, Hazlitt and Godwin – as well as the Novellos, who were frequent hosts to 'the brightest, most cosmopolitan assemblages' in 'artistic, middle class London'.[4] They partied, talked and sang endlessly, though Keats, shortly before severing his connection, wrote of being 'so completely tired' by 'a complete set to of Mozart and punning at the Novellos's that one senses that the jollity may have been a touch relentless'.[5] Charles was twenty years her senior but not discernibly a father-figure; later, when her fame outstripped her husband's, there is no evidence of discomfort on Charles's part, as there might have been had the relationship not been a sound and equal partnership.

The couple were not wealthy when they married in 1828, and in *My Long Life* Mary Cowden Clarke records that 'I resumed, more warmly than ever, my desire to earn some contribution to the our family income, as it was my parents' kind promise that I, as well as this new well-loved member ... should continue to reside with them'.[6] She began to publish brief articles at the same time as her mother, whose children were all out of the nursery, took up writing stories and novels herself. Twelve-year-old Clara was studying at the Paris Conservatoire, and her father was editing and publishing Handel and Purcell. Charles's popular literary lectures had not yet taken off, though he was later to become a star in that circuit. But he made a living as a free-lance journalist and drama critic, and Mary accompanied him on his visits to the theatre. Thus although her output at this stage was slender, they were a professional couple in a middle-class household. Perhaps they anticipated children, but the marriage was to be unproductive in this respect – a factor which tends to facilitate a woman's career when there are no regrets either.

Indeed, hers was a fortunate life: she came from a nurturing background and encountered no major hardships or unhappinesses. Most of the adversities which often seem to be characteristic of women's aspirational lives are absent here, or at least barely present. Nor is there much evidence that she felt seriously frustrated by any domestic or social restrictions. In her circle, where the cosmopolitan, liberal and unconventional values of her parents combined with Charles's dissenting, republican background and the often controversial achievements of their many friends, intellectual labour and public responsibility were expected of women as well as men. It was thus in a situation of emotional security, and no great financial stringency, with an excellent education behind her and a constructive intellectual environment to encourage her that Mary Cowden Clarke embarked on her monumental work in 1829.

The *Concordance* as scholarly labour

Just how monumental a labour it would be she probably did not know. At the start she was a doting amateur, who self-confessedly 'hardly knew there were such things as various readings, various commentators, various factions'.[7] Sixteen years of toil followed before the first of eighteen monthly parts was issued to a distinguished list of subscribers on 1 May 1844. It was not superseded for fifty years: a remarkable shelf-life for a work of scholarship. However, her 'affectionate veneration' for Shakespeare had begun not in study of the texts, but with that best-selling children's book from her own social circle, Charles and Mary Lamb's *Tales from Shakespear* (sic).[8] Like the Lambs, she saw her work on Shakespeare as a contribution to the gossipy, musical, bookish family life idealised by Victorian society. In the absence of a professional literary academy before the last third of the nineteenth century, much Shakespearean scholarship had accumulated, but it was neither the product nor the exclusive property of a professional enclave. Clergy, a Speaker of the House, merchant-heirs of the East India Company, a parliamentary reporter and a chess champion figure amongst Shakespeare's early editors, alongside poets and the compiler of a famous dictionary. As Gary Taylor has pointed out, 'Some were educated at Universities ... none were employed by Universities until the Cambridge edition of 1863–66.'[9] The plays were a standard fitting in every middle-class Victorian home: a what-not crammed with decorative oratory and a bottomless portmanteau of handy wisdom. Mary Cowden Clarke's ambition was to provide a labour-saving device: she undertook the Concordance to answer a 'regret ... that there should be no ready clue to his quotable sentences, though they were so constantly in request'.[10]

It was not, then, a project initially conceived in a spirit of objective scholarship, but a practical tool. The labour involved was formidable, and the proportion of mechanical drudgery very high. It took twelve years to extract and order her data, another four to check it against current editions and prepare it for the press. What gives the work its claim to the scholarly status it acquired in progress is its author's diligence and reliability. Its value consisted in its completeness, as it would in any comparable work today. However, it is not in fact quite as complete as its author claims because she left out what she considered insignificant terms in order to save space. Thus, as she wrote in her Preface, 'by omitting [let] as an auxiliary verb ... and retaining it merely in its more singular sense, the space gained is the enormous difference between 17 lines and 2184 lines, or six printed pages of three columns each'. We can notice, however, that the space-saving decision was only taken at a late stage, and may have been suggested by the publisher as she had obviously *recorded* all the instances of 'let' as auxiliary verb at some point in her labours. But how or when cuts were made, Mary Cowden Clarke certainly authorised them:

> *Come, look, marry, pray, truth, truly,* and *well,* when used merely inter-
> jectionally, and *still* and *well* as adverbs, are omitted. *Like,* as an adverb
> merely conveying a simile ... titles and a few verbs (to be, have, do) are
> omitted ... also oaths and exclamations of small importance, a few peculiar
> ones only, such as *aroint, avant* etc. being retained.

Clearly, there was a stronger idiosyncratic element in her choices than she admitted. On the other hand there is no bowdlerisation: indecencies are not omitted – but then, as much of Shakespeare's indecency consists of *double entendres* she was able to side-step this delicate issue. Nor was she entirely candid in her list of omissions which actually also included all pronouns and most prepositions. Because *when, whenever* and *until* are excluded, the *Concordance* cannot be used to investigate Shakespeare's treatment of time (a problem the Clarkes analysed in their later *Shakespeare Key*) and the exclusion of 'never' and 'if' ignore what are signature terms in *Lear* and *Macbeth* respectively. I shall suggest later that Mary Cowden Clarke shared with countless other bardolators an almost mystic zeal to discover an essential Shakespeare, and so it is perhaps ironic that what finally rendered her *Concordance* obsolete was not just developments in textual scholarship, but this omission of commonplace words, for it was eventually in the deployment of apparently insignificant terms that computerised analysis now tends to locate the unique fingerprints of an author.

Scholarship and feminine toil

However, in 1844 fame was instantaneous. The Preface was originally published with the last of the eighteen parts, so she was able to record the 'generous testimonies of sympathy and encouragement from many of the cleverest men of our age, between whom and myself I could never have hoped for any assimilation, had it not been for the mutual existence of profound veneration and love for the genius of Shakespeare'. She also thanked her 'co-mates and brothers in "labour"', the printers. Her long slog had won her a gratifying entrée to a world of men who were probably very glad that a woman had relieved them of this necessary but burdensome chore. Douglas Jerrold, best known as an editor of *Punch*, greeted it as 'the patient adoration of a woman'.[11]

Other responses imply that this kind of devoted labour has a specifically feminine quality. Indeed, this factor may have contributed to the disparagement expressed by a minority. A review of Bartlett's *Shakespeare Phrase-Book* referred to the *Concordance* as the 'stupendous result of sixteen years plodding toil' and lumped her work together with a kind 'to which we can[not] give unqualified approval': that is, the parade of Shakespearean 'beauties' which had begun with William Dodds's 1752 *Beauties of Shakespeare* and included Thomas Dolby's *Shakespeare Dictionary* (1832) which was not a dictionary at all.[12] Although this reviewer has nothing more specific to say about the *Concordance*, the following gives an inkling of the uses to which he or she imagines it might be put – and which, indeed, Cowden Clarke invited:

> The Shakespeare reader who remembers vaguely the beautiful passage in which perpetual maidenhood is compared to an ungathered rose, will find, on looking under the word *rose*, a reference, with the whole line, the same line in full will be found under the words *happy, distilled*, and *earthlier*.

This was unfair, though perhaps the reviewer's choice of a 'maidenly' example indicates a semi-automatic but erroneous association of this kind of compilation with women authors. Cowden Clarke's work was vastly more systematic and thorough than Becket's so-called *Concordance* of 1787, which cited Dr Johnson's opinion that 'the plays of Shakespeare are filled with practical axioms and domestic wisdom; and that a system of civil and economical prudence may be collected from them'. Becket's very arbitrary list of terms – 'basilisk, battle, bawcock, beauty' form a typical slice – are each illustrated by passages of 1–5 lines. Forty years later, the Rev. Samuel Aysgough's *Index/to the/Remarkable passages and words/made use of by/ Shakspeare* (sic); */calculated to point out the different meanings to which the words are applied* provides no explanation of what principles might have governed its meagre and haphazard selection. Compared with this kind of subjective amateurishness (and Aysgough was an Assistant Librarian at the British Museum), Cowden Clarke's work is a triumph of methodical diligence. In the 1881 edition she cited G. L. Craik's preface to his *The English of Shakespeare* (1857) which asked 'if any equally elaborate work, literary or of any other kind, so remarkable for exactness and freedom from error, ever before proceeded from the female head or hand ...' – a backhanded compliment, but welcome to a woman who later recorded her gratitude for the way in which 'distinguished Shakespeareans have treated me with a cordial *fraternity* [her italics] as one of their brotherhood'.[13]

The *Concordance* as 'labour of love'

Although the product of her labours could be seen as gender-neutral, there are several factors *surrounding* its production to which gendered values were attached: the quality of labour which went into it was feminised, and so was Cowden Clarke's pleasure in its success and a discernible emotional element in the reception of her work which plays up the femininity of its author. The *Concordance* was both marketed and received as a labour of love, but not quite the disinterested and dispassionate love of truth which is ideally supposed to characterise the pursuit of knowledge. Cowden Clarke's love for her subject was given an erotic blush. When a group of her American admirers presented her with a monumental chair carved with scenes from the plays and built-in writing desk the celebrated dictionary compiler Daniel Webster commented that 'She has treasured up every word of Shakespeare as if he were her lover' and she participated in the eroticising of her project. Not only did Clarke include this luscious tribute in her 1881 preface to the new and revised edition, she records herself writing it 'on the morning of Valentine's day ... to celebrate The Golden Wedding of my readers with their faithful servant'. (It was fifty years since

she began her task.) She 'must expect a kiss from Shakespeare', she had
been 'playfully' assured by Douglas Jerrold, 'when she should meet him in
Paradise'.

Back on earth, her sustained correspondence (1850–61) with Robert
Balmanno, another American fan, shows the same tint of whimsical
flirtation.[14] The letters (which were eventually published as a tribute
shortly after her death) began when Balmanno sent her some elaborate
pens to thank her for the *Concordance*, describing her as 'one of the most
estimable and extraordinary women that ever existed'. Her work exhibited
'the most wonderful instincts of female perseverance ever heard of' (2 April
1850), though he also wished to enquire 'whether it was not owing to the
sweet endearing kindness and encouragement of your beloved husband that
you did not often give up in despair'. Mrs Clarke was happy to provide an
intimate if jocular response. She tells him that her likeness may be deduced
by looking at Douglas Jerrold's *Punch* description of Shakespeare's wife (11
December 1847) and soon they were calling each other father-in-love and
daughter-in-love. While there may be something ludicrous (or plaintive)
about such charged friendships, it is also worth considering that they may
be an index of liberated feelings. Although neither participated in the
correspondence, both Mrs Balmanno and Charles Cowden Clarke seem
quite happy to have been implicated in what was already a *menage à trois*,
where Balmanno was the *voyeur* of Mary Cowden Clarke's *amour* with the
bard. This sexualisation of enthusiasm suggests a transgressive thrill in
crossing the border from the domestic sphere to the public.

In any case, an air of piety dispels any suggestion of impropriety in
this emotionalism. This is a familiar tactic in women's writing throughout
this period whereby potentially sexual feelings are dissipated or obscured
by quasi-religious ecstasy. So there is a strong flavour of the more saccharin
evangelism about this mutual admiration pact with Balmanno: *nihil nisi*
niceness must touch the beloved bard's shade: 'Surely if there be one thing
more than another to be derived from his works, it is a universal spirit of
toleration and gentleness' (15 July 1853). Thus Shakespeare shades into
gentle Jesus: 'We owe it to our master, and his divine philosophy of
forbearance, not to get into vexation of spirit about his writings. Let us be
worshippers, rather than partisans' (8 December 1853). Here, suffocating
Victorian notions of unsexual womanliness can be seen to be pressing in
on her, and the upswelling of liberated emotions which followed her public
success are immediately corseted in docile proprieties.

Although her professed aim was to compile a work of textual
reference, the *Concordance* turned out to be the foundation of a life-long
project to disseminate an extended, even intimate understanding of Shakespeare. At first, the claim to a devotional and even lover-like closeness

to the object of her scholarship may seem very obviously gendered, as it is
in the rhapsodies attending the reception of her great work. But the picture
turns out to be more complex, not least because the *Concordance* helped a
host of other enthusiasts, male and female, to disinter their own intimate
relationship with Shakespeare. Typically, an amateur bardolatrist (and,
with the exception of actors, they were all amateurs at first) would trawl
the work to discover whether Shakespeare had specialised knowledge of
his or her predilections or profession. I want to return to the question of
'her' profession later, but for the moment we can note how the Rev.
H. N. Ellacombe would have been enabled to look up carp, tench, gudgeon,
eels and minnows for his charmingly quaint dissertation on *Shakespeare as
an Angler* [15] and find out that bream, chubb and grayling are unrecorded.
This apparently tells us something about the streams the bard might have
fished. Clearly, Mr Ellacombe was not too heavily encumbered by his
clerical duties. His learning goes deep, but it is clear that his endeavour is
to enlist Shakespeare in the fraternity of scholar-fishermen and to claim
not just dispassionate insight but kinship as well. Whilst other objects of
scholarly enquiry may inspire the researcher to a degree of empathy, the
extent to which Shakespeare-researchers in the nineteenth and early
twentieth centuries wanted to get to know him in a quite personal sense
is astonishing. Indeed, until modern critical theory recently announced the
Death of the Author, the underlying purpose of much Shakespeare research
seems to have been biographical: to get to know not just his mind, art and
milieu, but his personal quirks, tastes and habits; to befriend and even
espouse him. *Letters to an Enthusiast* records the publication of 'Dr Bucknill's
"Psychology of Shakespeare"' (7 August 1859). Its author, writes Cowden
Clarke, who is 'now a superintendent of a lunatic asylum shows cause why
he [one almost expects 'He': she means Shakespeare] must have made brain
diseases his peculiar investigation. Glorious privilege of matchless genius!
It makes its own all that it touches!'

Thus the work enabled fishermen, physicians *et al.* to trace a
Shakespeare in their own image, but did not allow the texts to speak for
themselves. Advertising the 1881 edition, Mary Cowden Clarke was able
to quote several favourable testimonials such as that of W. J. Fox, author
of *Lectures on the Political Morality of the Plays* (1847) who claimed that
'These ... are all the allusions to Puritans which appear ... at least, they
are all I have been able to find with the help of the Concordance' and a
Dr Ingelby who, in the manner of testimonials to all kinds of nostrums,
begins 'It is now fifteen years since I first began to use systematically your
Concordance ... the completeness and accuracy of your book still seems
to me to place it on an eminence by itself.'

Shakespeare and feminine criticism

The *Concordance* played a key part in a burgeoning scholarly enterprise which began in the latter part of the eighteenth century, created a need for such a work of reference, and then swept on re-empowered by it. Early among the relatively haphazard compendiums of Shakespeare *sententiae* which the *Concordance* was to render obsolete was Elizabeth Griffith's *The Morality of Shakespeare's Drama* (1775) which assembled the bard's observations on 'domestic ties, offices and obligations'. Gary Taylor called it the beginning of 'specifically "feminine" criticism'.[16] But Cowden Clarke's approach and practice were not *exclusively* feminine; Becket's so-called *Concordance* of 1787 (cited above) was also an attempt to harvest from the plays 'a system of civil and economic prudence', and this principle was to gain even more widespread endorsement throughout the Victorian period from men and women alike. Such compilations were eventually to guarantee Shakespeare a central place in the post-Arnoldian curriculum, since they formed a gold mine of those 'touchstones' which the author of *Culture and Anarchy* had proposed as an index of shared values. But it had been clear since long before Matthew Arnold that as a source of moral 'portable property', Shakespeare rivalled the Bible. Carlyle had dubbed him Prophet and Priest; Mary Cowden Clarke worshipped 'our master'. In such a climate the text approaches the status of the Word, and editorial responsibilities and exegesis become a search for revelation. In 1829 one of the spurs to Mary Cowden Clarke's endeavour was the fact that although there was now a Concordance to the Bible, there was none to what she called 'the Bible of the Intellectual world'. Douglas Jerrold referred to her work as 'A concordance to the only author which would not seem to be a presumptuous rivalling with that concordance which belongs to the book most important to the human race'.[17]

The moralisation of Shakespeare was not exclusively the domain of women, yet when women combed Shakespeare's texts to detect his opinions on personal morality, rather than on fishing or brain disorders, it may have been because this is an area in which traditionally they could claim a specialised expertise of their own. We know that to become a 'woman', one had to be trained. Being a 'proper woman' required a degree of expertise and, in the Victorian period especially, a professed dedication to morality was virtually a 'professional' qualification for true womanhood. Such indeed is the principle which underlies *The Girlhood of Shakespeare's Heroines* (1850), the most durable by-product of the minute knowledge of the texts Cowden Clarke acquired during the compilation of the *Concordance*. Although the extraction of moral themes from Shakespeare's texts was undertaken by men as well as women, and although women from the

American Charlotte Lennox's collection of Shakespeare's sources in the
1750s and Elizabeth Montagu's riposte to Voltaire in 1769[18] and on to
Cowden Clarke herself in the 1840s had engaged in Shakespearean enter-
prises which it would be perverse to categorise as 'feminine', there is no
doubt that the popular part of Cowden Clarke's output during the rest of
her career was both heavily moralised, and not just 'feminine' but feminist.
I have elsewhere suggested that the fifteen 'girlhoods' point to a sophisticated and insightful reading of the plays, which registers some of the things
they do not say as clearly as what they more explicitly relate.[19] As reading
for girls, the tales form a manual of moral and sexual education which,
though too ponderous for today's tastes, are clearly the forerunner of the
sensible advice disguised in romantic format aimed at modern teenagers.
They offer a glimpse into one of the most mysterious of unrecorded
discourses: Victorian sex education. That this aim was understood by her
readers is just discernible in a long list of *encomia* from Britain and America
circulated by her publishers, 'We are glad to see in how brave and womanly
a spirit our authoress touches upon all womanly questions; and in
"Isabella ..." [*Measure for Measure*] she finds fit occasion to glance at the
darkest of them.'[20]

Though her awkward prose could hardly be called frank, her range
of concerns is indeed astonishing: Lady Macbeth's girlhood is distorted
because her birth killed her mother and failed to provide a male heir – a
predicament perhaps not uncommon amongst Mary Cowden Clarke's
young readers. Ophelia was neglected by another preoccupied single parent
and abused by her carers. In one of the very few passages of attention she
has received since Altick's biography, George C. Gross wrote that:

> her refusal to countenance the behaviour of the libertine any more than
> that of his victim, her insistence upon pity and understanding for fallen
> women, and her demands for social reform show that her glances backward
> fell upon Mary Wollstonecraft [whose daughter she had known] as well
> as upon Mrs Edgeworth's moralisms.[21]

Within the limits of her society she lived and proclaimed an equal
life – and her demand for a unified sexual standard was rooted in both her
marriage and her professional status. Charles was as enthusiastic as his wife
in declaring that, 'Of all writers, no-one ought to stand so high in the love
and gratitude of women [as Shakespeare] He has been the man to lift them
from the state of vassalage and degradation [and] with a prodigality of
generosity not infrequently placed the heroes at a disadvantage with
them.'[22]

For both Clarkes, Shakespeare's supposed feminism was part of a
gospel which as his acolytes they were duty bound to proclaim. Undeterred

by the prior existence of Mrs Jameson's *Shakespeare's Heroines: Charac-teristics of Women, Moral, Political and Historical* (1832) and pausing only to undertake a survey of *all* the characters in a series for *Sharpe's London Magazine*, 'On Shakespeare's individuality in his characters' (1848–51), Mary Cowden Clarke composed a series of pen-portraits of Shakespeare's women, where 'as in a mental looking glass, we women may contemplate ourselves'.[23] From there she broadened her scope to compose 'The woman of the writers' (four substantial pieces on Chaucer, Cervantes, Spenser and Richardson, again for *The Ladies' Companion* (1851) and an illustrated volume *World-Noted Women; or Types of Womanly Attributes of All Lands and Ages* (1858) ranging from Sappho to Florence Nightingale and studded with literary references. Released perhaps from the toils of the *Concordance*, the decade following its publication was prolific and high-profile. When Charles retired from the lecture circuit and the whole Novello ménage moved first to Nice and then to Genoa, husband and wife produced more in tandem. The major work of the next twenty years was to consist of two complete editions, both with Charles, and their combined work on the *Shakespeare Key* (1872), a 'companion to the Concordance' and massively detailed study of Shakespeare's stagecraft which formed a rare exception to the general tendency for sentimental appreciation. But Mary Cowden Clarke continued to mine the popular vein until her last years, and on 4 June 1887 published an admonitory article in *The Girls' Own Paper*: 'Shakespeare as the girl's friend'.[24] The first specific lesson is how to forgive erring lovers and husbands. Then, 'Another lesson, in minor morals and in discreet conduct, may be gathered by the young girl who is wooed by an urgent suitor when his previous life has not been all that her prudent parents approve.'

Shakespeare provided for forty years both the source and the buttress of her specialised womanly wisdom and professional expertise as the mentor of young girls – a status she could claim because of her reputation as Shakespeare's special friend and the compiler of his *Concordance*. A Vic-torian agony aunt is no less entitled to exploit the Shakespearean *oeuvre* in her own interests than a fishing vicar.

There is no space here for a history of the histories of Shakespeare criticism, but some recent approaches perpetuate the neglect of Cowden Clarke. In *Reinventing Shakespeare* (1990) Gary Taylor bundled her into a subsection of his chapter on *Victorian Values* 'in which our hero makes the acquaintance of a number of young ladies'. He begins with a choice snippet from the American Richard Grant White who claimed that women in general don't care for Shakespeare 'with the exception of a few who are not always the most loveable or the happiest of the sex'[25] and proceeds to erect on this generalisation a fearful composite: the virginal Shakespearecastrator. Taylor seized upon the fact that much of Dr Thomas Bowdler's *Family Shakespeare* was the work of sister Henrietta, and that the Lambs' *Tales* were more Mary than Charles. To these he added Mary Cowden Clarke's collaboration with 'her brother' Charles to produce their joint edition of the plays and declares that

> these women gave their siblings and their society a nineteenth century exemplar of ideal womanhood: what Shelley invoked as 'Spouse! Sister! Angel!' what Baudelaire addressed as 'Mon enfant, ma soeur,' a compound child-wife-sister. In return, a brother gave these women what they needed (a male patron) but did not burden them with the complications or subordinations of sex and motherhood.[26]

The poor dears also absolved themselves from the responsibility of appearing to understand Shakespeare's sexual references by sheltering behind their brothers' names. Thus hidden, they attacked. 'In the nineteenth century, as never before, women and children shaped the prevailing image of Shakespeare.'[27] But who had shaped the image of women and children? For once, Taylor's understanding of the wider cultural context has given way to grotesque distortion. He seems completely to have forgotten how much of women's production has immemorially been subsumed in that of their menfolk. Then after disempowering them with ridicule, he reinvests women with the power to shape the national hero. Of course the Victorian Shakespeare *was* a re-write; he was their contemporary as much as ours – or anyone's. But Victorian values were not unilaterally determined by women and children, though they were imposed in their name; and given the prevalence (even stranglehold) of such values, an unmodified Shakespeare would have been as unthinkable on the Victorian stage or in the Victorian curriculum as Restoration comedy.

In some respects women's literary labours seem to have been as nicely demarcated as the distinction between the foundry and the mill and, with the exception of Shakespeare, women critics concerned themselves much less with drama and playwrights than with other literary forms. Shakespeare alone seems to have escaped the ambiguous taint of the stage, but as we have seen he was attracting the attention of scholarly women from the mid-1700s – far too early for this to be a Victorian phenomenon. What is more, anyone who troubles to look at any of the examples of what Taylor dismisses may be surprised. Cleopatra might be expected to put a Victorian matron to the blush, but Anna Jameson coolly anticipated today's appreciation of the play's systematic self-reflectiveness to note the 'antithetical construction of the character, its consistent inconsistency ... [and] compound of contradictions of all that we most hate with what we most admire'.[28] Mary Cowden Clarke and Anna Jameson were by no means the only Victorian women to endorse masculine standards for feminine conduct whilst protesting about how men make it difficult to maintain them. But even where there is gender-bias in the readings of these authors it cannot be criticised as if the prevailing readings were gender-neutral. One only has to think of A. C. Bradley's magisterial pronouncement on *Anthony and Cleopatra* ('She destroys him') to realise just how much gender-bias in Shakespeare criticism was until quite recently the invisible norm.[29]

The scope of women's literary criticism and scholarship in the Victorian period seems to have been limited by the appropriateness of the subject for feminine scrutiny. Otherwise one might ask, if Shakespeare, why not Christopher Marlowe? Marlowe was virtually invented during the nineteenth century and might have offered women scholars plenty of career opportunities. Yet in *Rediscovering Marlowe* [30] Thomas Dabbs shows that no women took part in the endeavour. Whereas Shakespeare and his texts could be blurred with the scriptures, as we have seen, no such sentimental confusion was possible in Marlowe's case.

Although the 'facts' of his life are as unreliable as much of the Shakespeare biography, most of them were much more discreditable. Nor could his work be trawled for moral precepts or lofty aphorisms. As the subject of popular lectures he was praised for his mighty line, his dramatic power and a crude splendour which made Shakespeare seem all the more remarkable and refined. But no one was going to compile an essay on Marlowe's women, and their girlhoods were better undisclosed. There could be no place for him at the family hearth. The only female to feature in Dabbs's whole story was the entirely apocryphal 'well-meaning woman' who was blamed for insisting upon the removal from the first Mermaid edition of Marlowe's supposed self-indictment 'That all that love not Tobacco and Boies were fools'. Perceived moral restrictions limited the scope of women's labour just as much in the scholarly workplace as elsewhere.

Even without the operations of gender prejudice Cowden Clarke's scholarship would have been superseded. It has not just disappeared; it survives degraded as a faint but preposterous ghost of Victorian values. But even some of her contemporaries did not take her quite seriously. A caustic review of the *Girlhoods* commented on 'the young ladies of Mrs Clarke's seminary ... alas, poor dears, if they only knew what is to come!'[31] Her pioneering status in the *Concordance* and the *Shakespeare Key* with Charles might have been better respected today if she had not so wholeheartedly subscribed to the more popular tastes of her age as well as its passion for hard work. But it was surely because she was so well tuned to the temper of her times that she was able in old age to record that 'I have been blessed with a greatly privileged and happy life.'[32]

Subversion seems to have formed no conscious part of her

achievement. She seems to have been driven by a desire to belong to a masculine literary milieu. Perhaps the contrast between the obsessive gregariousness of her social circle and the lonely monotony of her sixteen years' labour on the *Concordance* made acceptability – and especially acceptability amongst men – the goal she sought. She called the printers her 'brothers'; she revelled in the acclaim of predominantly male fellow scholars. But she also allowed and encouraged a cult of personality to arise from the singularity of her achievement. Perhaps in her way she was one of the first multi-media scholar-superstars, a type which attracts even more envy and contempt today. She was prone to the notorious Queen Bee syndrome, attributed to personalities as diverse as George Eliot and Margaret Thatcher. Scholarship might seem to be nowhere more self-effacing than in the compilation of a Concordance, and self-effacement is proverbially the duty of a modest woman, but Cowden Clarke's achievement paradoxically catapulted her into a glamorous exposure which she relished. She seems, however, to have been instinctively aware of the glass ceiling where celebrity became notoriety for the Victorian woman, and safeguarded herself with a moral agenda endorsed by Shakespeare. She may have been unusual, smug or self-deluding, but the apparently easy-going conformity of her life was (and perhaps always is) a rare achievement. It is the same sense of swimming happily with the prevailing tide which both ensured her success and shortened her fame. She may have been too much of her time to survive it.

Notes

1   R. D. Altick, *The Cowden Clarkes* (Oxford, Oxford University Press, 1948), p. 7. Altick's biogaphy is the only modern account of a couple who both frequently figure in the letters and biogaphies oftheir contemporaries. Otherwise, little attention has been given to either in this century.

2   Mary Cowden Clarke, *My Long Life: An Autobiograhic Sketch* (London, T. Fisher Unwin, 1896), p. 37.

3   Cowden Clarke, *My Long Life*, p. 37.

4   Altick, *The Cowden Clarkes*, p. 31

5   Letter to George and Georgiana Keats, 6 December 1818–4 January 1819. H. E. Rollins (ed.), *The Letters of John Keats 1814–1821* Harvard University Press (Cambridge, Mass., 1958, vol 2, p. 11. Letter no. 137. Earlier in the same letter Keats writes of being 'devastated and excruciated with bad and repeated puns' at the Novellos.

6   Cowden Clarke, *My Long Life*, p. 44.

7   Altick, *The Cowden Clarkes*, p. 117.

8   *Shakespeariana*, vol. V, October 1888, no. LVIII, pp. 443–4.

9   G. Taylor, *Reinventing Shakespeare* (London, Hogarth, 1990), p. 185.

10 *Shakespeariana*, vol. V, October 1988, no. LVIII, pp. 443–4.

11   *Shilling Magazine*, January 1846.

12   *The Century Magazine*, vol. 4, New York, 1852.

13   Cowden Clarke, *My Long Life*, pp. 226–7.

14   A. U. Nettleton (ed.) (1902), *Letters to An Enthusiast* (Chicago, A. C. McClurg, 1902).

15   *Antiquary*, October 1881.

16   Taylor, *Reinventing Shakespeare*, p. 206.

17   *Shilling Magazine*, January 1846.

18   C. Lennox, *Shakespeare Illustrated* (London, A. Millar, 1753–54); E. Montagu, *Essay on the Writings and Genius of Shakespeare* (London, J. Dodsley et al., 1769).

19   C. P. Havely, C. P., 'Saying the unspeakable: Mary Cowden Clarke and *Measure for Measure*', *Durham University Journal*, 87:2 (1995), pp. 233–42.

20   The only reference given is 'New Monthly *Belle Assemble*'.

21   G. C. Gross, 'Mary Cowden Clarke, "The girlhood of Shakespeare's heroines" and the sex education of Victorian women', *Victorian Studies*, 16:1 (1972), pp. 37–58.

22   C. C. Clarke, *Shakespeare – Characters* (London, Smith Elder, 1863).

23   *The Ladies' Companion*, 1849–50, 1854.

24   *The Girls' Own Paper*, 4 June 1887.

25   R. G. White, 'On reading Shakespeare', in idem, *Studies in Shakespeare* (London, Sampson Low, 1885).

26   Taylor, *Reinventing Shakespeare*, p. 207.

27   Taylor, *Reinventing Shakespeare*, p. 209.

28   A. Jameson, *Characteristics of Women, Moral, Political and Historical*, 2 vols (London, 1832), p. 218.

29   A. C. Bradley, *Oxford Lectures on Poetry* (London, Macmillan, 1909).

30   T. Dabbs, *Reforming Marlowe* (Lewisburg, Pa, Bucknell University Press, 1991).

31   *Chambers Journal*, new series, XV (1851), p. 183.

32   Cowden Clarke, *My Long Life*, 3.

Women historians and documentary research: Lucy Aikin, Agnes Strickland, Mary Anne Everett Green and Lucy Toulmin Smith[1]

Anne Laurence

In 1851 a petition signed by eighty-three people was presented to the Master of the Rolls (who was responsible for the preservation of public records); signatories included Thomas Carlyle, Charles Dickens, Thomas Babington Macaulay, Harrison Ainsworth and three women: Lucy Aikin (1781–1864), Agnes Strickland (1796–1874) and Mary Anne Everett Green (1818–95). The petitioners called for payment for consulting public records to be waived for people engaged on serious literary or historical scholarship, arguing that the fees were set for lawyers who consulted only a few documents, while literary and historical researchers often needed to consult many as 'the only sure foundation of historical truth'.[2] The petition was successful and in 1852 fees for such researchers were abolished.[3]

These women were among many writers who signed the petition because of the importance they placed upon the use of historical documents to give authenticity to their historical writing. Their claims to write authoritatively about the past were grounded upon their use of the original materials of the past; their claims to have their work regarded as scholarly were based on their discovery and deciphering of documents; and their claims to have their work considered alongside that of men relied upon their presenting the evidence of their labours by printing hitherto unpublished historical materials. Their careers were not dissimilar from those of a number of male historians who made their livings as writers and literary figures. However, such careers became more difficult for women to pursue as a historical profession defined by doing historical research rather than by writing came into being during the nineteenth century.

The three women signatories were well known as authors. Lucy Aikin's most famous work was *Memoirs of the Court of Queen Elizabeth*, but she had retired from writing, being 70 at the time of the petition.[4] Agnes Strickland was celebrated for her *Lives of the Queens of England*, and, at the age of 55, was at the height of her powers. Mary Anne Everett Green, aged 43, had edited the *Letters of Royal and Illustrious Ladies of Great Britain*, and was working on *Lives of the Princesses of England*. A fourth woman, Lucy Toulmin Smith (1838–1911), who was particularly noted for her scholarly editions of late medieval texts for the Camden and the Early English Text Societies, continues the story into the twentieth century. The careers of these four women cover the century; they shared a concern for using original documents to reveal the 'authentic' voice of the people and ages of which they wrote, but the ways in which they used these documents, as well as their lives and careers, embody the changes that took place in the practice and profession of history during the nineteenth century.

History and historians

Before the nineteenth century history writing had characteristically been associated with male authors, in much the same way that history painting was seen as a largely masculine genre.[5] In the early part of the nineteenth century women writers took advantage of the public appetite for historical works on the women of the past, in a manner which might be said to conform to 'Thirsk's law'.[6] This appetite seems to have been created by the impending succession of the young Princess Victoria to the throne when a great flurry of books about queens and princesses appeared. Anna Jameson, for example, produced *Memoirs of Celebrated Female Sovereigns* (1831); and Hannah Lawrance published *Historical Memoirs of the Queens of England* (1838). Certain individuals, notably Elizabeth of Bohemia (the Winter Queen) and Mary Queen of Scots, were particularly popular subjects. Interest in women of the past continued after Victoria's accession and authors moved on to foreign queens with such works as Mrs Forbes Bush's *Memoirs of the Queens of France* (1843); Julia Pardoe's *Memoirs of the Queens of Spain* (1850) and Emma Willsher Atkinson's *Memoirs of the Queens of Prussia* (1858). Publishers seem to have felt that, by virtue of their femininity, women could write authoritatively about female historical characters, giving special insights into the private and domestic sides of the lives of public characters, especially of women of the past.

Thus, in the early nineteenth century, many women found recognition as historical writers. We might call them 'women of letters' who wrote on historical subjects, using the authority of original documents to substantiate their narratives. Some, such as Strickland, made a good living from such writing; others, such as Aikin, did it for interest and occupation, but recognition of their work by reviewers in the periodical press depended upon confining themselves to historical subjects judged suitable for women's attention, chiefly biographies and memoirs.[7]

These supplemented the historical narratives of such leading male practitioners as Edward Gibbon (1737–94), Thomas Carlyle (1795–1881), and T. B. Macaulay (1800–59), given the status of sages, and educated in the classics and in the amateur, liberal humanist tradition of the British universities, respectively Oxford, Edinburgh and Cambridge. Women writers provided accounts of the private lives of public characters, often dealing with subjects which male historians did not touch upon, the lives of women and children for example. No woman historian in the nineteenth century was accorded a similar standing or acquired so high a reputation as the celebrated, but quickly forgotten, republican Catherine Macaulay (1731–91) had had in the eighteenth century.[8]

The changes which took place in the practice and profession of history during the nineteenth century created both a new kind of history and a new kind of historian. History writing by both men and women was regarded in the early years of the century as a branch of literature and history was read for entertainment and moral instruction. Under the influence of German scholarship and, in particular, of the writings of Leopold von Ranke the study and presentation of history was transformed into a subject to be written according to neutral, 'scientific' principles.[9] Von Ranke's work itself was disseminated in Britain in translation, much of which was by women.[10] The intellectual authority of historical writing ceased to be regarded as a moral matter, and came to rely upon detailed and accurate reference to the materials of the past.

The demand for free and open access to public records was both evidence of and contributed to the changes which took place, changes which affected women in rather different ways from men. The consolidation of records in the Public Record Office, the establishment of the various record series (collections of printed documents) and of the Historical Manuscripts Commission in the 1860s and 1870s were part of a larger process by which a profession of people came into being who made their livings from full-time historical research rather than from the pursuit of literature. History was integrated into the formal curriculum of the universities and research into history was promoted by the foundation of historical societies. From the 1870s, practitioners' credentials were established by the training of a university degree in history, and by membership of historical associations, universities and record-keeping bodies. The creation of this 'academy' for history validated men's expertise and created a profession which largely excluded women except as assistants to men and confirmed their restriction to writing in particular historical genres.[11]

Everett Green's later career and Toulmin Smith's work took place under this new dispensation under which women were relegated to such tasks as the compilation of collections of documents, indexes, calendars and translations, which drew upon their supposed 'natural' talents for detailed, painstaking, meticulous work. Otherwise, they were restricted to writing historical works which were disregarded by the academy.[12] Women found new careers; but such careers were subordinate to those of men, were poorly paid and carried little status. Those women who wished to pursue serious historical studies had to service male historians in prestigious university posts by supplying them with the materials for writing 'academic' history, or had to write 'popular' history and children's books.

Women historians

Under these circumstances it might seem surprising that any women managed to make reputations for themselves as historians, but all four were well known during their lifetimes. Their posthumous reputations have fared rather differently. Few people now read the historical writings of Aikin and Strickland, even though they include quantities of unpublished correspondence; Strickland herself was inordinately proud of having rehabilitated Mary of Modena's reputation. Yet there is scarcely a historian of seventeenth-century England who has not consulted Everett Green's *Calendars* of the domestic state papers in the Public Record Office and Toulmin Smith's text remains one of the definitive editions of the *Itinerary* of the sixteenth-century antiquary, John Leland.

Natalie Zemon Davis, writing of earlier generations of women historians, has suggested that there are four preconditions for women to write history: a woman needs access to genres of historical writing and familiarity with modes of historical discourse; access to historical materials and enough of a public life to go out and make use of them; 'a sense of connection, through some activity or deep concern of her own, with the areas of public life then considered suitable for historical writing'; and, finally, an audience who will take her seriously.[13] In the lives and careers of all four women we can see how they negotiated these conditions.

Their education and family backgrounds were an important part of providing them with a knowledge of historical writing. All four were educated at home, largely at the direction of their fathers. They learnt foreign languages and read extensively in historical subjects, probably more widely and in greater depth than would have been the case had they gone to school. Of the two Strickland sisters who collaborated on the works which came out under Agnes's name, Elizabeth seems to have been the more proficient at research and she did much of the more difficult work; some doubt exists as to Agnes's linguistic abilities and she admitted to being unable to read fifteenth-century handwriting.[14] Everett Green had been better prepared, for after her marriage in 1846 to the painter George Pycock Green, she accompanied him abroad, using her time in Paris and Antwerp to read foreign historical materials.

As important as what these women actually learnt were their family backgrounds and connections, both in fostering the desire to write and, in some cases, providing opportunities for publication. The fathers of Aikin and Toulmin Smith were themselves well-known writers, both Unitarians, and Everett Green's father was a Methodist minister. These nonconformist connections were significant in their emphasis upon education for women, and for providing a favourable environment for the daughters' work. Aikin's father edited the periodicals the *Athenaeum* and the *Annual Register*, where her earliest published work appeared, and her aunt was the poet Anna Lætitia Barbauld. Lucy Toulmin Smith had long acted as amanuensis to her father, the writer and historian Joshua Toulmin Smith. Everett Green was named after her father's friend, the writer and historian of Methodism, James Everett. In contrast, the Anglican Strickland family had shown no previous disposition to writing, though other sisters and a brother later capitalised upon Elizabeth and Agnes's publishing success.[15]

If family connections could provide the opportunity for getting work published, filial piety could provide the impetus. In 1823 Aikin produced a memoir of her father and in 1826 a collection of miscellaneous works by her aunt, while Everett Green produced a privately printed memoir of her father. Toulmin Smith's early historical work was the result of her collaboration with her father; her first publication was an edition of deeds which he had been in the course of preparing at the time of his death in 1869, and her early solo publications carried on his work.[16]

As adults they all used the British Museum library, circulating libraries, and the extensive private libraries and manuscript collections of ancient families and of such antiquarian collectors as Sir Thomas Phillipps. Before the Public Record Office search rooms opened to the public in 1861, access to documents could be difficult. Trying to look at the State Papers in 1837, when the permission of the Prime Minister or Home Secretary was required, Agnes Strickland had 'met with an uncourteous repulse' from Lord John Russell, at which she was 'surprised and somewhat indignant'. Only after the intercession of various influential people was she successful.[17]

It was not enough to use and refer to documents; describing the search for sources was part of the process of establishing the historical

authenticity of these women's work. However, Strickland, the most gushing
of the four, sounds positively restrained by comparison with Carlyle. She
wrote of finding documents for her *Lives of the Queens* in 'repositories,
where they have slumbered among the dust of centuries, to afford their
silent, but incontrovertible evidence', while Carlyle, of collecting Cromwell's letters and speeches, wrote, 'I have gathered them from far and near;
fished them up from the foul Lethean quagmires where they lay
buried'.[18] Strickland perhaps made rather more of this than the other three
because she relied heavily on transcripts or edited versions made by others,
as, for example, the material on Mary Queen of Scots 'buried among the
almost inaccessible manuscripts of the Imperial Library at St Petersburgh'.[19]
Strickland was a tireless visitor to the sites of the events and lives of which
she wrote, believing strongly in the genius of place as a source of authenticity. For example in 1844 she went to the cathedral of St Denis to look
for the remains of Queen Henrietta Maria, and to St Germain to see
whether any traditions of the exiled court of James II and Mary of Modena
had survived.[20]

     Their publishing careers and their search for historical material gave
all four women a public life apart from their families. Strickland was
interested chiefly in mixing socially with the families whose royal and noble
ancestors she was researching. She was delighted to be treated 'like a
high-priestess' on visiting the Duke of Cleveland.[21] Her priorities in 1863
were summed up by her sister: 'Agnes, as usual, was in the whirl of society
in London; but being obliged to study at the British Museum, was glad
when she could get time for that purpose, not very easy for her to procure'.[22]
Agnes paid little attention to the work of other historians and did not seek
their approval; she was more concerned to be considered alongside women
of literary repute and sought the good opinion of such writers as Anna
Jameson and Lydia Howard Sigourney.[23]

     The other three women moved in rather different milieux. Aikin
and Toulmin Smith grew up in Unitarian families, mixing with people
with intellectual concerns and reforming interests. Amongst Aikin's oldest
friends was the Norwich nonconformist Taylor family, one of whom was
Sarah Austin, through whom she met Carlyle, Bentham and Mill. Aikin
remarked that she herself had had 'personal acquaintance with more or less
every literary woman of celebrity who adorned English society'.[24] Toulmin
Smith, two generations younger, had a wide acquaintance among literary
and historical editors and the men who had posts in the universities and
record-keeping bodies, as well as such younger historians as Mary Bateson.
Both her memorialist and her biographer noted the hospitality she offered
at her house in Oxford and her accomplishments as housewife and
gardener.[25] Everett Green held court at her house in Gower Street with

her son and three daughters, and was visited there by such people as Geraldine Jewsbury. She moved in the world of journalism, of which she did a good deal to make ends meet, though she became also very well known in the historical establishment.[26]

These women's sense of connection with the past had a variety of different origins. For Aikin and Toulmin Smith it is clear that their fathers' interests were significant. Agnes Strickland's fascination with the past was closely linked to her interest in her own distant ancestors, the northern Catholic Strickland family. She was also inspired by her identification with the character of Mary Queen of Scots. The romance of contact with historical materials (manuscripts are often referred to as 'precious' in her letters) and the opportunities for mixing with peers and their families in great houses fired her imagination. Her correspondence with Philip Howard of Corby Castle about his manuscripts includes her verses in praise of the Howard family.[27] Pride in ancestry played little part in Everett Green's interest in the past; in 1844 she wrote 'I have no high descent whatever to boast of', adding that as her father and grandfather had been Wesleyan ministers, 'their itinerant habits prevent their being personally associated with any particular locality', though she did compile a pedigree for the Sydenham family with whom she was connected.[28] She described coming to historical research as if it were almost accidental, saying that she and her artist husband: 'were engaged before I began to dabble in antiquities myself. However, we make a sort of compromise. I love pictures for his sake and he treats old books and manuscripts with all proper deference and respect for mine.'[29]

It is clear, however, that unlike Natalie Zemon Davis's earlier history women, making money was as important as a sense of connection with the past. Writing history or producing editions of historical documents allowed them to earn a living. Only Aikin came from such comfortable circumstances (both her father and her aunt had been very successful and widely-read authors) that income was of secondary importance; she also had relatively modest domestic needs, living with relatives for most of her life and observing in 1832, 'Profit I have no need of, and of reputation I have all I want'.[30]

The Stricklands' spur to writing arose from the financial straits in which the family found itself after Mr Strickland's death in 1818. While Agnes wrote, her domestic life was looked after by her mother and, latterly, by various sisters. She had initially pinned her hopes on selling her poetry, but she was more successful with the children's books and journalism which she and Elizabeth published during the 1820s and 1830s. Her historical writing arose directly from her journalism, for Elizabeth edited the *Court Journal* where she had published the lives of a number of female sovereigns.

Agnes then had the idea of turning these into a book. Initially, the sisters made little money from the *Lives of the Queens* but it soon became extremely successful, selling in large numbers in numerous different formats.[31] Elizabeth lived in a retiring fashion, but Agnes's social ambitions required a considerable income and her sense of achievement was crowned when, in 1870, she was granted a civil list pension of £100 a year.[32]

Both Everett Green and Toulmin Smith looked to their writing for an income. For Everett Green this was a pressing need when she had to take over as principal breadwinner when her husband became disabled. From 1853 she worked as a part-time assistant sorting and calendaring the mass of material arriving at the Public Record Office, work she continued to do for nearly forty years. She referred to her writing being done in her leisure, though much of it was paid journalism.[33] Toulmin Smith had to earn her living by her pen until, at the age of fifty-six, she was appointed librarian of Manchester College, Oxford, a Unitarian college associated with the university, a post she held until her death in 1911.

Their achievements in earning their living depended to a large extent upon their popularity as writers, which in turn demanded that there be an audience for their work. After the success of *Lives of the Queens of England*, Strickland showed her understanding of the value of her name to the sales of her work. Negotiating with Blackwoods to publish *Lives of the Queens of Scotland*, she wrote: 'I think the English tourists will carry off a vast number of copies in October, and that it is sure to be the drawing table book of the aristocratic and wealthy classes.'[34] All these women published their historical work under their own names following contemporary conventions for historical writing, though Everett Green sought the advice of her friend, the bibliomaniac Sir Thomas Phillips, on the delicate matter of whether, when she was married, she should publish under her maiden or married name.[35] This use of their real identities did not extend to all their literary output. They also published, anonymously, journalism, books, essays and poems on a variety of subjects, some of which they acknowledged as their own after the success of their historical works.

Their historical works often fared badly at the hands of reviewers, despite their large sales and popularity with the public.[36] Aikin was taken to task for her partisanship of Joseph Addison in a review in the *Athenæum*.[37] Macaulay was almost certainly the author of an article in the *Edinburgh Review* in 1847, attacking Strickland's lives of the Stuart queens in overtly gendered terms with the words 'ladies who assume masculine functions must learn to assume masculine gravity and impartiality'.[38] A satirical description in *Blackwood's Magazine* in 1851 referred to her as a 'literary woman of business and not the antique man of study'.[39] The editions of documents, lists and calendars produced by Everett Green and

Toulmin Smith did better, possibly because they exposed to public view the qualities for which women were praised and concealed those for which they were denigrated. A memorial notice for Toulmin Smith referred to 'the valuable masculine training' which emancipated her from the 'sloven-liness and easy going dilettantism' of English philology.[40]

Gender and genre

This stress upon the masculine functions of historical writing shaped the work that the four women published: it influenced the forms in which they chose to write; their subject matter; the language they used and the authorities by which they validated their accounts of the past. These concerns did not create a distinctively feminine genre of historical subject or expression, but they meant that the balance of women's historical writing was towards some forms and modes of expression rather than others. At the same time, these forms and modes of expression changed in response to the changes in the practice and profession of history in the nineteenth century.

We have already seen that women's published historical work consisted chiefly of biographies or memoirs recounting the private lives of public figures, commonly celebrated women. Men, too, produced such works; Peter Cunningham wrote a life of Nell Gwynne in 1852, for example. Likewise, collections of documents, another form of historical publication preferred by women, were not their sole province. Carlyle published the letters and speeches of Oliver Cromwell and the great historian of the seventeenth century, C. H. Firth, began his publishing career with a whole succession of collections of documents, acknowledging his debt to Everett Green.[41]

As writers, women studied historical sources and wrote on historical subjects, but they could only earn praise by keeping to the personal and the private, penetrating the intimate thoughts and domestic lives of historical characters, on which subjects they might claim authority by virtue of their sex. They could not earn respect for making larger historical judgements, especially about constitutional, legal and ecclesiastical matters or public affairs. Aikin and Strickland sought to validate their work by their appeal to historical sources, but in their subject matter and the audiences they sought to reach, they appealed to conventionally feminine models.[42] Aikin believed that 'it is from intimate views of private life in various ages and countries that the moral of political history is alone to be derived', regarding her work as a contribution to 'that class which forms the glory of French literature, – memoir'.[43] Strickland, while referring to the 'difficulties, the expense, the injury to health and the sacrifice of more profitable literary pursuits' of the 'documentary historian', also emphasised that she was writing about the domestic character of her subjects and their private as well as their public lives.[44] Everett Green's first publication was, she claimed self-deprecatingly, intended to 'aim no higher than a popular and [is] for the most part a lady's book' and 'since I could not have the vanity to suppose I could render my book acceptable to the antiquarians, I thought it wisdom to adopt in several aspects a more popular form than I had originally designed', though she had certainly consulted the originals of more of the manuscripts she quoted than had the Stricklands.[45]

However, Everett Green's later career and the career of Toulmin Smith show rather different characteristics. Instead of writing narrative histories including extensive quotations from documents, they edited and listed collections of documents, an activity which conferred authority on them and was work of the detailed, painstaking kind for which women were supposedly suited. Both used this as a way of writing on larger subjects. Everett Green had prefaced her edition of *Letters of Royal and Illustrious Ladies* by saying that she paid 'the strictest attention to fidelity in the transcripts and to correctness in the translations', but craved the reader's tolerance for having 'ventured upon a field usually occupied only by the learned of the other sex'.[46] The introduction to her *Lives of the Princesses* is similarly apologetic in its insistence upon her painstaking scholarship and verification of authorities.[47] But she came to write authoritatively of the committee structure and financial administration of the Common-wealth in the introductions to the calendars she edited for the Public Record Office.[48] She also often specifically mentions references to women, as for example the women who had to pay composition fines, or the petitions to Charles II of women royalists.[49] Toulmin Smith, re-editing Clement Mansfield Ingleby's volume of comments on Shakespeare's plays, acknowledged Ingleby's help, but 'all the more that I have been compelled to arrive at several conclusions entirely different from his'.[50] An edition of fourteenth-century accounts started by a German historian was translated and revised by Toulmin Smith, with 'a few corrections in expression, due to the English of a foreigner'.[51] And her edition of Leland's *Itinerary*, which she had 'reluctantly consented' to take on when the editor, Laurence Gomme, became clerk to the London County Council, follows his scheme but with 'some modifications and additions'.[52]

All four women had some contact with the historical and literary establishment of their time, but none was really of it. This marginalisation arose from the way in which their work was regarded. It was considered inappropriate for women to offer the vast moral judgements of the male sages, who celebrated or found wanting the great events, towering figures and cataclysmic movements of the past. Thus women lacked the oppor-tunity to attain the same intellectual authority.

Although concern for the moral lessons of the past is evident in all their works, none of these women used their historical work to further public causes as Charlotte Carmichael Stopes was to do in her book *British Freewomen*, which showed how women's position as citizens had been eroded since the middle ages and that granting them the vote would be no more than the restoration of ancient rights. However, they expressed their political and religious preferences and there is certainly evidence of a concern with contemporary public affairs.

Aikin's first published historical work was a translation into English of J. G. Hess's *Life of Ulrich Zwingli*, a subject of topical interest because of concern about the fate of Protestantism in Napoleonic France. Their common liberal, rationalist, dissenting background meant that both Aikin and Toulmin Smith were generally in favour of women's education. Aikin expressed her frustration that so few Englishwomen had been taught to think, and advocated that they be taught the Latin classics to inspire elevated sentiments.[53] But her concern with women's education was to make them suitable helpmeets to men, 'instead of aspiring to be inferior men, let us content ourselves with becoming noble women'.[54] Her commitment to social issues was theoretical rather than practical and she admitted in a letter in 1832 that she knew less of the English lower classes than of people in Peking: 'I have never seen enough to know at all how to address them'.[55] She was strongly in favour of parliamentary reform in 1832, but deplored political radicalism.

Toulmin Smith's concerns took a more practical form. Her *Manual of English Grammar and Language for Self Help* was intended for 'those who wished to supplement an education cut short by lack of time, or though other circumstances deficient', 'the clerk, the mechanician who goes to his daily business, may read a chapter on the train; the student of a Working Women's College may con a lesson of it for her class'.[56] Her father had been an ardent supporter of civil liberties for dissenters and was closely associated with John Howard the prison reformer. Toulmin Smith *père* had a particular interest in the history of Birmingham arising from his deep belief in civic virtue. Early civic history was a subject of great interest both to those who were involved in the franchise debate and to those involved in the early trade union movement. Lucy quoted from her father's notes on the worth of publishing old guild records to publicise the ancient principles of association embodied in them '[i]n the midst of the perplexing problems presented by modern Trades-unionism, and the dangers to enterprise and manly liberty threatened by its restrictive rules'. This was not an attack on trade unionism, but an expression of concern for the maintenance of its ancient principles of 'mutual self-help and manly independence'. We hear her voice in the comment that the majority of religious guilds were formed equally of men and women, 'which, in these times of the discovery of the neglect of ages heaped upon women, is a noteworthy fact'. Both she and her father expressed strongly the view that the book should be 'useful to the people'.[57]

It was the Tory, Jacobite, high Anglican Agnes Strickland (figure 12) who showed the greatest interest in conventionally feminine philanthropic activities. She took Sunday school when she was at home in Suffolk, and, adept at turning everything to advantage, she used the observations she made while visiting poor cottagers to write the sketches of rural life

12 *Agnes Strickland*, engraving (printed in 1848) by F. C. Lewis from a portrait by J. Haynes, 1846

published in *Old Friends and New Acquaintances*. She was not interested in larger social issues: both the Irish famine and the Chartist agitation left her unmoved. She lacked any sense of feminine solidarity or concern with women's causes, declining to sign a petition in favour of rescinding the Married Women's Property Act, on the grounds that legislation was no way to right such abuses and that the only way was to ask God to regenerate the hearts of wicked men.[58] One of her few politically motivated writings was her poem 'Demetrius' (1833), inspired by the struggle of the Greeks against the Turks. Both Strickland sisters were inadvertently dragged into controversy for their supposed Catholic sympathies. Agnes was reviled at a public meeting in Ipswich in 1848 where an evangelical member of her own church advised that women and children be prohibited from reading *Lives of the Queens of England*. The *Life of Mary Stuart* published with *Lives of the Queens of Scotland* gave rise to further criticism in 1855 which so wounded Elizabeth that she refused to join in writing the lives of the Stuart princesses which Agnes began in 1869. Agnes herself was such a fervent royalist that she declined to write the lives of the Brunswick queens on the grounds that to do so would be disrespectful to Queen Victoria.[59] Subsequently, Everett Green took on the task but never completed it.

These women confined their historical publications to particular forms and subjects, avoiding certain styles of writing and modes of expression. None of the four women is remembered for her rolling prose and heroic tales, while male sages self-consciously used orotund cadences to give their work authority. Aikin offered the view that mere antiquarianism was to be avoided, especially if it was 'void of that philosophical spirit which combines, which generalises, which infers', but she was equally opposed to the constraints of a metaphysical system.[60] There was little of the philosophical spirit in the work of the Stricklands, who showed no hesitation in putting words into the mouths and thoughts into the minds of those they wrote about. Of Henrietta Maria's return to England after the restoration of her son, King Charles II in 1660, Agnes wrote, 'the thoughts of Henrietta were soon forced back to those heavy sorrows which prove how little the world is, with all the vain distinctions, and pomps thereof, to a heart which has once been given to an object loved and lost'.[61] In Agnes's world, reverses were always tragic and attacks of rheumatism agonising. This is in marked contrast to Everett Green whose letters reveal a thoughtful and scholarly approach to disputed historical questions. Such phrases as 'I think I ought to have stronger evidence than that of a purely inferential character' and that a thesis was plausible but seemed to her 'too slight and shaky to warrant my admission' appear in her discussion of historical points.[62]

All four women made substantial careers for themselves as historians, and they were able to do so because of the use they made of two forms of scholarly practice. The first was their reference to original materials from the past. They drew attention to their expertise by emphasising, in Strickland's words, that materials they presented were 'only intelligible to persons skilled in the mysteries of documentary lore'.[63] They authenticated their expertise by describing the process of obtaining and deciphering documents. They exploited the belief that they were, as women, particularly good at the painstaking detailed work of transcribing and editing documents. The second was that they restricted themselves to writing on subjects where they might use the authority conferred by their femininity.

Collaboration or subversion?

None of these four historians, like many other women writing on historical subjects, fundamentally challenged patriarchal assumptions either in their writings or in their lives. None laid claim to the status of sage, though as published writers Aikin and Strickland aspired to be women of letters. Aikin rejected the heroic overtones of Carlyle's man of letters. Strickland, however, regarded herself as paying homage to the heroines of the past, and there was a dramatic, possibly even heroic turn to her accounts of gaining access to materials on the life of Mary of Modena, which were, 'guarded with such jealousy from the curiosity of foreigners, that nothing less than the powerful influence of M. Guizot [historian and sometime first minister of France] himself could have procured access to those collections'.[64] Her sister Elizabeth, by contrast, confessed her dislike of 'professedly literary' women, saying that she would rather be taken for a country gentlewoman than be classed among them.[65]

Aikin and Strickland drew upon historical documents to locate the authentic voice of the past; Everett Green and Toulmin Smith strove to provide accurate and authoritative editions and listings of historical materials. All four women worked within the restrictions placed upon them as women, though these restrictions changed their form in the course of the century with the emergence of a historical profession. But they were doing far more than passive elaborative work.[66] They worked within the forms available to them, not perhaps deliberately offering a challenge, but seizing the opportunities they could see were available to them. The pressing need to make a living was a greater stimulus than the desire to challenge patriarchy.

What Joan Thirsk has described as 'the biographical and documentary preferences of the history women', may have arisen from necessity rather than preference if their work was to be accepted.[67] They were not saboteurs of the prevailing culture, nor were they necessarily collaborators with it; they were, however, both complicit with it and subversive of it.

Notes

1   This essay owes much to conversations with Joan Thirsk over a number of years; to her Foreword to M. Prior (ed.), *Women in English Society 1500–1800* (London, Methuen, 1985); to her 'The history women', in M. O'Dowd and S. Wichert (eds), *Chattel, Servant or Citizen: Women's Status in Church, State and Society* (Belfast, Institute of Irish Studies, The Queen's University of Belfast, 1993); and to her lecture 'Not at the margins, but marginalised: women local and family historians' delivered at the Trevelyan Colloquium, Cambridge, 1995.

2   *The Thirteenth Report of the Deputy Keeper of the Public Records* (London, HMSO, 1852), pp. 37–8.

3   Philippa Levine, *The Amateur and the Professional: Antiquarians, Historians and Archaeologists in Victorian England, 1838–1886* (Cambridge, Cambridge University Press, 1986), p. 101.

4   Philip Hemery le Breton, *Memoirs, Miscellanies and Letters of the Late Lucy Aikin* (London, Longman, 1864), p. 173.

5   On history writing, see D. R. Woolf, 'A feminine past? Gender, genre, and historical knowledge in England, 1500–1800', *American Historical Review*, 102:3 (1997), p. 649. On history painting, see Wendy Wassyng Roworth, 'Kauffman and the art of painting in England', in Wendy Wassyng Roworth (ed.), *Angelica Kauffman: A Continental Artist in Georgian England* (London, Reaktion Books, 1992), p. 21.

6   Thirsk, 'The history women', p. 1.

7   Rohan Maitzen, '"This feminine preserve": historical biographies by Victorian women', *Victorian Studies*, 38:3 (1995), p. 371.

8   Bridget Hill, *The Republican Virago: The Life and Times of Catherine Macaulay, Historian* (Oxford, Clarendon Press, 1992), p. 131.

9   It has been pointed out that von Ranke's method was not 'scientific' in a positivist sense, so much as requiring new standards of evidence, accuracy and explanation. See Doris S. Goldstein, 'The organizational development of the British historical profession, 1884–1921', *Bulletin of the Institute of Historical Research*, 55 (1982), p. 190.

10 Mrs Sarah Austin, friend of Lucy Aikin, translated *The Ecclesiastical and Political History of the Popes in the Sixteenth and Seventeenth Centuries* (1840) and *History of the Reformation in Germany* (2nd edn, 1845); her daughter Lucie Duff Gordon translated *Ferdinand I and Maximilian II* (1853) and, with her husband, *Memoirs of the House of Brandenburg and History of Prussia* (1849); Mrs E. Foster translated *History of the Popes* (1846); Louisa Hay Kerr translated *History of Servia* (1847), all by Leopold von Ranke.

11 Levine, *The Amateur and the Professional*, pp. 9, 101, 119.

12 Women's supposed capacity for detailed, painstaking work is discussed by Cicely Palser Havely in chapter 6.

13 Natalie Zemon Davis, 'Gender and genre: women as historical writers 1400–1820', in Patricia H. Labalme (ed.), *Beyond Their Sex: Learned Women of the European Past* (New York, New York University Press, 1980), pp. 154–5.

14 Jane Margaret Strickland, *Life of Agnes Strickland* (Edinburgh, Blackwood, 1887), pp. 2, 5–6, 15; Una Pope-Hennessy, *Agnes Strickland: Biographer of the Queens of England* (London, Chatto and Windus, 1940), pp. 5, 138, 6, 183; Bodleian Library, Phillipps-Robinson MS d. 128, fo. 191; Eliza Lynn Linton, *My Literary Life* (London, Hodder and Stoughton, 1899), p. 90.

15   Jane Margaret Strickland wrote several children's books as well as her life of Agnes. Major C. M. Strickland published *Twenty-Seven Years in Canada's West*, edited by Agnes Strickland, in 1853. See Pope-Hennessy, *Agnes Strickland*, p. 5.

16   Lucy Toulmin Smith (ed.), *Lench's Trust: Copies of the Original Deeds* (Birmingham, privately printed, 1869); J. T. Toulmin Smith and L. Toulmin Smith, *English Gilds. The Original Ordinances of More than One Hundred English Gilds*, edited, with Notes by the late Toulmin Smith Esq ... with an Introduction and Glossary, &c. by his daughter Lucy Toulmin Smith (London, Early English Text Society, 1870).

17   Strickland, *Life*, pp. 26–7, 50. For a recent account, see Mary Delorme, '"Facts not opinions" – Agnes Strickland', *History Today*, 38 (February 1988).

18   Agnes Strickland, *Lives of the Queens of England*, 10 vols (London, Henry Colburn, 1845), vol. I, p. xiii; *Oliver Cromwell's Letters and Speeches with Elucidations by Thomas Carlyle* (London, J. M. Dent, 1907), p. 10.

19   Agnes Strickland, *Letters of Mary Queen of Scots and Documents Connected with her Personal History*, 3 vols (London, Henry Colburn, 1842–43), vol. III, p. xvi.

20   Strickland, *Lives of the Queens of England*, vol. 8, p. 257; Strickland, *Life*, p. 108.

21   J. A. Froude (ed.), *Letters and Memorials of Jane Welsh Carlyle* (London, Longmans, Green and Co., 1883), vol. II, p. 17.

22   Strickland, *Life*, p. 295.

23   Strickland, *Life*, pp. 84, 298; National Library of Scotland MS 4095, fo. 276v. An example of her lack of interest in other historians' work may be seen in her ignoring in her *Lives of the Tudor Princesses* published in 1868 (which included a life of Arabella Stuart) Elizabeth Cooper's edition of Stuart's letters which had appeared in 1866.

24   Le Breton, *Memoirs*, p. 7.

25   C. H. Herford, Memorial notice for Lucy Toulmin Smith, *The Inquirer*, 23 December 1911, p. 820; *Dictionary of National Biography* (entry by Elizabeth Lee).

26   C. H. Firth's obituary of Sophia Crawford Lomas, *History*, 14 (1929), p. 119; Phillipps-Robinson MS d. 136, fo. 264.

27   Phillipps-Robinson MS d. 128, fos. 184, 191; National Register of Archives Report 7034, Howard (Corby Castle) MSS.

28   Phillipps-Robinson MS c. 503, fo. 64; d. 134, fo. 85.

29   Phillipps-Robinson MS c. 503, fo. 60.

30   Le Breton, *Memoirs*, p. 268.

31   Strickland, *Life*, p. 23.

32   *Dictionary of National Biography*, Agnes Strickland.

33   Phillipps-Robinson MS, c. 503, fo. 56.

34   NLS, MS 4019, fo. 178, Strickland to Blackwood, 8 May 1850.

35   Phillipps-Robinson MS d. 135, fo. 81.

36   Maitzen, '"This feminine preserve"', pp. 372–3; Thirsk, 'The history women', p. 9.

37   *Atheneum* 812, 20 May 1843, 477.

38   Quoted in Pope-Hennessy, *Agnes Strickland*, p. 180.

39   Quoted in Pope-Hennessy, *Agnes Strickland*, p. 235.

40   *The Inquirer*, 23 December 1911, p. 820.

41   Carlyle's haphazard scholarship was revised and supplemented by Everett Green's niece, Sophia Crawford Lomas, who in 1904 produced a new edition of Cromwell's letters and speeches, based on Carlyle's, with an introduction by C. H. Firth.

42   Thaïs E. Morgan, 'Victorian sage discourse and the feminine: an introduction', in

Thaïs. E. Morgan (ed.), *Victorian Sages and Cultural Discourse: Renegotiating Gender and Power* (New Brunswick, Rutgers University Press, 1990), pp. 6–8.

43   Le Breton, *Memoirs*, p. 228; Lucy Aikin, *Memoirs of the Court of Queen Elizabeth*, 2 vols (London, Longman, 1818), vol. I, p. iii.

44   Agnes Strickland, *Lives of the Queens of England*, 12 vols (London, Henry Colburne, 1848), vol. XII, pp. xiv, xii.

45   Phillipps-Robinson MS d. 134, fo. 90v; c. 509, fo. 149; b. 179, fo. 56; d. 135, fo. 81; d. 136, fos 263, 267; c. 494, fo. 199; c. 503, fos. 58, 59; Mary Anne Everett Green, *Lives of the Princesses of England*, 6 vols (London, Henry Colburn, 1849–55), vol. I p. vi.

46   M. A. E. Wood, *Letters of Royal and Illustrious Ladies*, 3 vols (London, Henry Colburn, 1846), vol. I, pp. vi, xi.

47   Green, *Lives of the Princesses*, vol. I, p. vi.

48   See her introductions to the *Calendar of the Proceedings of the Committee for Compounding 1643–60*, 5 vols (London, HMSO, 1889–92), vols I, V; *Calendar of the Proceedings of the Committee for the Advance of Money 1642–56* (London, HMSO, 1888), vol. I; *Calendar of State Papers Domestic 1649–50* (London, HMSO, 1875).

49   *Calendar of the Committee for Compounding*, vol. 1, pp. xviii–xix; *Calendar of State Papers Domestic 1660*, p. x.

50   C. M. Ingleby, *Shakespeare's Centurie of Prayse; Being Materials for a History of Opinion on Shakespeare and his Works AD 1591–1693*, 2nd edn revised with many additions by Lucy Toulmin Smith, New Shakspere Society, series IV, no. 2 (1879), p. xxiii.

51   *Expeditions to Prussia and the Holy Land made by Henry Earl of Derby (afterwards King Henry IV) in the Years 1390–1 and 1392–3*, Camden Society, NS, LII (1894), pp. v–vii.

52   Lucy Toulmin Smith (ed.), *The Itinerary of John Leland in or about the Years 1535–1543*, 5 vols (London, George Bell, 1907).

53   Le Breton, *Memoirs*, pp. 126, 258.

54   Lucy Aikin, *Epistles on Women exemplifying their Character and Condition in Various Ages and Nations* (London, J. Johnson and Co., 1810), p. vi.

55   Le Breton, *Memoirs*, p. 268.

56   Lucy Toulmin Smith, *Manual of English Grammar and Language for Self Help* (London, Ward Lock, 1885), pp. v–vi.

57   Toulmin Smith, *English Gilds*, pp. xiii, xix, xxx, lv.

58   Pope Hennessy, *Agnes Strickland*, pp. 173, 39, 242; Strickland, *Life*, pp. viii, 40, 249.

59   Strickland, *Life*, pp. 17–18, 164, 233, 149.

60   Le Breton, *Memoirs*, p. 142.

61   Strickland, *Lives of the Queens of England*, vol. 8, p. 227.

62   Phillipps-Robinson MS d. 134, fo. 90v; d. 136, fo. 263.

63   Strickland, *Letters of Mary Queen of Scots*, vol. I, p. xiv.

64   Strickland, *Lives of the Queens of England*, vol. 9, p. vii.

65   Phillipps-Robinson MS d. 128, fo. 232 verso, Elizabeth Strickland to Sir Thomas Phillipps, 5 November 1840.

66   Deirdre David, *Intellectual Women and Victorian Patriarchy* (Basingstoke, Macmillan, 1987), p. 4.

67   Thirsk, 'The history women', p. 5.

13 Frederick Sandys, *Portrait of Margaret Oliphant*, 1881

Margaret Oliphant, 'mightier than the mightiest of her sex'[1]

Joan Bellamy

Margaret Oliphant (1828–97) (figure 13), one of the most prolific and successful of writers of her day, worked in a wide range of genres, including literary histories, biographies, translations. She wrote at least ninety-seven novels (very few of them now available), and, from 1854 to 1897, about four hundred critical reviews. This essay considers a selection of her reviews, mainly from *Blackwood's Edinburgh Magazine*, and her *Literary History of England*,[2] considering her role as a female critic and some contemporary gendered views of that role.

Reputation and frustrated ambition

As with so many nineteenth-century women writers her achievements have virtually disappeared from history. Yet at the height of her career Oliphant was regarded as an important novelist and influential critic. However, praise was frequently qualified by considerations of her gender. In a draft note, prepared for the appeal to erect a memorial to Oliphant in St Giles Cathedral, William Blackwood, the publisher, wrote, 'Her position among English *women* of letters is assured, and she will rank in future as one of the foremost *women* workers of the century'[3] (emphases added). A. W. Kinglake, historian of the Crimean War, praised her 'thoroughly feminine tact'.[4] But hostility could border on mysogyny. Henry James (1814–1916), commented, 'I should almost suppose in fact that no woman had ever, for half a century, had her personal "say" so publicly and irresponsibly.'[5] James resented such outspokenness in a woman. He acknowledged her energy and her 'liberal' and 'heroic' production but in a tone of superior irony.

Throughout her life Oliphant worked regularly for Blackwoods. They published many of her novels and employed her as a major contributor to the *Blackwood's Edinburgh Magazine*. John Blackwood (1818–79), described her somewhat patronisingly, as 'a wonderfully clever (little) woman', but also declared, 'George Eliot and Mrs Oliphant are able to hold their own against all male competitors.'[6] Oliphant was 'one of his skilled hands', and 'mightier than the mightiest of her sex'.[7] This qualified support extended to praising her skill as a translator from the French and the Blackwood family turned to her to write the history of their publishing house.[8]

Oliphant's self-image reveals her response to the conflicting press-ures of literary and professional ambition, domestic sentiment and responsibilities. Her life demonstrates the difficulties experienced by a woman working in a male-dominated profession and reacting to changing concepts of woman's role and nature. Responding to William Blackwood's request for advice, she once defensively downgraded herself as 'a trades-woman'.[9] She also described herself as 'a sort of general utility woman on *Blackwood's*',[10] while frequently insisting on respect for her work and her authority as an experienced and successful literary woman.

Virginia Woolf, in *Three Guineas*, identified Oliphant's predicament when she asserted that she 'sold her brain, prostituted her culture, and enslaved her intellectual liberty in order that she might earn her living and educate her children', a view echoing Oliphant's own agonised self-criticism.[11] But Oliphant, like many women writers who worked to support their families, believed she had no choice and that her first responsibilities were to her children and other dependants.[12]

Though the Blackwoods apparently valued Oliphant highly they never gave her permanent employment. In the early days of reviewing for them she had modestly assumed there would be only a limited field of work available to her.[13] But as she grew more experienced and confident she felt frustrated at failing to achieve the financial stability she needed to meet her family responsibilities. 'I wish there was only any chance for a woman of a situation in which one could have a settled income and steady work. I should not be afraid as far as that goes of competition.'[14] She felt by 1880, that she had the experience for an editor of a periodical; she writes:

> I am very anxious as you know to get regular work which I can arrange beforehand and which will bring in regular payment. Though I have always done very well yet there is an element of precariousness in literary work which is at once against economy and against comfort, and I am very much bent on some occupation of a continuous character, editorship or otherwise. In the meantime if you should know of any editorial situation that is going begging think of me.[15]

In 1886, proposing a series of regular articles on literary developments and related matters, she referred to her disappointed hopes of a permanent editorship, and recommended her idea as a plan 'which if I had once had a magazine in my own hands as I once thought I should, I should certainly have adopted'.[16] Her skills are evidenced by two series of translations of foreign and ancient classical literature which she edited. She also made many suggestions to Blackwoods for articles, and for books to be reviewed. She wrote estimates of the manuscripts of other writers which were submitted to her, and she expressed concern for quality in the magazine and a sense of responsibility for its influence. Her claims to critical authority derived from her own successful practice in writing novels, criticism, other literary *genres*, and from her extensive knowledge accumulated through unremitting application to work over many years.

Nevertheless she felt disadvantaged by influential male networks, complaining to George Craik, the publisher, 'The only way your good thoughts could come to practical benefit would be to find me something like an editorship such as his friends have more than once found for Leslie Stephen – but then he is a man.'[17] Visiting London, John Blackwood enjoyed meeting 'his' (male) writers at convivial dinners where political and literary matters were discussed. After one dinner with, among others, Thackeray and Charles Reade where he 'had capital fun', he drove out to see Oliphant in the domestic setting of her Windsor home, thus drawing attention to the different sorts of professional relationships forged between male and female writers.[18] Oliphant complained about the influence of cliques and groups of like-minded friends who promoted one another on 'the horrible mutual admiration principle'.[19] Defending her review of a book by Augustus Hare she wrote:

> The tremendous applause which has greeted this very worthy performance is a good specimen of the sort of thing which I am anxious to struggle against. These fictitious reputations got up by men who happen to be 'remembered at the Universities' and who have many connections among literary men.[20]

The paradox is that though Oliphant felt her exclusion from this kind of male society and saw herself as battling unaided in the struggle to earn a living, she was, in fact, greatly assisted by John Blackwood.

Criticism and moral responsibility

Blackwood's was one of the most prestigious of the many opinion-forming periodicals of the nineteenth century, catering for a middle-class readership. The profession of journalism expanded with the growth of periodical publishing, offering opportunities to women as well as to men. It could be practised in the home, needing only pen, paper and flat surface to work on. Though women's formal educational opportunities were restricted, many (like those men who were self-educated), were able to achieve publication.

Until the 1860s periodical articles were generally anonymous, a practice which was increasingly challenged. It was argued in its favour that the anonymous work carried the total weight of authority of the given periodical but the dangers of irresponsible writing were obvious. Though it was not intended to advantage them, anonymity allowed the middle-class woman to earn money discreetly, she could also enter into the sphere of public debate; anonymous, she could assume a male persona and the weight of male authority. The practice did, however, impede the development of journalism and a recognition of women's abilities as effective and authoritative reviewers and commentators. As late as 1890 Oliphant expressed her approval of anonymity on the grounds that 'the paper [should] stand on its own merits' and not adopt 'devices' to gain publicity.[21] Her own series *The Old Saloon* was anonymous, the title implying a male voice.

The serious periodical played an important part in the education of the middle-class reader, contributing also to the development of critical practice. As well as evaluating contemporary works serious critics needed a sense of literary history, as did their readers. Over the period June 1871 to February 1876 Oliphant produced for *Blackwood's* a series of long articles under the title *A Century of Great Poets*, followed by historical surveys, in 1882 and 1892, respectively, *The Literary History of England in the End of the Eighteenth Century and Beginning of the Nineteenth Century* and *The Victorian Age of English Literature*.

Matthew Arnold often complained of the insularity of British culture, a charge which could not be applied to Oliphant, who was sure that there was an important readership for the works of foreign writers. She vigorously promoted Blackwood's Foreign Classics series which she herself had proposed and edited. She consciously took on the role of teacher, believing the series had an educational value for a public which would need careful explanations of background and allusions.[22]

Serious periodicals such as *Blackwood's* and critics such as Oliphant contributed to the scholarly critical practice adopted in newly established university departments of English in the last decades of the century and later. She was among those literary journalists, men and women, who were seeking to establish objective standards of responsible criticism of current literary works. They were beginning to identify narrative strategies, structure, the quality of the prose and other formal aspects. Some critics regarded fiction as beneath serious critical treatment, but Oliphant was among those who helped to raise its status as demanding serious attention.

Though *Blackwood's* had been founded specifically to counteract the

Whig influence of *The Edinburgh Review*, and advocated Tory politics, it reflected John Blackwood's concern for non-partisan standards of literary criticism, uninfluenced by personal favouritism or the interests of publishers. Oliphant shared these principles. Scattered through her letters to Blackwood are frequent expressions of concern for standards and her awareness of the journal's potential influence on readers. 'Please to recollect that it is fair criticism without fear or favour that I want to go in for.'[23] The following month she suggested that background information about the works might be provided in the review, writing 'I think it might be worthwhile to try if sound criticism could be helped out of the mire in this way.'[24] During a disagreement with Blackwood she declared, 'I can hold my tongue – but if I do speak it must be according to my own judgement'.[25]

In the same year, seeking to exercise her influence more effectively she wrote to Blackwood:

> I am so riled (?) by the want of anything like real criticism that I wish very much you would give me room every month or every alternate month for a general review of books of all kinds under any title or form you please – I get infinitely impatient of the newspapers, in which – even the best of them one can place no dependence whatever.[26]

Defending her independence she advised William Blackwood not to interfere too much with his contributors and advocated the freedom John Blackwood had allowed.[27] She reminded him occasionally that she didn't agree with the politics of the magazine, 'I don't you know like your politics',[28] but she also congratulated him on maintaining the magazine's high literary standards.

Oliphant shared the general critical view of literature as moral education. She drew a clear distinction between the literature for the middle-class market, directed to informing and morally educating, and that for the uneducated and toiling classes who, she believed, in their rare moments of leisure wanted escapist literature, such as melodramas and stories about high life. She deplored representations of sexual desire especially when portrayed in women and attacked the 'sensation novels' of the 1860s exemplified by the work of Mary Braddon (1835–1915), and Rhoda Broughton (1840–1920), and which depicted women gripped by sexual passion or defying conventional norms of behaviour, encouraging illusions and fantasies about love and relations between the sexes. Oliphant looked for stories about credible characters in recognisable social situations working out their problems in a 'lifelike' way and closing with an uplifting or salutary moral conclusion. While she reveals an awareness of the novel as a genre with continuously evolving preoccupations, she regarded moral values as immutable.

Her article, 'The Anti-Marriage League', published in January 1896, with its furious attack on *Jude the Obscure* is widely seen to have damaged her reputation. Hardy thought she was motivated by jealousy; undoubtedly she was seriously troubled by its depiction of sexuality, unstable marriage, cohabitation, and the 'new woman'. Although this article was highly critical, she had reservations about whether she was authoritative enough to write on it. In a letter to Archibald Blackwood, she reflected,

> I have been thinking over Hardy's book and I don't feel sure that it might not be my duty to treat it and a few others of the same kind seriously, putting my name to the article. If I do it at all I think I should do this. Consult Mr. Allardyce or any other friend you are accustomed to rely on about this. For I am not quite [clear?] not whether it would be right to do it but whether I am the person to do it. The evil is very great – I only doubt if my voice is authoritative enough to denounce it.[29]

Oliphant's reviews are long (she herself generally referred to them as 'papers'), often offering an overview of the given topic and carefully constructed to unify a number of related themes. Treating formal aspects Oliphant often adopts the vocabulary of the graphic arts; the Cross biography of George Eliot 'is like a mural painting or sculpture in very low relief'.[30] Her review refers to portraiture, silhouettes and background. A review of Trollope's *Last Chronicles of Barset*,[31] similarly refers to such pictorial concepts as 'high tone of colour', 'garish light', 'sketches', 'tint', 'line'. She writes a fluent, varied prose style with a clear systematic structure based on a wide range of references and experience, expressed in a natural, cultivated voice. She described her own style in the gendered term 'feminine phraseology' but provided no examples.[32] She probably had in mind the contrast between the writing near to the rhythms and vocabulary of educated speech and the weightier styles of writers such as Macaulay or Carlyle inspired by the patterns of classical rhetoric. George Eliot's style she defines as 'less definable in point of sex than the books of any other woman who has ever written'; it is marked by an 'absence of timidity often varied by temerity, which, however disguised, is rarely absent from the style of women … her scientific illustrations and indications of a scholarship more easy and assured than a woman's ordinary furtive classical allusions no doubt added greatly to this effect'.[33]

Literary and gendered networks

If nineteenth-century men developed professional and personal networks, women also enjoyed mutually beneficial friendships, albeit as selective as the rivalries and resentments existing among male groups. Mary Howitt (1799–1888), committed to campaigning for women's rights and active in a literary partnership with her husband, was very helpful to Oliphant who, in turn, helped Dinah Mullock (1826–87) (whom she once described as 'a sister novelist'), to achieve the publication of *John Halifax Gentleman*. She was a very supportive friend to Gerardine MacPherson (d. 1878), Anna Jameson's niece, and over the years approached Blackwoods recommending MacPherson's work. Oliphant reviewed her friend's *Memoirs of the Life of Anna Jameson*,[34] which she had, herself, seen through the press after the author's death. Between her and Anne Ritchie (1837–1919), novelist daughter of Thackeray, there was a warm and supportive friendship. Ritchie wrote the volume on Madame de Sévigné in the Foreign Classics series which Oliphant edited. In old age Ritchie declared, 'Mrs. Gaskell and Mrs. Oliphant were my torch-bearers in youth as afterwards.'[35]

Oliphant worked on a large number of reviews of books by women. In an outstanding survey article, 'Modern novelists – great and small', as early as May 1855 in *Blackwood's*, she declared, 'this is quite distinctly the age of female novelists'. She comments on a number of works but her main concern is with *Jane Eyre* (Brontë had died a few weeks before), published eight years before, with its 'vixen of a heroine' and its 'hero of singular animal force'. For Oliphant this is a revolutionary work, overturning novelistic conventions and giving expression to a 'grossness such as could only be perpetrated by a woman'. The 'revolutionary' elements are identified by Oliphant as its challenge to 'old-fashioned deference' towards women, which implicitly assumes their inferiority, the battle between the heroine and hero, conversations between them which 'no man could have dared to give – which could only have been given by the over boldness of innocence and ignorance trying to imagine what it could never understand, and which are as womanish as they are unwomanly'.[36] This enigmatic comment hints at an instinctive, feminine knowledge which both conforms to contemporary stereotypes of the chaste, sexually innocent, 'womanly' woman and suggests a liberating 'boldness and innocence'.

Despite her belief that literature should exert a conventional moral influence, we see here Oliphant's generous sympathy for a woman writer and her own pragmatism and openness to the work's full power. Though she uses the term 'coarseness', echoing the attacks which greeted the novel on its first appearance, she nevertheless surrenders to the work, and acknowledging her own conflicting reactions to it, discusses its power of creating atmosphere, describing landscapes, and the extraordinary 'force which makes everything real – a motion which is irresistible. We are swept up in the current, and never draw breath till the tale is ended' (pp. 558–9). The article closes with a reference to Brontë's death, praises her powers and points to her influence. This undogmatic response to *Jane Eyre* perhaps held the seeds of Oliphant's later, albeit slow, adjustment to some of the

developments of the women's rights movement and changes in the assumptions about women's work, their abilities and status.

How slow and partial this adjustment was is to be seen in *Blackwood's*, September 1867, when she returned to a discussion of Brontë's
work and its influence, in a review article deploring the publication of
'sensational' novels.[37] Oliphant claims that the English novel, unlike the
French, had hitherto been remarkable for its wholesomeness and suitability
as family reading which is endangered by novels showing women driven
wild with love and presenting a 'fleshly and unlovely record'. She suggests
that Brontë initiated the change with *Jane Eyre* and (p. 259) cites
(unfortunately erroneously) a scene in *Shirley* where a curate's daughter
deplores her lack of opportunity of meeting with a suitable man she might
marry. (Her memory is at fault here.) Oliphant foresees such novels being
kept away from the young with consequent, cultural divisions within
families. Furthermore, she deplores the influence of the sensation novels
on the grounds that they are not 'true' and that young women might be
influenced to believe that they have the same desires as the fictional
heroines. She blames the women's rights movement for suggesting that
women have duties more important than their duty to be 'pure' (presumably
chaste):

> Women's rights and women's duties have had enough discussion, perhaps
> even from the ridiculous point of view. We have most of us made merry
> over Mr. Mill's crotchet on the subject and over the Dr. Marys and Dr.
> Elizabeths; but yet a woman has one duty of invaluable importance to
> her country and her race which cannot be over-estimated – and that is
> the duty of being pure. (p. 275)

Oliphant never hesitated as a critic to differ from generally received
opinions in her evaluations of writers, George Eliot being a case in point.
From 1858, when *Scenes from Clerical Life* appeared, each new novel by
Eliot was widely acclaimed, but Oliphant did not share the enthusiasm and
was reluctant to deal with Eliot's work. In her review, *Two Cities – Two
Books*, she combined an interesting discussion of the two Georges – Eliot
and Sand – and their novels *Romola* and *Consuelo* – with the two cities,
Florence and Venice, where the stories are situated.[38] She admires Sand's
generosity, her affection for her characters, but feels that Eliot has essentially
created an unsympathetic heroine in Romola, 'the noble, lofty, limited,
narrow and splendid being' (p. 78) but rigid and uncompromising. She had
earlier written to Blackwood in connection with *Middlemarch*: 'These
superior heroines are very awful people I wish George Eliot (however),
would not be so hard on all her mediocrities – for after all mediocrity is
the rule and only a few of the human race can be superior.'[39]

The two women had the same publisher but never met. While Oliphant recognised Eliot's genius she was repelled by her moral code in living with the already married George Henry Lewes.[40]

Resentfully, she compared her own personal situation as lone bread-winner for her family and the reception of her novels, with the extraordinary support Eliot enjoyed from Lewes. When she reviewed the biography of Eliot by the latter's widower J. W. Cross, Oliphant seized her opportunity for an extensive evaluation of Eliot and her work in *The Edinburgh Review*, April 1885. She characterised it as 'a great disappoint-ment' (p. 516). 'A gigantic silhouette, showing her figure against a dull background. Background and figure are alike dull' (p. 517). Deploring its hagiographic tone, she challenges aspects of Eliot's reputation and raises the problem of how, given the claims for Eliot as a moral teacher in her fiction, she was able to avoid ostracism and condemnation for living with Lewes. 'In her later life she put on something more than the professor's gown, something like the camel's hair of the prophet. And from the beginning she secured for herself quite exceptional personal as well as literary eminence' (p. 516). Oliphant suggests that Eliot succeeded because she became skilled at constructing new personas for herself as new circum-stances arose, and always with a high opinion of her own actions and motives.[41] She was sheltered from adverse criticism of both her life and her work by the protective cocoon created by Lewes who stood between her and the world. In her *Autobiography* Oliphant contrasted her own situation with Eliot's:

> How I have been handicapped in life! Should I have done better if I had been kept, like her, in a mental greenhouse and taken care of? This is one of the things it is perfectly impossible to tell.[42]

Oliphant seeks to construct a biography and character study of Eliot from characters and situations in the novels. While describing the early 'rural' novels as 'noble' and conceding Eliot's genius she nevertheless offers a powerful and troubling challenge to Eliot's integrity when she refers to Eliot's agnosticism and accuses her of exploiting those very religious sentiments of her readers which she herself disavowed. Of course Oliphant was swimming against the tide, not so much in her estimate of Cross's work but in her view of Eliot's personality and achievement.

Biography, femininity and women's rights

Oliphant recorded that she enjoyed reviewing biographies and auto-biographies. In *Blackwood's* of April 1874, in 'New books', she compares the autobiography of J. S. Mill (1806–73), with the memoirs of Mary

Somerville (1780–1872), much to Mill's disadvantage.[43] She was hostile to Mill, disliking what she regarded as displays of intellectualism and she had already attacked his support for women's suffrage. She was unsympathetic to his mournful account, which she describes as a 'pale suggestion of a life, which might have been but was not' (p. 443). She warmed to Somerville as a Scot, like herself. Compared with Mary Somerville, Mill would appear to have had enormous advantages and Oliphant is drawn to the woman scientist's modesty and simplicity and full of admiration for the persistence with which she educated herself, despite early hostility to her intellectual interests. Somerville was not only a genius but, Oliphant emphasises, a good woman, who seemed not to know how remarkable a person she was, while Mill seems to be always conscious of a superiority to other people. Oliphant and her readers were more comfortable with Somerville than they were with Mill. Somerville, though intellectually brilliant, remained 'womanly', unthreatening, while Mill with his radical ideas offered challenges to women's social and moral position. Oliphant's critical work on other women writers, as well as the practical assistance she offered them, suggests an instinctive, but non-political, feeling of 'sisterhood' and female solidarity.

As the century progressed debates on women's rights became increasingly prominent. Some women writers questioned dominant perceptions of woman's nature and their role in society, contributing to the pressure for change. When Oliphant reviewed *The Memoirs of the Life of Anna Jameson* in *Blackwood's* in February 1879 along with Fanny Kemble's *Records of a Girlhood*, she praised these working women who pursued their careers and professional commitments without engaging in controversy about women's work, and she complains:

> For our own part, we are much disposed to believe that the greatest and most fundamental wrong done to women in this world is the small appreciation ever shown – at least in words – of the natural and inevitable share of the world's work which they cannot avoid, and which no one can say they do not fulfil unmurmuringly. (p. 206)

She accepts as 'natural' that women's work is to be housekeepers and mothers and to live as the dependants of their husbands. She ignores the arguments raised by women's rights activists on issues of domesticity and the constraints of dependency. Devoted to her children and with a deep debt of gratitude to her own mother, she believed motherhood was 'the most honoured and holiest of names' deserving of the utmost respect,[44] a view she later reiterated to John Blackwood, asserting that it was wrong 'to teach our boys that their mothers, or even, if you like, their maiden aunts, are "fair game"'.[45]

Though responding to women, who, like herself, worked independently and successfully, Oliphant had no sympathy with political activism. As a woman, she was not alone in claiming to take no interest in politics. As women were largely excluded from political life it is hardly surprising that many of them took no active interest in it. For most people it seemed simply 'natural' that politics were not matters for women to busy themselves with. She advocated the conventional views about woman's place in the home and society and believed in an essential feminine nature, but she herself filled the traditional masculine role of earning money as a busy, professional worker. Thus her own practice subverted the very stereotypes of the ideal woman which she recommended. In 1856 she refused to sign the petition for a Married Women's Property Bill and offered to Blackwood an article replying to the pamphlet of 1854, A Brief Summary in Plain Language of the Most Important Laws Concerning Women by Barbara Bodichon (1827–91). Oliphant's article appeared anonymously, in April 1856 as 'The laws concerning women'. It asserted that marital arrangements were partly embodied in the law which were dictated by 'nature' and should be inviolable and could not be changed without endangering social stability. She blames women's rights campaigners for raising problems which concern only a minority of women.

In Blackwood's, in February 1858, she replied to Bodichon's Women and Work of the previous year in an article entitled 'The condition of women'. Contrary to Bodichon's view, Oliphant argues that the problems of women seeking employment are no worse than those for men. She claims that many well-educated men cannot find employment, and conditions which would be demeaning for a man are accepted by women. She argues again that the idea of inequality is an invention of a small minority of dissatisfied women and that there is equality but the sexes have their different spheres. Middle-class families train their daughters well for their appointed roles in domestic life and as assistants in their businesses. She fails to engage with the actual situation which the Langham Place Group of women's rights campaigners and the Governesses' Benevolent Society had uncovered. There were thousands of middle-class women seeking work as governesses or companions, badly paid, insecure, often suffering acute poverty in sickness and old age.

In Blackwood's, in September 1866, Oliphant published her article, 'The great unrepresented', attacking J. S. Mill's Parliamentary Bill which proposed to extend the franchise to spinsters and widowed householders. Oliphant writes that she herself does not want the vote, and the thrust of the article is hostile to the idea of women's suffrage. The tone is ironic and anti-intellectual. She argues that Mill might be a clever man but he has no common sense. She is happy to be a woman and needs no protection or championing from Mill:

> We are used to being women. On the whole, strange as it may seem, we like it. Girls may object, and do object, to the disabilities which are sometimes rather hard upon them; but by the time a woman has come to the mature age at which she can understand herself and her destiny, she has in most cases got to see the justice of it, and learned to identify herself distinctly in the world. (p. 376)

She suggests that the whole campaign is merely the beginning of a wider extension of the franchise to young women. Having secured the vote some may even want to be Members of Parliament.

Oliphant never generalised from her own experience to identify with the politics of the women's movement, although she resented the disadvantages she suffered as a woman. She believed she was deliberately ignored by male critics. At the same time she asserted that with sufficient effort, strength of character and dedication, everybody, including women, could achieve their ambitions and independence. The very nature of her work as a writer encouraged her sense of solitary, individual effort as the recipe for success. Oliphant had commented as early as 1855 in a Blackwood's article: 'Fiction depends entirely on the individual powers of its professors.'[46]

However, despite her opposition to the women's rights campaigns Margaret Oliphant was not immune to the slow, gradual changes of attitude brought about by the debate on 'the woman question'. She reacted vigorously against suggestions that women writers were somehow unnatural, not really womanly women: 'Who is your friend who is so sweetly patronizing to women in the last number? It is very comforting to be told that we may write for our living without being monsters, but isn't it a trifle out of date to say so just at this particular moment?'[47]

Eight years later she protested to John Blackwood about a story he had published, '1895: The lady candidate' which, purporting to look to the future, made fun of women wanting to enter Parliament and she wrote:

> This sort of glib nonsense has by degrees brought me round to the conviction that however indifferent I may be personally to political privileges the system which supposes me incapable of forming a reasonable opinion on public matters is very far from a perfect one – theoretically at least, whatever the practical difficulties in amending it may be, and as all women are not girls of twenty, and some of us are reasonable beings it is worth while considering I think whether perpetual impertinence of this kind may not have an effect quite the reverse of that which I suppose its originators intend. I am almost sorry to say that I don't feel myself much sillier than the majority of men I meet, though perhaps that may be because the men in Windsor are not lofty specimens. Forgive me, but I think this sort of thing is a mistake – especially when not very well done.[48]

Even her views on women's suffrage were modifying. By May 1880 she was declaring in *Fraser's Magazine*, 'I think it highly absurd that I should not have a vote if I want one.'[49]

In her two-volume survey of *The Literary History of England in the End of the Eighteenth and Beginning of the Nineteenth Century*, of 1882, Oliphant discusses a number of women writers including Mary Wollstonecraft, whom she read for the first time as she worked on this book. Her attitude to Wollstonecraft reflects the shifts in her reaction to the women's movement. She describes Wollstonecraft's early years, and her unsatisfactory father, and comments that the women's rights movements can be seen as the consequence of women being 'compelled by the hard stress of circumstances to despise the men about them'. She discusses with great sympathy Wollstonecraft's willing assumption of family responsibilities. The parallels in this respect with her own life cannot have escaped Oliphant, neither can the similarities in the help Wollstonecraft received from her publisher Joseph Johnson and that provided by John Blackwood to herself. She also envisages Wollstonecraft at her literary drudgery while, rather like herself, hoping to write a great work. She reassures the reader that *The Vindication of the Rights of Woman* is 'of the mildest description' and praises its 'generous vehemence' in urging better education for women and the rejection of false values in relations between the sexes. She sees Wollstonecraft as a faithful wife to her lover Imlay, victim of her own generous and trusting philosophy. She is singularly unjudgemental about Wollstonecraft's relations with Godwin, but obviously marvels at his naïvety in revealing intimate details of their relationship which subsequently gave Wollstonecraft the reputation of immoral revolutionary. What Oliphant saw in Wollstonecraft was a hard-working, talented woman, betrayed by her own generosity and idealism and by weak men. Oliphant minimises Wollstonecraft's significance for the later nineteenth century, seeing no links between Wollstonecraft's ideas and the demands of the women's rights movement, most of whose leaders were anxious not to be identified with Wollstonecraft. Nor did Oliphant see any connection with the 'The new woman' of her own latter years.

Oliphant worked to earn a living for her family under complex conditions. She carried the responsibilities of the breadwinner, traditionally the male role, while fulfilling the traditionally female role of care for her children and dependants and supervision of the household. She was a conscientious and shrewd critic, always feeling under pressure to maintain a place in a male-dominated profession, yet unable to achieve her editorial ambitions. While she brought to a wide readership the fruits of her own literary skill, knowledge and dedication, she found it difficult to resolve the tensions created by changes in women's social status, the growing

acknowledgement of women's sexuality and new social relationships between men and woman. Her considerable legacy of critical work, which
has been too long hidden and calls out for new evaluation, contributed to
developing critical practice. By her example she helped to expand the
opportunities for women in the fields of journalism and literary production.

Notes

1   I am indebted in the writing of this chapter to the work of Elisabeth Jay, *Mrs Oliphant: 'A Fiction to Herself'* (Oxford, Clarendon Press, 1995), and idem (ed.), *The Autobiography of Margaret Oliphant* (Oxford and New York, Oxford University Press, 1990); and to Merryn Williams, *Margaret Oliphant, A Critical Biography* (Macmillan, London, 1986).

2   Margaret Oliphant, *The Literary History of England in the End of the Eighteenth Century and the Beginning of the Nineteenth Century* (London, Macmillan & Co., 1882).

3   Handwritten draft by William Blackwood for the Appeal Committee, undated. National Library of Scotland, Blackwood MS 4664. Letters from the National Library of Scotland dated before 29 October 1879 are to John Blackwood, afterwards to William Blackwood or Archibald Blackwood.

4   Mrs Gerald Porter, *Annals of A Publishing House* (Edinburgh, Blackwood, 1898), vol. 3, p. 114.

5   Henry James, *Notes on Novelists With Some Other Notes* (London, J. M. Dent & Sons Ltd, 1914), p. 358. Cited in Jay, *Autobiography of Margaret Oliphant*, p. xvi.

6   Porter, *Annals*, pp. 73, 164.

7   Porter, *Annals*, pp. 174, 188.

8   Porter, *Annals*, p. 339.

9   Blackwood MS 4476, fo. 167, 23 March 1885.

10 Porter, *Annals*, vol. 2, p. 475, cited in Williams, *Margaret Oliphant*, p. 23.

11 Virginia Woolf, *The Three Guineas* (Harmondsworth, Penguin, 1977), p. 106.

12 See Jay, *Autobiography of Margaret Oliphant*, pp. 15–16.

13 'I am afraid a feminine critic must find but a limited orbit possible to lie about her': Blackwood MS 4111, fo. 253, 1855.

14 Blackwood MS 4251, fo. 147, 12 February 1869.

15 Blackwood MS 4410, fo. 178–9, 18 February 1880.

16 Blackwood MS 4490, fo. 93–4, 27 November 1886. 'The plan' became 'The Old Saloon' series. For a discussion of Oliphant's efforts to obtain an editorship of a magazine see Jay, *Mrs Oliphant*, pp. 248–50.

17 Macmillan MS, 10 October 1885, cited in Williams, *Margaret Oliphant*, p. 140. The first woman to be appointed to a staff post in journalism was probably Eliza Lynn Linton, who worked on *The Morning Chronicle* for two years from 1849. Harriet Martineau in 1837 refused the offer of the post of editor of a proposed economic journal: see H. Martineau, *Harriet Martineau's Autobiography*, 3rd edn (London, Smith Elder, 1877), vol. 2, p. 109.

18 Porter, *Annals*, p. 94.

19 Blackwood MS 4266, fo. 58, 15 July 1870.

20 Blackwood MS 4309, fo. 72, 6 February 1873.

21 Blackwood MS 4558, fo. 169, 15 June 1890.

22 Blackwood MS 4380, fo. 80, 28 January 1878.

23 Blackwood MS 4266, fo. 40, 1870, 'March' pencilled in.

24 Blackwood MS 4266, fo. 42, 9 April 1870.

25 Blackwood MS 4266, fo. 71, 21 October 1870. Oliphant was not the only critic disturbed by low standards and even unscrupulousness. In her autobiography Mary Howitt, a friend of Oliphant, referred to the 'wretched and degraded state of criticism': Mary Howitt, *An Autobiography*, 2 vols (London, W. Isbister, 1889), vol. 1, p. 221.

26 Blackwood MS 4266, fo. 100–1, 1870.

27 Blackwood MS 4410, fo. 191, 3 July 1880.

28 Blackwood MS 4437, fo. 123, December 1882.

29 Blackwood MS 4635, fo. 265, 28 November 1895.

30 Blackwood MS 4476, fo. 158, 29 January 1885.

31 *Blackwood's*, September 1867, pp. 277–8 and in D. Smalley (ed.), *Trollope, The Critical Heritage* (London, Routledge & Kegan Paul, 1969), p. 303.

32 Blackwood MS 4163, fo. 147, 1861.

33 J. Cross (ed.), *George Eliot's Life as related in her Letters and Journals* 3 vols (Edinburgh, Blackwood, 1885), reviewed by Oliphant in *The Edinburgh Review*, April 1885, p. 543.

34 *Blackwood's*, February 1879, pp. 206–24.

35 Anne Ritchie, *From the Porch* (London, Smith, Elder & Co., 1913), p. 6. Presidential Address delivered at the Annual General Meeting of the English Association, 10 January 1913: English Association Pamphlet, no. 24, p. 2.

36 'Modern novelists – great and small', *Blackwood's Edinburgh Magazine*, May 1855, pp. 555, 557, 558.

37 'Novels', *Blackwood's*, pp. 257–80.

38 *Blackwood's*, July 1874, pp. 72–91.

39 Blackwood MS 4280, fo. 226, 2 December 1871.

40 'I hope you don't think me so utterly stupid as to have any doubt about the perfection of George Eliot's writing': Blackwood MS 4213, fo. 96, 30 June 1866, and also: 'I will do Savanarola and compliment George Eliot too, if you like with the most sublime indifference to her deserts in this particular – though having just received a slight but forcible sketch of the former history of Mr Lewis (sic) from the graphic lips of Mrs Carlyle, I can't help a sensation of disgust at anything connected with him, Romola included': Blackwood MS 4184, fo. 109, 1863.

41 This opinion was shared by Eliza Lynn Linton: 'She grew to be artificial, *posée*, pretentious, unreal. She lived an unreal life all through, both mentally and socially; and in her endeavour to harmonise two irreconcilables – to be at once conventional and insurgent – the upholder of the sanctity of marriage while living as the wife of a married man. She was a made woman – not in the French sense – but made by self-manipulation, as one makes a statue or a vase. I have never known any one who seemed to me so purely artificial as George Eliot.' Cited in Lynn Linton, *My Literary Life, Reminiscences of Dickens, Thackeray, George Eliot* (London, Hodder and Stoughton, 1899), pp. 97–8.

42 Jay, *Autobiography of Margaret Oliphant*, p. 15.

43 M. Somerville, *Personal Recollections from Early Life to Old Age of Mary Somerville With Selections from her Correspondence*, by her Daughter, Martha Somerville

(London, J. Murray, 1873); J. S. Mill, *Autobiography*, ed. Helen Taylor (London, Longmans, 1873).

44   Blackwood MS 4111, fo. 266–7, 1855.

45   Blackwood MS 4349, fo. 68–9, 10 May 1876.

46   'Modern novelists', pp. 554–68.

47   Blackwood MS 4238, fo. 35, 1 October 1868. It is not clear what 'this particular moment' means; it could refer to the agitation for women's suffrage, or the prestige of women writers.

48   Blackwood MS 4349, fo. 116–17, 1876.

49   Cited in Williams, *Margaret Oliphant*, p. 108.

Hints on Household Taste and *The Art of Decoration*: authors, their audiences and gender in interior design

Colin Cunningham

'Most fashionable people, women especially, conceive that they possess the faculty of distinguishing good from bad design in familiar objects':[1] Charles Locke Eastlake neatly asserts that women have the principal role in discerning the rightness of their domestic surroundings. His assumption of a standard gendered view throws into sharp focus a problem in the development of taste and 'home-making' that was particularly acute in the later decades of the nineteenth century – the role of women in interior design and the status of their work. Additionally, in writing about taste, he raises a further gender issue – who should arbitrate in this 'women's' sphere. Eastlake, a leading art critic and Director of the National Gallery, was the author of *Hints on Household Taste*, first published in 1868, a book of guidance that is still often regarded as the most significant such manual of its time.[2] The success of his book established him as the arbiter of taste in interior decoration, a position which seemed to be amply justified by his scholarly knowledge of furniture history, and his close understanding of design.

The enterprise of scholarly study of the history and principles of interior decoration, as distinct from the knowledge amassed by designers, was relatively new in the mid-century. Yet only thirteen years after East-lake's book appeared, another followed, that to judge by the number of editions was at least as popular. This was Mary Eliza Haweis's *Art of Decoration*.[3] The gender issues underlying the move from a book by a male author, clearly aimed at a female readership, to a similar manual by a woman in little over a decade, prompts this enquiry into the ways in which

Mary Eliza Haweis, or MEH as she preferred to be known, negotiated the ambiguities of establishing herself as an expert in a field, in which design and production, if not consumption, were very largely male dominated. There were no special qualifications to which she or any other writer could point; and writings on taste were largely in the hands of the male art critics. Yet Haweis managed to secure for herself wide acclaim as an arbiter of taste; and she did so partly by justifying her opinions by reference to the better established discipline of history. Hers is a work that was able to draw on the first institution established for the study of design, or art manufactures, the South Kensington Museums;[4] and she achieved a success in print almost equal to Eastlake's, in spite of the fact that she had no public position from which to operate.

She was born in 1848, the eldest daughter of Thomas Musgrove Joy, a fashionable portrait painter, who nonetheless failed to reach the accredited elite status of Royal Academician.[5] Her upbringing thus involved exclusion from the professional élite at the same time that it included a good practical training in painting and drawing. That she was talented is shown by her success in having a picture accepted for the Royal Academy Summer Exhibition at the early age of eighteen.[6] At nineteen she married the Rev. Hugh Reginald Haweis, rector of St James, Westmoreland Street, Marylebone, a position which brought in an income of around £200 per year.[7] Hugh Haweis was already launched on a career that made him the most fashionable preacher in London, but in 1867 the future was far from bright. Although by marrying her clergyman Mary had acquired a respectable status, she had not escaped from financial worries, a situation that only worsened when her children were born. Her work has, therefore, to be seen against the background of a real need to ensure a sufficient income. However, by the late 1870s she was well known as a prolific author and an authority on dress, taste and household decoration.

At that date it was 'the woman of the home' who, it was generally assumed, had to assemble the objects and choose the patterns that would provide her family, and especially her husband on his return from work, with that oasis of calm and beauty that was the ideal of the High Victorian middle-class home. Frances Power Cobbe, generally regarded as a progressive commentator, summed up the prevailing view:

> The making of a true home is really our peculiar and inalienable right, –
> a right which no man can take from us; for a man can no more make a
> home than a drone can make a hive ... a woman, and only a woman, –
> and a woman all by herself, if she likes, and without any man to help
> her, – who can turn a house into a home.[8]

Cobbe accepts the sphere of specifically female authority in home-making, although the role had been previously defined by male commentators. Ruskin, for instance, had expressed the conventional view in 1864, claiming, 'the man's work for his own home is ... to secure its maintenance progress and defence; the woman's to secure its order comfort and loveliness'.[9] And Robert Kerr, one of the leading exponents of domestic design, had explained that 'the more graceful sex are generally better qualified, both as respects taste and leisure, to appreciate the decorative element in whatever form of development'.[10] The field about which Haweis was to write was therefore clearly established as the preserve of women. On the other hand the sphere of critic, the actual writing itself, was by no means as clearly available to women. The same was true of the practice of designing that provided the field for criticism.

By the 1870s several schools of design had opened classes for women in London [11] and the provinces and the first professional female interior designers were already at work in America.[12] However, instruction manuals still presumed that the woman's role was largely that of a consumer, selector and assembler of the objects that constituted the home surroundings. Yet these were particularly interesting years for interior design. The exuberance of the Great Exhibition of 1851 was absorbed and replaced by the more orderly display of its products and other goods that made up the South Kensington Museums. Nonetheless it remained almost exclusively the role of men to design, to direct and train those who would make the selection for their home, although schools of design were increasingly opening their classes to women. The field of architecture, which increasingly encompassed furniture and interior design, was still overwhelmingly the preserve of men. It was they who provided the teachers in the major institutions such as the South Kensington Art Schools, and, of course, it was men such as Arthur Lazenby Liberty, Messrs Maples, William Morris and his friends, who dominated the production and marketing of design.

That Haweis managed to establish herself as an expert in this field, dominated by critics such as Charles Locke Eastlake was something of an achievement. She was not the first woman in this field, but she was certainly one of the most prolific.[13] However, it is significant that she began her career in print not by any direct assault on the conventionally gendered preserve of the critic, but through the equally gendered leisure activity of drawing and illustrating. As the child of a painter, this may have been both a natural and an easy progress: it also answered a need that she recognised as a mother in the education and training of her children, another gendered occupation. The fact that she chose to go into print as an illustrator of children's books was evidence of her need for paid work to secure the family income in the face of her husband's rather precarious stipend. The specific type of book illustrated resulted from her concern for quality in educational material, precisely the concern that underlay her principal work as a design critic.

The experience of providing pre-school education for her first child led her to publish *Tales From Chaucer*, with her own illustrations to make this text, acknowledged as 'great literature' available to children. In doing so she was able to draw on skills she had developed as a child in her father's studio, and was following a route that had been available to women for several generations. But book illustration was not the same as authoritative discourse on dress and decoration. The former was an acceptable activity, and only a small advance on what was conventionally regarded as a necessary accomplishment in young women. Scholarly discourse and criticism were, it was felt, more serious matters; and the field was dominated by male writers. Haweis's own activities gave her a good deal of practical experience in book design, fashion and in home-making, which she combined with a more 'scholarly' concern with education.

These conventionally gendered activities were crucial, first in forming her own views, and second in gaining the reputation that allowed her to be accepted as an expert. Her absolute determination to secure precisely what she wanted was an essential quality, and probably one that helped her in her battle for public recognition as a critic. She had very particular and often original views on house decoration, which she began to put into practice as soon as she moved into her first home at 16 Welbeck Street. To break away from the grimy monotony of the London streetscape, she painted the facade moss green, relieved with black and red in the window reveals.[14] The colour scheme was startling enough; but even more unconventional was the fact that Haweis apparently did the painting herself in utter disregard for social convention. She describes how she attracted a crowd of onlookers as she perched on her ladder, like 'a regular raree show'; but what really mattered was that she set a fashion. As the wife of a fashionable preacher, she was expected to be regularly seen in public by a wide range of leading society figures; and her skill as a maker of costume consequently provided another field for action. Not surprisingly, therefore, her first book in the field of taste was *The Art of Beauty*, whose frontispiece (figure 14) of a girl with a dashing red skull cap started a vogue described as 'à la Mrs Haweis'.[15]

In the fashion-conscious world of London society it was important to be able to give a lead. But there was a good deal more to Haweis's dress than merely determined individuality. Her financial position precluded spending large sums in the many fashionable milliners' shops. 'I have often told you', she wrote to her mother, 'that we are living beyond our means and look a great deal richer than we are, and so every pound is of consequence'.[16] Accordingly she was forced to improvise and to create

14 Mary Haweis, frontispiece to *The Art of Beauty*, 1878. The drawing is signed with the monogram MEH, which Haweis designed for herself. The girl's red skull-cap was copied as a fashionable accessory in a mode described as 'à la Mrs Haweis'.

many of her own costumes. This practical experience of dressmaking was the common lot of those at the lower end of the scale of gentility, and fiction provides frequent images of young ladies whose prospects of marriage and/or social success depended partly on their skill with the needle. However, Haweis was able to manage her own dressmaking, not only because she was practised in the art of needlework, but also because she spent a great deal of time studying historic costume in paintings and in the South Kensington Museum.[17] Although the field was a relatively new one, this sort of study involved some scholarly activity; and there is no doubt that Haweis acquired a thorough understanding of the history of dress. Part of the evidence for this is the way that both *The Art of Beauty* and *The Art of Decoration* are illustrated with her own sketches of historic costume.

Her detailed knowledge afforded her a justifiable arrogance; and she was certainly outspoken in her criticism of others. Something of this is preserved in the memoir her husband wrote after her death; and the historical justification for her criticism is significant of her intention to be thought of as a scholar rather than merely a woman of taste:

> That sleeve did you say? Why it is a revival of a fourteenth century mode, but the loop has not been understood. The modiste had no idea for what it was originally meant. Besides it really belongs to another period. Those slashes? Quite absurd! The whole meaning of the slash was to reveal a rich under-garment, and here there is none. I dare say that great lady over there with the lappet and pouch-like thing is not aware that it is a survival of the serf-costume of Henry II's time and is really a badge of servitude.[18]

Haweis's academic position, then, was justified by long study of sources in paintings in the national collections, and by close inspection of furnishings in great houses that she was able to visit either when they were opened to the public or as the wife of a well-known preacher. This detailed knowledge of costume and furniture allowed her to assume the role of expert. However, what may be considered her first scholarly book, *The Art of Beauty*, could be dismissed as a document concerned almost exclusively with womens' interests. It deals largely with dress, and it is difficult to imagine that the readership was anything other than female. She began the book with the claim that: 'The culture of beauty is everywhere a legitimate art'; but continued: 'A woman's natural quality is to attract, and having attracted to enchain; ... We may add, therefore, that the culture of beauty is the natural right of every woman'.[19] The matter of dress was widely seen as a woman's concern; and it would have been possible to dismiss writing on the subject as merely the distillation of a practical expertise, rather than the result of expert knowledge. In Haweis's case it was both. Her expertise gave her the confidence to make authoritative statements; but she was careful to support these with historical justification. Eastlake took a rather different view of this particular field of design. Although he devoted a whole chapter of his *Hints on Household Taste* to dress and jewellery, he avoided laying down any principles on the grounds that 'the subject is impossible for the simple reason that the rapid changes of fashion make it useless to approve or condemn'.[20]

If, however, we were to argue that Haweis, in publishing her *Art of Beauty*, was doing no more than work within the dominant view of desirable femininity, her book is nonetheless comprehensive, with a historical survey of costume and, perhaps most interesting, a final section of advice to young girls that goes beyond mere clothing. Haweis deals with her subjects by character – the Nonentity, the Shy Girl, the Stupid Girl, the Plain Girl – and so on. Here it seems that she is talking as a mother – she had one daughter with whom she did not get on well – and to that extent the book could rightly be seen to be unacademic and prone to oversimplification. She was several generations too early for the science of child psychiatry and the study of interpersonal relations. Her passion for study is, however, apparent in the way she aims her severest criticism at the Ill-Educated Girl: 'educate yourself – somehow to some extent, … you cannot join in, you can only interrupt a conversation; but books are so cheap, and your leisure probably so large that there is little to prevent an effort to redeem lost time'.[21] It seems not unreasonable to read into this a passion for learning and scholarship, which was the means of justifying her own position as an authority.

Haweis's concern for education was undoubtedly the main purpose of *The Art of Decoration* that was aimed at instructing the, probably, young home-maker. As Harriet Beecher Stowe had commented: beauty was of positive benefit in the home, 'having a constant wholesome power over the young and contributing much to the education of the entire household in refinement, intellectual development, and moral sensibility'.[22] The difficulty (figure 15), however, arose in the matter of selecting beautiful objects, for there was a bewildering choice that presented the sheltered product of a mid-Victorian upbringing with real difficulty. The huge expansion of the market for furniture and fittings, the 'art manufactures' of the Great Exhibition, was in part a response to growing middle-class wealth. It provided an important element in the growing social mobility, for different social strata had access to some of the same objects with which to display taste and power. Not only did the young housewife have to match her purchases to her husband's income,[23] but she also had to cope with the pressures of competition in display, the multi-layered conventions of status and the intractable problem of 'taste'. From the perspective of the twenty-first century the launching of untrained and largely uneducated young married women into this maelstrom may seem socially manipulative. The assumption that the man of the house might have few opinions and less ability in choosing his own surroundings seems equally blinkered. It was less apparent at the time, though there were several commentators who were aware of the problems; and it was this dilemma that Haweis set out to resolve.

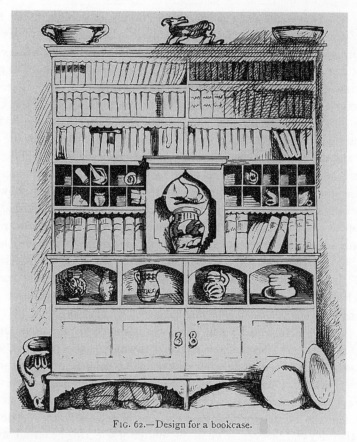

Fɪɢ. 62.—Design for a bookcase.

15 Mary Haweis, sketch for a library bookcase from *The Art of Decoration*, 1881. The design demonstrates Haweis's recipe for mixing 'china', *cloisonneé*, or German glass to avoid the 'joyless' appearance of solid books

Haweis's book, like Eastlake's, was intended to provide a reasoned basis for choice, so that her readers, whether newly wealthy or conventionally genteel, could be confident that in following her advice they would commit no solecisms nor end up living in discomfort. In so doing, she was attacking the intractable problem of 'taste'. This essay is not concerned with the complex issues that underlie and contribute to definitions of taste, except to recognise the range of factors involved. The question of period specificity is certainly relevant, with individual opinions more highly valued at some periods than others. Issues of class and social mobility are also central, and were important throughout the nineteenth century when 'good taste' was assumed as an élitist value. Finally, questions of gender were crucial, particularly at the divide between the individual's exercise of taste and the 'expert's' authoritative advice. If it was assumed that taste in household matters was a feminine attribute, the corollary was that male understanding had no part to play. Yet men dominated the process of design and manufacture, and the majority of mid-century critics were male. There was ample scope for blurring of boundaries; and it is significant that some nineteenth-century arbiters of taste, such as John Ruskin and Oscar Wilde, transgressed the conventionally gendered bounds of their sex. Haweis's achievement was in establishing the link between the 'feminine' role of the home-maker and the previously 'masculine' preserve of the authoritative critic.

She was addressing an audience that was already provided for by Charles Locke Eastlake, and it is interesting to see how her approach differs from his. He wrote from the standpoint of the professional,[24] that is to say he was the occupant of a paid position at the peak of the art establishment. His views, therefore, when published, had the status of his directorship of the National Gallery; and they need to be taken as those of the establishment. They are also those of an educated and sensitive man, with a strong feeling for construction in furniture, qualities that were a part of his qualification for his RIBA post in the first place. He attempted to provide a reasoned and consistent set of standards by which a client might furnish a house. He was committed to the Gothic Revival style, and argued a case for well-constructed furniture that accorded with the tenets of the Arts and Crafts movement. Among the designers he cites are Pugin, A. W. Blomfield, Charles Heaton, E. J. Tarver, and his own work is illustrated on several occasions. This selection merely underlines the male dominance of design. Indeed most of the favoured designers of furniture in the Gothic Revival style were architects,[25] rather than specialist furniture designers. His book, *Hints on Household Taste*, therefore, reflects the gendered divide between making and consuming.

Eastlake begins with the problem of judicious selection, and attacks the plethora of poorly designed furniture available. However, the tenor of his language throughout assumes that his audience will be female, and, although he nowhere states specifically that his subject is 'women's work', he does adopt a noticeably patronising tone:

> while a young lady is devoting at school or under a governess, so many hours a day to music, so many to languages, and so many to general sciences, she is all this time unconsciously forming that sense of the beautiful, which we call taste.[26]

> When Materfamilias enters an upholsterer's warehouse, how can she possibly decide on the pattern of her new carpet ... The shopman remarks of one piece of goods, that it is 'elegant'; of another, that it is 'striking'; of a third, that it is 'unique', and so forth. The good lady ... is utterly unable to explain why she should, or why she should not, like any of

them ... In this dilemma the gentleman with the yard-wand again comes to the rescue, imparts his firm opinion as to which is most 'fashionable', and this at once carries the day.[27]

Eastlake was very much a prisoner of the way in which the various spaces of the Victorian home had become identified as 'masculine' or 'feminine' territory. He deals with both types of space, so presumably he accepted that some of his readers would be men; though it might also be assumed that a wife could be involved in the furnishing of any room. The book is arranged with descriptions of the average house, room by room; and thus reflects the gendered divide of function and ambience that was already standard.[28] The text is not exhaustive; and a number of the specialist rooms, such as the male preserve of the Billiard Room, are not mentioned, because the book is designed for the average middle-income family rather than for the wealthy upper middle classes. However, a masculine (or masculinist) assumption does seem to be apparent in the way that the Library, another male preserve, is picked out for approval: 'Of all the rooms in a modern house, that which is used as a library is the one least likely to offend a fastidious taste by its appointments. Here at least the furniture – usually of oak – is strong and solid. The silly knicknacks which too frequently crowd a drawing room table, chiffonier or mantel-piece, are banished from this retreat'.[29] The sentence reveals much of Eastlake's unconscious prejudice, though it is ostensibly directed at the mass produced and over-ornamented goods of the mid-century. However, the underlying assumption seems to be that masculine taste is superior.

There is a further gendered assumption that women are likely to be beguiled by the 'silly knicknacks', which Eastlake castigates as 'the cheap vulgarities of Tottenham Court Road', presumably a sideswipe at Maples's new store. There is also an element here of the progress of taste in the acceptance of new fashions. By 1870 it was fashionable to decry the productions of the mid-century, the sorts of objects of which Walter Crane said:

> the furniture is afflicted with curvature of the spine, and dreary lumps of ormulu repose on marble slabs at every opportunity, where monstrosities of every kind are encouraged under glass shades, while every species of design-debauchery is indulged upon carpets, curtains, chintzes and wall-papers, and where the antimacassar is made to cover a multitude of sins.[30]

Eastlake writing in the late 1860s was voicing a conventional taste for work such as the honest sturdy productions of Morris and Co. However, if he appears to be in the mainstream of the development of later nineteenth-century design, it must also be recognised that what he objects to is apparently what his readers preferred. By 1870 the new taste for Queen

Anne, more delicate and ornamental, was becoming established. A careful reading of Eastlake's text suggests that he felt that the new style represented a desire for fashionable novelty, something which he appears to have found both distasteful and essentially feminine. In making the usual distinction between the 'male' dining room and the 'female' drawing room, he attributes the difference to the relative solidity of the furniture:

> we sit down to dine upon an oaken chair before an oaken table, with a Turkey carpet under our feet, and a red flock paper staring us in the face. After dinner the ladies ascend into a green-and-gold papered drawing room, to perform on a walnut-wood piano, having first seated themselves on walnut-wood music stools, while their friends are reclining on a walnut-wood sofa, protected from the heat of the fire by a walnut-wood screen.[31]

He is most exercised by the desire for prettiness and the excessive clutter of drawing rooms and boudoirs, and, in short, represents the common sort of unconscious chauvinism that set out to educate the housewife, who was assumed to be about as feckless and incapable as Dickens's Dora in *David Copperfield*. Sense and discrimination, as opposed to taste, seem, from his language, to reside in men. In this he reflects the assumptions and gender roles that were the contemporary norm. His position secured him a hearing and established his taste as worthy of attention; and the fact that his book went through six editions in twelve years is evidence of its popularity. Indeed, given his preference for the sort of furniture that was produced to match the Gothic Revival, its continuing popularity at the end of the 1870s is quite remarkable, since the Gothic Revival was by then clearly outmoded. Yet, although it is addressed principally to a female audience, the gendered assumptions that underlie his book was seen as entirely unremarkable.

The reason seems to lie partly in the broader systems of design, manufacture and marketing. The involvement of women as professional designers seems to have been minimal throughout the nineteenth century, in spite of the increase in the numbers of women studying design, and the emergence of important practitioners such as Margaret (1864–1933) and Frances MacDonald (1873–1921) in Glasgow. Women were certainly involved in 'fancy work' as Eastlake recognises;[32] and it is well known that it was the female students of the South Kensington Art Schools who painted the tiles designed by Sir Edward Poynter for the Grill Room in the South Kensington Museums (at least until the work was taken over by Minton Campbell & Co.'s Art Studios).[33] It seems also to have been quite acceptable for genteel 'young ladies', and presumably also for young housewives, to undertake some ornamental decoration for their home. Fringes and antimacassars might as often be made as bought; but there were probably also many young ladies, like the daughters of Roundell Palmer at Blackmoor, capable of painting designs on ornamental tiles for their fireplaces.[34] However, as Juliet Kinchin has pointed out: 'gendered distinctions ... remained surprisingly consistent throughout the nineteenth century despite the increasing plethora of styles and goods from which consumers could choose'.[35]

How does Haweis as a woman negotiate such authoritative views? In her later years she was an ardent supporter of women's suffrage, so there can be no doubting her later sympathies. She has also been described as one who was 'never anxious to please everyone, troubled herself little enough with other peoples prejudices and was quite immovable in her prejudices',[36] an intolerance which may well have been born out of the struggle to achieve recognition as an expert. Achieve that status she certainly did, and was probably more popular in the 1880s than Eastlake in the 1870s. She wrote extensively in magazines such as *The Queen* and the *Contemporary Review*, and then produced two books on the furnishing of homes, *Beautiful Houses* and *The Art of Decoration*. Both make interesting contrasts with *Hints on Household Taste*, but both also have interesting parallels.

Beautiful Houses is interesting because it represents a woman's view of what was to be admired in contemporary design. It is immediately apparent that Haweis is also trapped in the conventional gendered view that the leaders of taste and practitioners of design were men. She describes twelve houses, only one of which is noted as belonging to a woman. The list is not altogether surprising in that it includes the houses of Frederick Leighton, William Burges, Alma Tadema, G. H. Boughton, Alfred Morrison, Reuben Sassoon and J. J. Stevenson. There is a strong predominance of the artistic and literary community, who are tacitly accepted as arbiters of taste. The list is completed with the British Embassy in Rome, Mr Haseltine's rooms in Rome, Ashley Park in Surrey[37] and the Villa Campana, a quartet which underlines the interest of Queen Anne designers and their followers in the early Renaissance. The only woman's house is listed simply as 'A Bijou House', but turns out to be the home of a Miss Hozier. However, the dominance of male practice is apparent even here: 'it is one of the smallest abodes in Wilton Place, belonging to Miss Hozier, and has been entirely decorated by the rising young architect, Mr William Wallace, of Old Bond Street'.[38] Clearly the sorts of product and the schemes of decoration to be admired are most likely to be designed by men; even if women are still acknowledged as likely to be the possessors of a superior sense of taste.

No figures have been recovered for the size of the edition, so it is unclear how widely the book was read. The popularity of the *Art of*

Decoration can be judged to some extent by the number and speed of the editions, but it is significant that neither of the two books was reviewed in the *Contemporary Review* for which Haweis wrote, and of the major publications only *The Academy* carried a review of *Beautiful Houses*[39] and the same journal failed to review the *Art of Decoration*. More interesting is the sarcastic tone of this review, which castigates *Beautiful Houses* as 'an example of the real "too too" in literature' and expresses a 'doubt whether some of our modern Della Cruscas of art will be able to refrain from tears as they read some of its most precious passages'.[40] The (presumably male) reviewer deals with the book as acerbically as W. S. Gilbert did with Bunthorn in *Patience*; and the suggestion is barely concealed that the book was of little importance.[41] The implication seems to be that the established literary world considered this first attempt at analysing design and interior decoration as only of interest as women's chit-chat. One reason might be that there is no academic justification for the choice of the twelve houses, but that was not a mistake Haweis would repeat. The *Art of Decoration* is both more exhaustive and more determinedly scholarly.

The book was written by a woman who was obliged to pursue a career as a writer and who sought to break into the male-dominated world of art and design criticism. We need to consider whether, in so doing, she presents a differently gendered view. Like Eastlake she addresses the consumer, and she makes a strong plea, like him, for consumer power that should dictate what is produced. 'Changes must emanate from the public,' she argues. 'not from their servant, the producer: for it is they who pay for it, not any elect body.'[42] The whole passage assumes the existing situation of male dominance of craftwork;[43] but the attempt to confirm the customer's confidence in his/her opinion is put even more strongly than in Eastlake. This important difference in Haweis's approach is both more pluralistic and more eclectic. She sets out to argue that what matters is individual taste, rather than obedience to a set of rules, claiming that 'the rules of taste are wide, not narrow, and will admit all tastes'.[44] Her subsequent text indicates both her awareness of the importance of the Gothic Revival and the Arts and Crafts movement as well as a more fashionable appreciation of the Aesthetic movement. It is revealing that she refers on several occasions to Whistler's Peacock Room. She also speaks well of Morris designs, particularly the wallpapers; though she complains that his carpets 'fade detestably soon',[45] a criticism borne, it would seem, from practical experience as a housewife.

Unlike Eastlake, however, Haweis builds her book round a historical survey of furniture, giving her suggestions the same foundation in scholarship as she had used for her advice on dress. The historical basis of her description is used not only to explore the range of different fashions available, but also to instruct her readers in what constituted 'quality' in design. The work is based on a close study of numerous examples in museums and this is the key to her claim to authority. The museum collection stands as a justification for her own taste, and a means of supporting her views by reference to accepted precedent. She was certainly well placed to make such claims. Her first recorded visit to the South Kensington Museums was in 1856, when she was eight and, living in London, and she had ample opportunity to visit and revisit the collections as they developed.

Her opposition to the dictates of fashion is fairly predictable, but it is less conventional in that she sneers at the current 'aesthetic' taste as determinedly as Gilbert and Sullivan in *Patience*.

> Right and delightful as it is to cultivate beauty, it is no doubt possible to carry the 'lust of the eye' too far like other things. Those 'aesthetic' folks who worship Signorelli, and sit among blue china and green paper mourning over the 19th century and yearning for the Past like the lost Children in the Wood for the departed uncle, sometimes make us think we might be cloyed with beauty (if this be its haunt), till we would hail tripe and onions on Judson-dyed china for a relief. There are other colours in the rainbow besides green and blue.[46]

She also regularly castigates professional designers who 'do' rooms by rote.

> All these fashionable rooms resemble each other. The Queen-Anne-mad decorators (some conspicuously) have but one idea and drive it to death. One hears that Mr Brown or the Misses Smith have decorated So and So's house. We know without ever entering it what that house is like. That house is a bore. There is not one original thought in it, from its inconvenient entrance to its last dark and aesthetic cranny.[47]

Here Haweis cites both male and female designers. The assumption is that there was nothing out of the ordinary in having your house 'done' by the Misses Smith, even though it seems likely that they might be more in the nature of (paid) advisers rather than commercial professionals.[48] However, she makes no gendered distinction in dismissing those who take over the decoration of another's home and replace their individual choices with a recipe. This is slightly surprising in view of her clear admiration for the architects and firms she lists in her introduction. But, as she makes clear in *Beautiful Houses*, it is allowance for the individual that marks out a good designer: 'All the houses decorated by Mr William Wallace have a certain soft, rich, dainty tone about them, quite individual, and absolutely different from the now-vulgarized "*Empire*" frigidities; and (what is very important) Mr. Wallace does not deprive the inhabitants of all voice in their own decoration.'[49]

Haweis's insistence on the rightness of individual taste is important, and marks a development on the position adopted by Eastlake. In this she is doing much more than press the claims of the succeeding Aesthetic movement, for all its deliberate quirkiness and conscious elitism. In fact in *The Art of Decoration* she continues her attack on commercial decorators by returning to her anti-aesthetic theme in a manner that is ambiguously gendered:

> For the most part, these houses reflect no inmate's character, no natural need or requirement – they contain no thought, no sweet little surprise – no touch of genius, nor even of ability. Yet they are 'aesthetic'. A recent writer in the 'Contemporary Review' explained with some humour the condensed farfetchedness which in China constitutes 'good literary style', but he did not say whether the aesthetic practice of obscure speech is traceable to aesthetic worship of Nankeen pots and plates. But though our unregenerate hearts may sigh for relief and something neither blue-green or green-blue, we must not be unjust. These rooms are so convenient, after all! They are less offensive than the old red and gold business. You can move easily among the sparse furniture. The little joints and inlaid spots are very 'nice' and the little emasculated legs vibrate sympathetically at a touch, so slight they are – poor little naked, shivering things! There is something weakly and feminine about this style, which goes to the heart, surely.[50]

The delicacy of the aesthetic furniture is seen as feminine; and, although Haweis clearly despises the fashionable aesthetic art-furniture, the current Japanese taste, she does admit its convenience. Yet her equation of certain styles with femininity, and beyond that with prettiness is important, and in many ways close to Eastlake. And this is a central element in her recipe of good taste. At the beginning of her book she praises 'prettiness': 'In summer, some bay window or shady niche might be the best nucleus, where the flowers in gayest pots, the curtains of softest folds, might be grouped: and in some such spot of main brilliancy the inhabitants, who would be sure to gravitate thither, would be the better thrown up and set off.'[51]

Here Haweis is apparently talking of the drawing room, one of the 'feminine' spaces. Yet there are a number of points in her book where she appears deliberately to ignore the conventional gender divide. Her comments on the study and library, both conventionally 'masculine' spaces, are particularly interesting.

> I prefer the furniture of a study or library a little gay in colour, because a mass of books, even gilt backed, unrelieved, always tells dark and heavy; I once knew a bookworm who, feeling the want of colour, painted his wall blood-red, his doors arsenic-green; A soft light-red and a kindly

moss-green such as a wood grows in midsummer, would have a different effect; but most colours are painful in too large a mass, and should be relieved by variations in the mouldings, or by pictures in parcel-gilt frames – filigree are the best – and a little china, or *cloisonné*, or German glass, sturdy and quaint. The books in one place and the china in another, each in its own glazed case, appears to me a joyless arrangement. Marry the gay colours of the one to the sober coats and bright thoughts of the other; mix pots and books in such a manner as that neither shall interfere with the other; and you get an artistically good effect.[52]

and slightly earlier:

The colour of a bookshelf is not necessarily dark; the wood may be inlaid, incrusted with pieces of metal or stone, or painted. In pale blue, white, or green, varnished and thoroughly dried before the books are put in, bookshelves may be made a real addition in beauty. The colour should depend on that of the walls and ceiling.[53]

Haweis is most probably reflecting her own colour preference, which would be entirely consistent with her advocacy of individual taste. In terms of gender, such a course would, however, be likely to reinforce the contemporary distinctions in home furnishing, since the consumer to whom her words were addressed was most likely to be a woman. And there is some confirmation of this dilemma in her summary of the home-maker's involvement. She is quite clear that the woman of the house would not do the basic decorating herself and would need to rely on male decorators or designers. Her approved designers are the predictable, but it is interesting that, in referring to Walter Crane and Randolph Caldecott as book designers, she makes no mention of Kate Greenaway. The omission is curious unless she disliked Greenaway as a professional rival. She talks about glass, mirrors and windows, recommending that women decorate the panes:

This mode of decoration would, I think, have the additional merit of being inconspicuous enough not to tire the eye by perpetually attracting it; and the upper part of the window might be left untouched if preferred so as to show the whole sky, if any be visible, from the position of the house. This would also offer a pleasing employment to idle young ladies at home, who could trace a pretty device in opaque enamel from a transparent pattern pasted outside the pane, whether they have much idea of drawing or not, and it would be better than making cardboard mats or gumming gold paper around photographs.[54]

Haweis accepts without question the gendered view of 'quiet housewifely grace' and the leisure to indulge in such pastimes. Yet she is generally careful, unlike Eastlake, to avoid a consistently gendered language in her text. 'He' occurs about as often as 'she'. Occasionally she adopts a convention that has become the norm today, for instance in criticising a type of chair: 'For instance, a chair stuffed so as to receive the shoulders comfortably, but leaving a hollow in the middle of the spine (a common fault) is adapted to very few positions, and soon so further tires a tired body that *he or she* (my italics) soon quits the chair to try another.'[55] For the most part, however, she refers to her readers as 'people'. Yet this apparent sensitivity is not maintained consistently, and much of her text makes similar assumptions to Eastlake in the involvement of women. She writes, for instance:

> A sensible woman will always have her sitting room light, for many reasons of health, convenience, and work – but not too light. A woman who is 'getting on' will not sit with her back to the light, that negress-effect [sic] is not pretty, but she will sit a respectable distance from the light.[56]

Or, in a section on Comfort and Beauty there is even a hint of the voyeur and of woman as the object of vision:

> a beautiful woman reclining on a sofa becomes for a time a part of the sofa, and the sofa part of her. Is it not best that the sofa should therefore be beautiful, so as at least not to add an ugliness to her during the transient association, though it may be unable to contribute a charm? It *will*, however, generally contribute a charm in the eyes of a cultivated spectator.[57]

Like Eastlake, Haweis attempts to cover the whole house, down to the china and plate. Unlike him, however, she does not deal with the individual spaces one by one. Instead she keeps the practical advice to the third part of her book, under the title General Applications. Although she intended to reinforce her dictat of appropriateness, her interest in prettiness and delicacy, conventionally equated with the 'feminine', is apparent. Here there may have been a problem of understanding on the part of her readers, who themselves were also prisoners of gender stereotypes. In *The Art of Beauty* she had apparently tried the same approach, and been criticised, as she rather ruefully admitted. 'In my book "Art of Beauty," the suggestion that surroundings ought to be adapted to persons, and the colours of rooms to their inhabitants, was much misunderstood. A great deal of small fun was made out of my supposed assertion that ladies should dress up to their rooms, or redecorate them to suit every new dress, or refuse to dine out without a warranty of the colour they were expected to sit against.'[58] She had already stated that 'furniture is a kind of dress, dress a kind of furniture, which both mirror the mind of their owner, and the temper of the age; which both minister to our comfort and culture, and they ought to be considered together'.[59] And this was clearly important to her. Yet in a period when male attire was restricted in both colour and form, this attitude would have the effect of focusing immediately on the contribution, and interests, of women. Indeed in her survey of periods, even where she does consider male dress, this bias is apparent.

Her enthusiastic descriptions of female historic costume seem to underline her preference for prettiness, delicacy and rich materials and soft tones. In that she was also arguing for the primacy of individual taste, she was entirely entitled to her own preference. But her individual preference, if that is what it is, supports remarkably closely the conventional gendered divide between the association of sober, solid and dark as 'masculine' attributes in design and delicate, light and fanciful as 'feminine'. In spite of her apparent attempt to address both sexes, and her blurring of the gender divide in certain categories of room or certain items of furniture, she avoids the attempt to overthrow the conventional views that she found established. Indeed the gendered approach to her subject is positively reinforced by her drawing of a willowy girl, with a few lines of poetry about Nature which forms the frontispiece to her book. In this sense her text, following a decade after Eastlake's, represents a fashion for 'individuality' in design and a greater eclecticism rather than a change of direction. In the field of interior decoration change was a great deal slower in coming than in literature or social reform, and although Haweis was accepted as an authority, she was, it seems, unable to defeat the popular stereotype. Her book is curiously retrograde step at the moment when women designers, most notably the 'Glasgow girls', were emerging as leaders of taste in their own right. Possibly this accounts for the way it passed into obscurity, while Eastlake's equally conventional text has survived as a typical Victorian document, gendered in a typically Victorian way.

Notes

1   Charles Locke Eastlake, *Hints on Household Taste*, 2nd edn (London, Longmans, Green & Co., 1869, 1st edn 1868), p. 7.

2   Charles Locke Eastlake, 1839–1906, Secretary RIBA 1866–77, Director National Gallery 1878–98.

3   Mrs H. R. Haweis, *The Art of Decoration* (London, Chatto & Windus, 1881); see also her other titles: *The Art of Beauty* (London, Chatto & Windus, 1878); *Beautiful Houses* (London, Sampson Low & Co., 1882); and *The Art of Housekeeping: A Bridal Garland* (London, Chatto & Windus, 1889).

4   The South Kensington Museums were established under the aegis of the Department of Science and Art in the wake of the Great Exhibition of 1851. The collections of objects were housed in buildings on the estate of the Commissioners of the Great Exhibition, and by the end of the century were renamed the Victoria & Albert Museum.

5   See *Dictionary of National Biography* and Graves, *Royal Academy Exhibitors* (1906) pp. 293–4. Joy is recorded as an 'Honorary Exhibitor', but in spite of an

acquaintance with William Powell Frith PRA, was not even elected an Associate member.

6   See Graves, *Royal Academy Exhibitors*, p. 293. The work was an illustration of a literary theme from *Jean Ingelow*, and was Eliza Mary's only RA exhibit. It was submitted shortly after her father's death; and, according to MEH's *Thought Book* was a part of her determination to earn a living. See B. Howe, *Arbiter of Elegance* (London, Harvill Press, 1967), pp. 62ff.

7   St James, Westmoreland Street was Crown appointment, and had no parish. The stipend was entirely made up from pew rents.

8   Frances Power Cobbe, *The Duties of Women* (1881), quoted in Jenni Calder, *The Victorian Home* (London, Batsford, 1977), p. 102.

9   J. John Ruskin, *Sesame and Lilies, II Of Queen's Gardens* (lectures delivered at Manchester in 1864, reissued London, J. M. Dent, 1907), p. 72.

10   Robert Kerr, *The Gentleman's House* (London, 1871), p. 86, quoted in Juliet Kinchin 'Interiors: nineteenth-century essays on the "masculine" and the "feminine" room', in Pat Kirkham (ed.), *The Gendered Object* (Manchester, Manchester University Press, 1996), p. 20.

11   In London the establishment of the Central School of Design in 1836 was followed by the founding of 'The Female School of Design' in 1842. See F. Graeme Chalmers, *Women in the Nineteenth Century Art World: Schools of Design for Women in London and Philadelphia* (London, Greenwood Press, 1998).

12   See, for example, Jane S. Smith, *Elsie de Wolfe* (New York, Athenaeum, 1982).

13   In 1878 under the editorship of W. R. Loftie a series of booklets appeared under the title *Art at Home*. Although Loftie himself wrote *The Dining Room*, dealing with that conventionally male space, volumes on *The Drawing Room*, *The Bedroom and Boudoir* and on *House Decoration in Painting* were contributed by Mrs Orrinsmith, Lady Barker and the Misses Agnes and Rhoda Gartret respectively.

14   This is described in Haweis, *The Art of Decoration*, p. 388, as painted in 1873 in 'moss green relieved by red and black in the reveals of the windows and the balcony'. Curiously, perhaps, Mary does not describe it as 'my house' but as the home of 'Rev. R. H. Haweis'.

15   Howe, *Arbiter of Elegance*, p. 137.

16   Letter to Mrs Thomas Joy, January 1876, quoted in Howe, *Arbiter of Elegance*, p. 131.

17   Her first recorded visit to the South Kensington Museums was in 1856.

18   H. R. Haweis (ed.), *Words to Women: Addresses and Essays* (with a memoir) (London, Bernard & Isbister, 1900), quoted in Howe, *Arbiter of Elegance*, p. 149.

19   Haweis, *The Art of Beauty*, p. 1.

20   Eastlake, *Hints on Household Taste*, p. 237.

21   Haweis, *The Art of Beauty*, p. 268.

22   Catherine E. Beecher and Harriet Beecher Stowe, *The American Woman's Home*, (Boston, 1869), p. 84, quoted in Maurice Howard and Michael Snodin, *A History of Ornament* (London, 1995), p. 149.

23   Until the Married Women's Property Act of 1873, it really was her husband's income and entirely his to dispose.

24   At the time he wrote he was Secretary of the RIBA, and was shortly to follow his uncle as Director of the National Gallery.

25   The architectural profession was still almost exclusively male. The first women architects appeared in the census for 1861, though it is widely assumed they were

widows carrying on their late husband's business, most likely in the role of managers rather than draughtsmen.

26   Eastlake, *Hints on Household Taste*, p. 7.

27   Eastlake, *Hints on Household Taste*, p. 10.

28   This has recently been discussed in detail by Juliet Kinchin in 'Interiors', pp. 12–29.

29   Eastlake, *Hints on Household Taste*, p. 113.

30   Quoted in E. P. Thompson, *William Morris: Romantic to Revolutionary* (London, Lawrence & Wishart, 1955), p. 124.

31   Eastlake, *Hints on Household Taste*, p. 65.

32   See, for instance Eastlake, *Hints on Household Taste*, pp. 88–9.

33   See Charlotte Gere and Michael Whiteway, *Nineteenth Century Design* (London, Weidenfield & Nicolson, 1993), p. 138. The involvement of 'young ladies' in this particular branch of art manufacture is clearly related to the regular use of women as painters in the pottery industry as a whole.

34   It has not proved possible to verify this story preserved in the family's oral tradition, but the tiles are of a particularly unusual design so it is not impossible. They were probably painted in biscuit, and then glazed and fired by W. B. Simpson.

35   Kinchin, 'Interiors', p. 24.

36   Howe, *Arbiter of Elegance*, p. 16.

37   Ashley Park, Surrey, home of Sir Henry Fletcher, and known for its great gallery and collection of furniture, demolished 1925: (see Howard Colvin, *A Biographical Dictionary of British Architects 1600–1840*, 3rd edn (New Haven and London, Yale University Press, 1995), pp. 745, 1027.

38   Mrs H. R. Haweis, *Beautiful Houses: Being a Description of Certain Well-Known Artistic Houses*, 2nd edn (London, Sampson Low & Co., 1882), p. 99.

39   The periodicals searched for reviews are: *The Athenaeum, Quarterly Review, Blackwood's Magazine, Contemporary Review, Saturday Review, Nineteenth Century, Cornhill Magazine, Edinburgh Review, The Academy*. The years searched were 1881 and 1882, the years of publication of the two books. I am grateful to Madeline Thompson for this research. A review of *The Art of Beauty* is noted in the New York *Ellective Magazine* for 1878. I am grateful to Professor Carol Krinsky for searching the New York libraries for this for me. However, none of the major libraries in New York appear to hold this periodical. Both this absence from major collections and the implied status of the magazine indicate gendered attitudes to Haweis's original publication.

40   *The Academy*, 540, 9 September 1882, pp. 191–2.

41   It is possible that Haweis was more favourably received in America, for her earlier book, *The Art of Beauty*, was at least reviewed in the *Ellective Magazine*, 1878, p. 472.

42   Haweis, *The Art of Decoration*, pp. 20–1.

43   In her introduction she gives a partial list of key designers, all of whom are male: Sir Jeffery Wyatville, Joseph Paxton, Crace, Evans of Shrewsbury, Clayton & Bell, W. J. Aitchison, Gillow & Co., Minton & Co., Owen Jones, Pugin, Whistler, Cottier & Co., Powell & Co., William Morris, Burne-Jones, Walter Crane, Charles Eastlake, William Burges, Helbronner & Co. and James Fergusson: Haweis, *The Art of Decoration*, p. xxiii.

44   Haweis, *The Art of Decoration*, p. 11.

45   Haweis, *The Art of Decoration*, p. 294.

46   Haweis, *The Art of Decoration*, p. 17.

47   Haweis, *The Art of Decoration*, pp. 52–3.

48   I know of no detailed study of the women involved in decoration in this way. It would be interesting to know how many were at work in the capital in the later 1870s. The best-known parallel case is probably that of Gertrude Jekyll in her role as garden designer.

49   Haweis, *Beautiful Houses*, p. 106.

50   Haweis, *The Art of Decoration*, pp. 53–4.

51   Haweis, *The Art of Decoration*, pp. 10–11.

52   Haweis, *The Art of Decoration*, p. 306.

53   Haweis, *The Art of Decoration*, p. 304.

54   Haweis, *The Art of Decoration*, pp. 244–5.

55   Haweis, *The Art of Decoration*, p. 266.

56   Haweis, *The Art of Decoration*, p. 352.

57   Haweis, *The Art of Decoration*, pp. 269–70.

58   Haweis, *The Art of Decoration*, p. 23.

59   Haweis, *The Art of Decoration*, p. 17.

Women, translation
and empowerment[1]

Lorna Hardwick

The notion that knowledge of Greek texts is somehow empowering has
persisted to the present day. Even though the nineteenth-century pattern
of a classical education is no longer with us, mature women students who
wish to learn Greek sometimes say to me: 'I've always wanted to do this.
My brother did it at school but I couldn't.' In the early and mid-nineteenth
century, women's education was even more differentiated from men's, and
even among educated women many accepted that this should be so.[2]
Nevertheless, some did learn Greek. Why and how they did this, the use
to which they put it and how their work was regarded are questions which
underlie this study. I have chosen to focus on two women scholars, Anna
Swanwick and Augusta Webster. Both produced translations of Greek
tragedy, had an interest in women's education and supported the Suffrage
movement, but their work also displays significant contrasts in outlook and
in literary activity.

Recent research has shown increasing awareness of the importance
in the cultural history of subsequent ages of the history of classical scholarship and the broader reception of the ideas and images of antiquity.
Attitudes to and reworking of the literature and art of the ancient world
provide a significant strand in nineteenth-century social and cultural
history and in particular provide an index for the analysis of change in
scholarly, educational and artistic conventions. The question of initial
access to classical learning and the uses to which it might subsequently be
put reveals important areas of gender and class exclusion and enables us
to identify and analyse the relationships between challenge to and complicity with dominant traditions. Competition to appropriate the classical
canon (and the moral force associated with it) made classical texts part of
the battlefield of social change.[3]

The early nineteenth century saw a shift from Rome to Greece as a source of political and poetical inspiration. The focus on Greece was seen as breaking with previous stress on Roman examples of moral and political rectitude.[4] The new emphasis on appropriation of ancient Greek culture, perhaps stimulated by the struggle for Greek independence in the early part of the century, seemed to offer a richer choice and there is evidence of a gradually emerging double consciousness.[5] Greek culture might be reconstructed as a model of elite taste. It might equally well yield material which appeared to sanction democracy, political debate and social reform or even perhaps to threaten the values associated with Christian monotheism.

This essay aims to illuminate one aspect of this nexus of cultural relationships and to demonstrate how consciousness of the empowering possibilities of ancient Greece operated in different ways in different contexts. The upsurge of interest in Greek culture led to an increase in demand for translations. In the 1820s the number of translations from original texts trebled (fifty-five as opposed to eighteen in the previous ten years). There was a further spurt in the 1860s in response to school and university needs. As a result of these demands there were more opportunities for translators from outside the traditional aristocratic and academic fields to publish their work.[6]

Both Anna Swanwick and Augusta Webster were prominent translators in their own time but have since largely slipped from notice. Although both were Greek scholars, there are significant contrasts in their background and education, in the ways in which their literary output was communicated and received and in how they used it to advance the authority of their ideas on gender and social morality. There is enough common ground between them to enable analysis of the implications of this divergence. In assessing the relationship between their work as translators and their work for women's empowerment three main areas are crucial: their scholarship and the authority derived from it; the relationship between their translations and their other literary work; their treatment of power relationships (both material and moral) in their work as a whole.

Neither fits cosily into the 'educated women as helpmate/subversive' stereotype which emerges from nineteenth-century fiction by women.[7] The two most compelling images are perhaps those of Dorothea Brooke in George Eliot's Middlemarch and Caroline Helstone in Charlotte Brontë's Shirley. Dorothea combines a desire to serve with a desire for wisdom, 'but it was not entirely out of devotion to her future husband that she wished to know Latin and Greek. Those provinces of masculine knowledge seemed to her a standing-ground from which all truth could be seen more truly'.[8] Of course, she discovered that the 'Key to all Mythologies' didn't bring wisdom, let alone happiness.[9]

A more radical attitude to the key-holders is shown by Caroline Helston's claims in relation to St Paul,

> I dare say, if I could read the original Greek, I should find that many of the words have been wrongly translated, perhaps misapprehended altogether. It would be possible, I doubt not, with a little ingenuity, to give the passage quite a contrary turn; to make it say, 'Let the woman speak out whenever she sees fit to make an objection – it is permitted to a woman to teach and to exercise authority as much as may be. Man, meantime, cannot do better than hold his peace', and so on.[10]

My concerns here pick up two aspects of the Dorothea/Caroline polarity. First, what kind of 'wisdom' did my chosen scholars hope to find in the Greek texts and communicate through translation? Furthermore, if Greek is a means to power, how did they exercise this power? This second point raises further questions about the women's relationship with mechanisms, networks and institutions through which power was in practice exercised. Underlying both issues are questions concerning the philosophy and practice of translation which they developed. There seem to have been two distinct types of audience which they had in mind. The first was made up of those who knew Greek, would be critical of the translator's scholarship and, if impressed, would accept the translator as someone whose opinions were worth attention. The second type of audience consisted of those who would be 'improved' by access to the canon of classical texts. This audience raised very different issues for the two translators, particularly in respect of judgements about who would be suitable for 'improvement' and how this might be achieved. In this context, it is necessary also to consider their relationship to Sage discourse. Because of its status in moral and political debate, recent research has treated Sage writing as a specific genre within the field of Victorian studies.[11] Characterisation of the genre ranges from the inclusive (covering essays and fiction in addition to more obviously didactic writing) to the more narrowly typological, such as non-fiction prose drawing on the structure and language of biblical prophecy.[12] Both Swanwick and Webster produced important work in addition to translations and Swanwick's works of criticism and moral precept and Webster's essays on social issues bring them within the Sage genre. The generic and intertextual complexity of Sage writing prompts investigation of the relationship between their translations and the other kinds of writing they produced since the 'woman question' (along with the 'condition of England' question) permeated Sage discourse written by both men and women.

In recent years, translation has become more widely accepted as a coherent part of literary output and in the case of Swanwick and Webster provides a point of convergence in work which is in other respects widely diverging. Furthermore, in the case of both women, it is necessary to consider the mutual relevance of their translations and their other work in order to analyse their sense of the relationship between Greek ideas and society and those of their own time.[13] Their formulation of this relationship usefully clarifies several aspects of their Sage writing and adds a dimension to broader analysis of the variety of tone and ideology to be found in the genre.

So in many respects, there are parallel sets of questions to be asked about female Sages and female translators. In respect of translation, what was the relationship between translators and the paradigms of male scholarship? Were women assimilated into the norms of classical scholarship rather than becoming forces for challenge? Were there distinctively female scholarly discourses on a par with, but differing from, the male or was it (like Elizabeth Barrett's character) 'lady's Greek, without the accents'.[14] To put it bluntly did women scholars become accomplices/complicit in the exclusive aspects of appropriation or did they join in order to subvert?[15]

Both Swanwick and Webster followed the example of Elizabeth Barrett and started their work on translation from Greek with Aeschylus' *Prometheus Bound*, a play which dramatises issues of obligation, community, freedom, tyranny and oppression of woman. Subsequently, the choice of Greek texts is indicative of the direction taken by their other work. Swanwick stayed with Aeschylus and found in the *Oresteia* a trilogy resonant with issues of political and social conflict, the emergence of democracy and the sanctioning power of religion. Webster chose Euripides' *Medea*, not only as a study of the psychology of a wronged woman but also a stimulus to explore the interaction between material circumstances and gender relations.

Anna Swanwick

Although she was judged to merit an obituary in *The Times* (Saturday, 4 November 1899) which described her as, 'in her time a well-known woman of letters as well as a leader in social and educational reform movements' (figure 16), Swanwick has largely slipped from notice in the twentieth century. Apart from the brief summary by Elizabeth Lee in the Supplement to the *Dictionary of National Biography* (*DNB*), the major source for Swanwick's life is the memoir by her niece Mary L. Bruce.[16] It is hagiographic in tone, but provides a careful record of Swanwick's main areas of activity in her long life and preserves verbatim versions of some of her speeches.[17]

Swanwick was born in Liverpool in 1813, the youngest daughter of a merchant and descended from a nonconformist divine. The family was

16 Photograph of Anna Swanwick, 1890s (?)

liberal in politics and Unitarian in religion. She was deeply influenced by
the Unitarian ethos which held that it was necessary for both men and
women to develop intellectual powers in order to achieve a corresponding
development of moral and religious character.[18] However, although she
went to what she later described as 'the best girls' school in Liverpool' it
failed to respond to her desire to learn more about mathematics and she
left at the age of thirteen. Late in life, in an address to the students at
Bedford College, she said, 'I often longed to assume the costume of a boy
in order to learn Latin, Greek and Mathematics, which were then regarded
as essential to a liberal education for boys but were not thought of for girls.' [19]
    After she left school, Swanwick studied German with her sister in
order to read Schiller and later Goethe. When she was eighteen she met

the Rev. James Martineau (brother of Harriet) when he was appointed minister at the Unitarian Chapel in Paradise Street, Liverpool. His lectures on mental and moral philosophy had great influence on the young people in the congregation. In 1838 Swanwick moved to Tavistock Place in London. Shortly afterwards she visited Germany to study Greek as well as German, 'as she wished to read the New Testament in the original'.[20] She studied in Berlin and was soon engaged in translating Plato into German. She also learnt Hebrew and read Kant and Fichte. At this stage in her life she was a strict sabbatarian and refused to attend concerts on Sundays.

Her personal and intellectual development in these years is a good example of the results of exposure to the influential interrelationship between German and classical culture, fostered by the German Romantic movement in the work of scholars and poets such as Schlegel.[21] Indeed, Swanwick's first publications were translations from Goethe and Schiller.[22] She had independent means and did not need to write for a living.

Translations from Greek

Subsequently Swanwick continued to develop her interest in translation from Greek encouraged by Baron Bunsen and F. W. Newman. In 1865 she published her translation of Aeschylus' *Oresteia*. The translation took her four years to complete and in general had very favourable reviews, except for her adoption of blank verse for the iambics and rhyme for the lyric metres. Letters of congratulation came in, including those from F. D. Maurice and from Gladstone, who wrote to A. Swanwick, Esq., via the publishers.[23] She replied and they became friends. She subsequently attended many of his Thursday breakfasts where she was sometimes the only woman present apart from Mrs Gladstone and they 'discussed Homer, Aeschylus, Dante, Shakespeare and Ireland'.

In 1873 her translation of the complete works of Aeschylus was published, illustrated by Flaxman, followed in 1900 by her translation of *The Agamemnon* of Aeschylus.[24] This was performed as part of the emerging tradition of the Cambridge Greek play.[25]

Critical response to Swanwick's translation

Two comments on Swanwick's translations indicate the direct and indirect use to which they were put. First, there was the way in which her work opened up wider access to classical culture. Dr Butler of Trinity (contributing an appreciation at the end of her life) wrote, 'it was for the general reader that she laboured rather than for professional scholars. She was anxious that the noble dramas of the age of Pericles should become, in their thoughts, if not their language, familiar to readers of all classes in England.' Butler also stressed her religious purpose, while Sir Richard Jebb noted 'a genuine sympathy with the original; much poetic feeling; disciplined command of expression; and a fine literary tact'.[26] Secondly, there was the way in which her work created respect for women's scholarship. A good example is the enthusiastic but perhaps patronising review by the Rev. P. H. Wickstead (a friend) in the dreaded Saturday Reviler (as Bruce termed the *Saturday Review*), 'here is fit cause for the advocates of the rights of women to gather together and chant a paean in commemoration of their advanced prospects and position'.[27]

This link between (male) perceptions of women's scholarship and the credibility of the movements for women's education and suffrage was made at greater length in an article titled 'Capacities of women' in the *Westminster Review* in 1865.[28] The article considered recent work by Bessie Rayner Parkes, Anna Swanwick and Frances Power Cobbe and discussed them as diverse examples of women writers who, evidently, encountered some hostile reviews. As the reviewer put it,

> at least they will show how much their talents and their sound accomplishments deserve respect: how unjust and how superficial is that tone of disparagement so easily (we had almost said, so naturally) assumed by an anonymous reviewer, whose task it is to write down a woman, or the cause which she is maintaining.

This raises two significant points – first, the gendering of the language of critical review and second, the association make by critics between a woman's literary production and the causes for which she stands or is supposed to stand.

There are numerous examples of the ways in which the language of review encoded a gendered 'evaluation' of women. For instance, George Stillman Hillard wrote of Elizabeth Barrett's translation of *Prometheus Bound*:

> The version of the great work of Aeschylus, a daring enterprise for a young lady, and one which could not have been attempted, without a degree of learning highly creditable to her industry and perseverance, is not a very successful one … we like her preface much better than the work it introduces. That is written in vigorous and manly prose, and shows a power of independent thought, discriminating criticism and a good deal of masculine learning, if the ladies will pardon us the expression; we mean by it, that kind of learning usually monopolised by gentlemen.[29]

The comic extremes of gendered reviewing were well illustrated in 1868 when an anonymous reviewer in *The Athenaeum* commented on Augusta Webster's translation of the *Medea*: 'the subject if not grand, is one of general interest, being confined to no time, place or class of society. It is also one which a lady might naturally be expected to handle with success as she must be able to enter fully into the feelings of the unfortunate heroine in her distressing condition.' [30]

That 'writing down' a woman's scholarship or ability served as a means of writing down her cause was well understood by the reviewer in the *Westminster Review* of 1865 who likened gender-based exclusions to those based on national or religious chauvinism: 'Men who are not person- ally conceited, often display conceit, at once offensive and injurious, in the claims which they make for their church, their country, their race or (we will add) for their sex.' [31] The reviewer's emphasis is on the scholarly nature of Swanwick's work and extracts from her translation of the *Agamemnon* were placed side by side with the same passages in Blackie's version. Significantly, the reviewer assumed that not all readers will be familiar with the Greek text of the Aeschylus but the play also allowed a direct comparison between male and female scholarship. The reviewer praises Swanwick's faithfulness to the original, adding that, 'the things which the reader may perhaps wonder to find in Blackie and miss in her, are not in Aeschylus'. Furthermore, 'not only in tenderness, dignity, weight and in that *masculine attribute terseness* but also in understanding and intimate feeling of the Greek, the lady need not fear comparison with the Greek professor' (italics added). Finally the verdict on her scholarship is 'it is everywhere conscientious in the extreme. She is fully possessed with the principle avowed in her preface, that "any wilful or unacknowledged deviation from the original is tantamount to a breach of trust". Every line bears the mark of honest laborious thought with delicate sense of the Greek.' [32]

The same praise is not extended to Frances Power Cobbe of whom is written, 'Miss Cobbe's learning, though very extensive on the subject of human religion, and as such commands our high respect, is not accurate in respect to the Latin and Greek languages. Has no kind friend pointed it out?' Finally the telling point is that 'since the number of Englishmen who can understand an easy Latin sentence is very large and those who can judge of a metaphysical controversy are very few, Miss Cobbe damaged her book extremely by such absurdities: for those who see her haste and inaccuracy in Latin quotations will be apt to impute a like inaccuracy to her fundamental philosophy'. [33]

The reviewer is clearly opposed to Cobbe's religious ideas and Kantian philosophy as well as to her Latin and Greek usage. Swanwick escapes more lightly although she, too, had strong religious convictions and had studied Kant. Somewhat surprisingly the reviewer skates over her long introduction to the Aeschylus ('an ample, elaborate and learned essay on the growth and improvement of Greek religion in outline its truth is questionable', and instead comments on its (Grotean) closing sequence, in which Swanwick discussed the moral uses of poetry and arts as national educators.[34] The reviewer is almost certainly Swanwick's friend and mentor F. W. Newman.[35] Newman was at that stage of his life an opponent of conventional religion. His willingness to bypass Swanwick's long and somewhat tedious religious discussion in her introduction to the *Oresteia* testifies not only to his regard for her translation but also to her success at networking among males.[36]

I shall return later to the way in which Swanwick's scholarship empowered her in her practical work, by allowing her voice to be heard and her deliberations to be effective. However, first I want to look at an area which the reviewer bypassed – her approach to translation and its potential conflict with her social and religious ideas.

Mary Bruce's memoir quotes at first hand Swanwick's own methods.[37] First, she aimed to acquire a thorough knowledge of the original (being able to repeat it by heart). Second, she emphasised accuracy. Third, she tried to develop a metre as close to the original as the language would permit. This last is in contrast to methods which concentrated on fluency in English. Together with the influence of F. W. Newman, whose translation of Homer's *Iliad* she frequently cited with approval, this approach inclined her away from the 'domesticating' method of translation which canonised fluency and encoded dominant English cultural values into the translation. In contrast Newman, the author of *Four Lectures on the Contrasts of Ancient and Modern History* (1847) was associated with the 'foreignising' method which aimed to register the linguistic and cultural differences of the original text.[38]

The debate between proponents of the 'domesticating' and the 'foreignising' methods of translation rests on an assumption that there is a stable notion of what the English language is and represents. Swanwick's lengthy introduction to her Aeschylus translation does not focus on issues of domestication and foreignisation in relation to translation, but it does confront the issue in relation to religion. In the preface she refers to the need for 'faithfulness to the original [text] in spirit as well as form'. Deviation was seen as a 'breach of trust'. Yet she also had to address the problem presented by the fact that while Greek culture might in some respects be perceived as admirable, its religion was pagan.

Religious ideas in Aeschylus were, according to Swanwick, developed from the primitive and the primeval and marked the second great stage of human progress, a prelude to Christianity 'a dim but most wonderful foreshadowing' (p. xxviii). In her view the translation thus required both fidelity to the original and logically, as well as in terms of scholarship, a 'distancing' from nineteenth-century values. A lack of such distance would, she considered, be offensive to readers' moral and religious sensibility as well as to scholarship. This can be seen, too, in her choice of political language, for example her use of the quasi-medieval 'lieges' as a translation of *polis*-related terms.[39]

Swanwick was also fond of terms like 'primeval' and 'germ'. She used 'Germ' to signify Apollo's description of parenthood:

> Not parent of the embryo but nurse
> Is she, the so-called mother of the child
> The father is the source, as stranger, she
> For stranger rears the germ if heaven blight not.
>   (Swanwick, lines 627–30)

This is a bowdlerised rendering of Aeschylus' *Eumenides*, lines 658–61:

> The mother is no parent of that which is called her child, but only nurse of the new-planted seed that grows. The parent is he who mounts. A stranger she preserves a stranger's seed, if no god interfere.[40]

Swanwick's translation also employs in places a Christianised religious discourse: 'salvation', 'trespass', 'sin', for example:

> Chorus
>
> Thee thou shalt see in durance drear,
> 'Gainst God, or guest, or parents dear,
> Like thee who sinn'd, receiving their due need.
> For Hades, ruler of the nether sphere,
> Exactest auditor of human kind,
> Graved on the tablet of his mind
> Doth every trespass read (Swanwick, lines 259–65)

In contrast the Aeschylus, lines 271–5, focus on impiety:

> and watch the rest of the mortals stained with violence
> gainst god or guest
> or hurt parents who were close and dear,
> each with the pain upon him that his crime deserves.
> Hades is great, Hades calls men to reckoning
> there under the ground,
> sees all, and cuts it deep in his recording mind[41]

Swanwick acknowledged, too, the influence of doctrines about development and progress in religion which she acquired from German scholars and most notably from the ideas of the Oxford Professor Max Müller on the derivations of Greek religious symbols and language.[42] Although much of Müller's best-known work was not published until the 1890s, Swanwick's introduction to her *Aeschylus* translation indicates she was thoroughly

familiar with his main lines of thought and especially his stress on the study
of the development of the human mind as part of historical research. Very
roughly, Swanwick used Homer as a benchmark from which to chart the
'progress' of Greek religious ideas towards those expressed three centuries
later in Aeschylus, especially the *Eumenides*, in which religious and legal
sanctions were harmonised.

The development of a link between moral worth and divine favour
is, according to Swanwick the distinguishing mark of 'progress' between
Homer and Aeschylus. She wrote that in this way ancient poetry 'records
the religious life of humanity'. These views were also set out in her later
monograph *Evolution and the Religion of the Future* (1893).

She was an enthusiastic attender of scientific lectures and her
development of a kind of intellectual and religious Darwinism lies behind
the importance she attached to poets as 'the interpreter of their age'. Her
book *Poets the Interpreters of their Age* (1892) attracted the attention of the
Saturday Review which commented, 'In the season of guide-books a guide
to Parnassus is no bad thing for those who want time or inclination for
independent studies.' [43] In this work the chapter on Homer contains some
interesting critical observations on the poetic representation of women,
notably her discussion of the plight of captives and of Andromache's lament
over Hector and her fears for her son.[44] She also comments on the imagery
of the swimmer used to convey Penelope's joy at Odysseus' return in
Odyssey, noticing how the exchange between husband and wife of traditionally masculine and traditionally feminine images enlarges understanding of
women's emotional power and resourcefulness.[45]

Swanwick regards such passages as a redeeming feature of the heroic
age described by Homer, showing 'the strength and tenderness of the
domestic affections as exhibited in the conjugal, the parental and the filial
relations'.[46] However, her discussion also conveys the extent to which
Homeric epic is also concerned with brutality, exploitation and greed and
she shows less tendency than some other Victorians, such as Gladstone,
to sanitise the political and moral ethos of the poems.

Swanwick's book was, she says in the introduction, prepared in
response to requests from those who had attended popular lectures. It
responds, perhaps, to the hopes expressed in a passage at the end of her
Aeschylus introduction, in which she quotes from Grote's *History of Greece*
on the vitality and importance of the Greek tragic theatre, 'All this
abundance found its way to the minds of the great body of citizens, not
excepting even the poorest'.[47] Swanwick added that, as in Athens, the
thoughts of the great poets should be 'brought to the hearts and minds of
our people'.

The women's movement: suffrage

The inspiration for Swanwick's support for the suffrage movement came when Lucretia Mott, who had travelled from Massachusetts to attend the World Anti-Slavery convention in London in 1840 was, with other women, denied participation in the convention. When they protested, the vote went against them and it was decided that women could sit in the gallery and listen but not offend against good taste by speaking in public. Unitarians supported the protesters by offering a meeting room and some male delegates showed solidarity by taking their seats with the women 'behind the bar'. The event proved to be a watershed in provoking awareness of the parallels between slavery and gender oppression.[48]

In 1865 Swanwick signed the petition on women's suffrage organised by Barbara Bodichon and the Langham Place associates and presented to Parliament in 1866 by J. S. Mill. In 1873 she spoke in public for the first time at the age of sixty. Frances Power Cobbe recorded that Swanwick was asked to second a resolution on suffrage because of her 'Sage' status as 'so learned a women and one so universally respected'.[49] Swanwick in fact made what the Birmingham Daily Post described as 'the speech of the evening' and sat down to thunderous applause.

The women's movement: education

Soon after moving to London in 1838, Swanwick started an evening school for poor girls at her house in Woburn Square, then she rented rooms for them. She recruited students by approaching poor women in the slums. Her classes were then incorporated into the Portland British Schools by James Martineau when he moved to London. Swanwick then developed evening classes for young men to deter them from hooliganism (and, according to Mary Bruce, from Chartist excesses). She joined with F. D. Maurice, Charles Kingsley and others in establishing working men's clubs and institutes, leading to Morley College.

Her work for women's education also continued. In 1849 Queen's College in Harley Street was started by Maurice and his group, followed by the college in Bedford Square with which Swanwick's connection lasted fifty years. She became one of the first students 'to encourage others' and her name appears on the register of students between 1849 and 1859 with details of the classes she attended and the fees she paid.[50]

She also attended F. W. Newman's classes on maths as a Lady Visitor, 'responsible to the Council for the maintenance of order and discipline'. Greek was soon added and she said Newman's guidance helped with her later work on Aeschylus. She was a member of the College

Council from 1857–61. In 1878 she presented the first women graduates from Bedford College and in 1884 was the first woman to be elected Visitor (1884–89), presiding over the Jubilee Conference in 1899.

She was active in the development of Somerville College, Oxford, and of Girton College, Cambridge, which insisted that the Cambridge curriculum should be the same for male and female students. She also did substantial work on the committee allocating grants from the Pfeiffer bequest for women's education which distributed money to Girton, Newnham, Bedford, Queen's, the School of Medicine for Women, Maria Gray Training College, Somerville, Women's Halls at Trinity College Dublin, Edinburgh, Cardiff, Aberystwyth, University College London and the College for Working Women.[51]

Her advice on curriculum matters included recognition of the difference between Greek and Victorian values and she had definite views on the place of Greek in courses of study:

> I yet hesitate to recommend it as a part of the curriculum of boys or girls unless it can be taken later and with more concentrated determination to master the extremely difficult grammar than is usually given to school lessons It is to be remembered, moreover, that in the literature of Greece and Rome there are no works adapted expressly for the young. The ancient classics, written by adults for adults, are beyond the intelligence of immature minds while in regard to the moral lessons to be drawn from them, the superiority in my opinion is vastly in favour of more modern writers.[52]

Education and social issues

This strict moral tone is evident in other speeches and papers. Ironically, it led to a modification of her early sabbatarianism. At the Social Science Congress in 1875 she read a paper which asserted 'would that every gin palace could be transformed to a library or palace of art' and in her role as Vice-President of the Sunday Society campaigned for the popular promotion of education and culture on Sundays as an alternative to drink shops as well as offering a relief from toil. These ideas were developed in her book *An Utopian Dream and How It May Be Realised* (1888). She also campaigned for free libraries, on the grounds that the cost to society would be less that that of the crime resulting from the unoccupied masses getting drunk (*Books, Our Best Friends or Our Deadliest Foes*, printed privately, 1886).

Those who appreciated her influence spoke of the quietness of Swanwick's hospitality and her 'salon' welcomed many of the leading figures of the day, including Tennyson and Browning as well as Gladstone.

However, she clearly had a formidable side. Her association with Professor
F. W. Newman began when she attended one of his classes on mathematics
and 'on perceiving that he had made a slight error in the exposition of a
problem when the lesson was over she ventured to call his attention to
it', while in the *History of Bedford College* it is claimed that she 'was probably
the most learned woman associated with Bedford College at this time –
was indeed one of the few learned women of the day. A Greek and Hebrew
scholar, a devotee and translator of Goethe, she was dreaded in her world
as a blue stocking.'[53] Swanwick's translations provide significant evidence
of the strategies adopted by Victorian Hellenism in mediating Greek values
and religion to audiences in their own society. Her translations and the
scholarly regard in which she was held in turn gave authority to her
practical work.

Augusta Webster

Augusta Webster (1837–94), the other distinguished woman translator
acknowledged with Swanwick by *The Athenaeum* in 1868, provides an
almost total contrast in background, lifestyle, prose style and scope of
literary output.[54] Augusta Davies (as she then was) was educated in
Cambridge where her father became Chief Constable, attended the Cambridge School of Art, taught herself Greek to help a younger brother and
under the pseudonym Cecil Home published two volumes of poetry and a
novel. After her marriage to a Cambridge law lecturer and solicitor, she
published as Augusta Webster a translation of *Prometheus Bound* (1866)
followed by *Medea* (1868) and *Portraits* (1870), a collection of dramatic
monologues. Later, she wrote for the theatre, including *In a Day* (1882)
produced in 1890 with her daughter in the lead role (she was one of the
few leading writers who was also a mother). She also wrote a blank verse
play about the deranged Roman Emperor Caligula, *The Sentence* (1887).

Social and political perspectives

She was twice elected to the London School Board where she campaigned
for technical training and education for women. Webster advocated her
causes with vigour, mainly in *The Examiner*. Her 'Essays on suffrage' were
reissued by the Women's Suffrage Union in 1878 and a collection of essays
on issues related to married women were reprinted from *The Examiner* in
1879 as *A Housewife's Opinions* (Macmillan). The volume included pieces
on 'University degrees for women', 'University examinations for women',
'Protection for the working woman', 'Dull people', 'Parliamentary franchise
for women ratepayers', 'Husband hunting and match making' (opening

sentence 'People think women who do not want to marry unfeminine: people think women who do want to marry immodest ... this is hard upon marriageable women.'). Nor did she neglect the male interest. Her essay, 'The cost of a leg of mutton' ruthlessly exposes 'hidden' domestic costs and advocates co-operative supply and preparation of food.[55]

Webster described the then current suffrage arrangements as 'the blind leading the dumb', supported Frances Cobbe's work for battered wives, devoted an essay entitled 'An irrepressible army' to ridiculing the opponents of women's suffrage, and argued for accuracy in translation from an analogy with gin (which the Trades Descriptions Act required to be neat, not adulterated with sugar and water).[56]

Her 'sagacity' is, therefore, of a completely different kind from Swanwick's and is characterised by the inclusion of sharply analytic and polemical writing in occasional and sometimes apparently trivial pieces. Her favoured technique involves the manipulation of perspectives by transposing accepted arguments and descriptions to unexpected situations. Thus beneath her reputation for plain speaking there is a complex intelligence. She exploits the perceived simplicity of the female voice and concerns as a means of destablising certainties and changing agendas.[57]

Translation theory and practice

She devoted two essays to considering the nature of translation and here too mocked some aspects of the prevailing wisdom. The shorter essay 'The translation of poetry' questions the mutual exclusiveness of two opposed theories of translation ('the letter' and 'the spirit'), arguing that there cannot be one without the other. The second, longer and major essay is 'A transcript and a transcription' in which she contrasted two translations of Aeschylus' *Agamemnon*. The first (by Morshead) was of the flowing literary 'readable' variety, which she lambasts as un-Aeschylean. The second was by Robert Browning – 'the hail-fellow of Aeschylus, who spends his vigour in unflinching self-restraint and will not be lured from his dogged fidelity as a translator by any temptation to achieve a beautiful passage or a well-rounded stanza'.[58] As always with Webster's criticism there is a sting in the tail. She respected Browning's theory of translation which is 'to be literal at every cost except that of violence to our language', but argued that his *Agamemnon* failed to meet that aim and was hardly recognisable as a work in English, 'the reader who knows no Greek at all will be left bewildered and incredulous ... difficult poet as Aeschylus may have been he could never have puzzled Greeks as Englishmen must be puzzled by this ... without Aeschylus to translate Browning, how can they track out the meaning?'

Her critique of Browning can be read as a satire on and challenge to the dominant paradigm of masculinity in translation techniques.[59] She challenges the paradigm in two ways. First, she demonstrates that a translation which is robust, terse and undecorated (all considered masculinist virtues) may achieve this at the expense of readability. Second, she claims that in good translation a knowledge of Greek (and appreciation of its subtlety and allusiveness) must go together with appreciation of the equivalent qualities in English.

She focuses on detailed examples of Browning's diction and her idiom is characteristically down-to-earth, 'It is not amplification to allow the Greek words a sufficient number of English correspondents to state the literal meaning plainly, even if the English words should be twice as many as the Greek, anymore than it is over-payment to give two sixpences to discharge a debt of a shilling when you have not a shilling in your purse.' The butt of her criticism was Browning's attempt to compress together the Greek pedigree of a word plus its Aeschylean accretions. Her parting shot is, 'We could wish nothing better for literature than that Mr. Browning, having translated the *Agamemnon* of Aeschylus, should go on to translate the *Agamemnon* of Robert Browning.'[60] Beneath her robust writing and apparent plainness of diction (her style was described by reviewers as 'masculine and vigorous') lies a sense that a translation, too, has a poetic identity of its own which has to be open and pliable in order to excite the imagination in a way equivalent to the voice of the source text.

Poetry as critique

Webster is nowadays more widely known for her poetry than for her essays and translations.[61] However, the ideological and discursive relationship between the different aspects of her work suggests they should be considered as a whole. In contrast, the late nineteenth century largely marginalised her poetry perhaps because her ruthless exposure of the force of class wealth and power did not easily accommodate the fashionable focus on the emotions of the individual. Nevertheless she was well regarded by female writers such as Christina Rossetti, who considered that together with Elizabeth Barrett Browning she combined 'masculine' and 'feminine' qualities in her poetry. Rossetti rated her poetry, 'decidedly higher than George Eliot's', considered her voice one of the most formidable of women writers, and complained that Gladstone omitted Webster from his list of poetesses (unfortunately most of the Rossetti/Webster correspondence has not survived).[62]

Unlike Swanwick, who used academic textbooks and tracts as a vehicle to disseminate her social ideas, Webster encoded social criticism in creative writing. A crucial element in this was the dramatic monologue which she developed in directions which undermined the conventional notion of the simplicity and sentimentality of woman's voice. She used the dramatic distance of this form to challenge social and gender conventions, notably in *A Castaway* and in *Circe* and *Medea in Athens*.[63] These monologues give a voice to the morally ambivalent. *A Castaway* articulates a feminist social analysis of the plight of the contemporary commodity, the 'ruined' woman, placing prostitution alongside other occupations such as journalism or marriage.

Circe and *Medea in Athens* use images of woman from canonical Greek texts as a springboard for imagined responses to situations (sexuality, revenge and the material and emotional realities of loneliness) which are not bounded by classical time and space. In *Medea in Athens* the epithet 'ruined' is transposed to the de-heroised Jason. In exploring sexuality, Webster recognises and challenges the limits of both Greek and Victorian social conventions, providing a variant on the way in which comparison of new work or translation with the source text can provide an indication of the power of compulsory or voluntary cultural censorship, in both source and receiving traditions. In Homer, audience and reader identification with the female figures works either as a means of promoting resubjugation (Penelope, for example) or as a ploy to get the reader to participate in the denigration of women, such as Circe, who transgress the norms which promote dependency. Swanwick's Homer criticism is complicit with this approach. In contrast Webster not only gives Circe a voice but leaves her in control of the narrative and the emotions it creates.[64] Thus alongside her use in her essays of dramatic irony to subvert conventional perspectives, the female figures from Greek texts allow her in her poetry to develop new cultural formations as a means of critique. The dynamics of both essays and dramatic monologues are informed by the knowledge of formal and discursive techniques which she developed in her translations and by her sense of the relationship between material circumstances and gendered ideology which was stimulated by her work on Greek tragedy.

Swanwick and Webster: contrasts and convergence

There is a variety of nineteenth-century perceptions of the possible relationship between Greek texts and contemporary readings. Swanwick's approach shows a tension between on the one hand her sense of the force of Greek political ideas concerning community and democracy, and on the other hand her view that the Greeks, being pagans, could only be *progressing* towards a fully Christian perception of religious and political morality.

Webster's approach was different. She combined an interest in exploring Greek thinking about the female personality and the self with her examinations of contemporary ideas and assumptions. Furthermore, her interest in the relationship between these ideas and the material context of living (whether Greek or Victorian) led her in her poetry to 'translate' figures and situations between chronologically distanced cultures, thus creating a dynamic of mutual interrogation.[65]

Both Swanwick and Webster in very different ways contributed to Sage discourse. Swanwick's Sage writing centred on religion, the condition of England question and on education. On the 'woman question' it was more a matter of Sage speaking and doing. The surviving evidence indicates that she was skilled in her use of networks of associates and quietly influential in Establishment circles. Webster's Sage writing is more popular in tone and more obviously related to everyday life.

There is a clear link between scholarly authority and Sage effectiveness for both Swanwick and Webster.[66] However, both were writing towards the end of a period when independent intellectuals and scholars had been significant contributors in the field of classical studies. A perhaps unforeseen effect of their work to improve women's educational opportunities was to support the growing expectation that the most significant scholarly work would be done by professionals, most of whom would be male.[67]

In order to achieve recognition, both women worked within the conventions of a scholarship which was still male dominated. However, from a somewhat different ideological perspective, each used scholarship as a means of refining her own ideas and ensuring that they were communicated to a new and more varied readership. Webster's was the more radical voice in social analysis and it is significant both that it was in her creative writing that this emerged and that her most committed poetry draws on the insights she obtained from her work on Greek texts. Her poetry dropped from view in the last part of the nineteenth and most of the twentieth centuries. This suggests that while a translation of a canonical text may be regarded as non-threatening, a translation of the issues and insights of that text into another cultural context may be perceived as either 'strange' or even subversive, especially if it subverts easy assumptions about the role of women in art and culture.

In their determination that women scholars had a role to play in the transmission of learning, their commitment to improved educational and political opportunities for women and their exploitation of canonical Greek texts as a means to achieving these aims, Swanwick and Webster negotiated roles which were both part of and counter to the dominant culture.

Notes

1   This essay was developed from a paper presented at a research conference on Nineteenth-Century Appropriations of Classical Texts at the University of Reading in June 1995 and I am grateful to the organisers Dr Fiona Macintosh and Dr Edith Hall for their encouragement. I also thank Madeline Thompson for her invaluable research assistance in the early stages of the work, the members of the Women in the Humanities Research Group, Sophie Badham (Archivist to Royal Holloway and Bedford New College), Edward Chitham, Carol Gillespie, Kate Penny (Archivist to Girton College, Cambridge) and Christopher Stray.

2   For example, see the quotation from Maria Edgeworth cited by Madeline Thompson in chapter 2. R. L. Edgeworth evidently recognised the subversive potential of classical study since in a letter to the Committee of the Board of Education (*Parliamentary Papers 1813–14*) he claimed that some abridgements of ancient history for school use were 'certainly improper' since 'to inculcate democracy and a foolish hankering after undefined liberty is not necessary in Ireland'.

3   For detailed studies of particular aspects of appropriation see M. L. Clarke, *Classical Education in Britain 1500–1900* (Cambridge, Cambridge University Press, 1959); R. Gilmour, *The Victorian Period: The Intellectual and Cultural Context of English Literature, 1830–1890* (London and New York, Longman, 1993), esp. ch. 1 and ch. 4; R. Jenkyns, *The Victorians and Ancient Greece* (Oxford, Blackwell, 1980); M. Liversidge and C. Edwards, *Imagining Rome: British Artists and Rome in the Nineteenth Century* (London, Merrell Holberton, 1996); C. A. Stray, *Reconstructing Classics: Schools, Universities and Society in England 1830–1960* (Oxford, Oxford University Press, 1998); F. M. Turner, *The Greek Heritage in Victorian Britain* (New Haven and London, Yale University Press, 1981); F. M. Turner, 'Antiquity in Victorian Contexts', *Browning Institute Studies*, 10 (1982) pp. 1–14; F. M. Turner, 'Why the Greeks and not the Romans in Victorian Britain?', in G. W. Clarke (ed.), *Rediscovering Hellenism: The Hellenic Inheritance and the English Imagination* (Cambridge, Cambridge University Press, 1989), pp. 61–81; F. M. Turner, *Contesting Cultural Authority* (Cambridge, Cambridge University Press, 1993).

4   Turner, 'Why the Greeks'.

5   Gilmour, *The Victorian Period*, pp. 42–5.

6   See K. K. Collins and F. Williams, 'Lewes at Colonus: An early Victorian view of translation from the Greek', *The Modern Language Review*, 82 (1987), pp. 293–312, esp. 293–5.

7   R. Fowler, 'On not knowing Greek: the classics and the women of letters', *Classical Journal*, 78 (1983), pp. 337–48.

8   G. Eliot, *Middlemarch*, book 1, ch. 7 1st pub. 1871–72. Quotation taken from Penguin English Library edn, ed. W. J. Harvey (Harmondsworth, Penguin Books, 1965), p. 88.

9   The literary effects of George Eliot's education in Greek have been explored in P. E. Easterling, 'George Eliot and Greek tragedy', *Arion*, 3rd series, 1:2 (1991), pp. 60–74; Laura McClure, 'On knowing Greek: George Eliot and the classical tradition', *Classical and Modern Literature*, 13:2 (1993), pp. 139–51.

10 Charlotte Brontë, *Shirley* (Oxford, Clarendon, 1979), p. 371.

11 Thaïs E. Morgan (ed.), *Victorian Sages and Cultural Discourse: Renegotiating Gender and Power* (New Brunswick and London, Rutgers University Press, 1990).

12 Dorothy Mermin, *Godiva's Ride: Women of Letters in England, 1830–1880* (Bloomington and Indianapolis, Indiana University Press, 1993), has a chapter on the

female sage. Swanwick is not mentioned at all. Webster appears only in other chapters.

13   On the relationship between a writer's translations and other work see, for example, the demonstration of interdependence in Timothy Webb's study of Shelley's writing, *The Violet in the Crucible* (Oxford, Oxford University Press, 1976).

14   Elizabeth Barrett, *Aurora Leigh*, II, 76 (1st pub. London, 1857. Edition used here is ed. Margaret Reynolds (Athens, Ohio, Ohio University Press, 1992)).

15   This topic also raises theoretical issues, especially concerning the methodological relationship between analysis of social and literary history and analysis of discourse: see, for example, Eleni Varikas, 'Gender and experience', *New Left Review*, 211 (1995), pp. 89–104.

16   *Dictionary of National Biography*, Supplement 1900 (Oxford, Oxford University Press, 1909), vol. xxii, pp. 1246–7; Mary L. Bruce, *Anna Swanwick: A Memoir and Recollections 1813–1899* (London, T. Fisher Unwin, 1903).

17   The justification for the substantial memoir (261 pages) was said by Mary Bruce to be 'her literary work and the part she took in the advancements of women's education "plus" the love and esteem felt by all' (Note to the reader, pp. ix–xx).

18   For a full discussion of the paradoxical relationship between Unitarian principles of gender equality in education and their practice of patriarchal power structures in business and in the home, see Ruth Watts, 'Knowledge is power – Unitarians, gender and education in the eighteenth and early nineteenth centuries', *Gender and Education*, 1:1 (1989), pp. 35–50 and Kathryn Gleadle, *The Early Feminists: Radical Unitarians and the Emergence of the Women's Rights Movement* (London, Macmillan, 1995).

19   Quoted in Bruce, *Anna Swanwick*, p. 19.

20   Since at that time British academic institutions excluded Unitarians, Germany provided an important alternative.

21   A. W. Schlegel (1767–1845) translated extensively from Shakespeare and the Romance languages and influenced Goethe and Scheleirmacher. Germany at the turn of the eighteenth and nineteenth centuries was the scene of a striking confluence of translating activities. The choice and execution of verse form became an important criterion for evaluation of translation. Schlegel thought that there was greater metrical resonance between Greek and German than between Greek and other languages.

22   For example, A. Swanwick, *Selections from the Dramas of Goethe and Schiller* (London, 1843), *Faust*, parts 1 & 2 (London, G. Bell & Sons, 1879, revised edition 1888) including *Iphigenia*. Gleadle comments on the links between radical Unitarianism and German culture and suggests that it allowed the transformation of religion into a richer kind of belief. More traditional Unitarians, in contrast, found that German scholarship challenged their emphasis on biblical authority.

23   A. Swanwick is conjecturally but wrongly identified as Swanwick's father, who had been dead some years, in H. C. G. Matthew (ed.), *The Gladstone Diaries*, VI, 1861–1868 (Oxford, Clarendon Press, 1978), p. 373 note 7.

24   The complete Aeschylus went to a 4th edition in 1884 (revised 1890, London, George Bell and Sons) which she wished to be seen as her completed work.

25   For the cultural and social context, see P. E. Easterling, 'The early years of the Cambridge Greek play: 1882–1912', in Christopher Stray (ed.), *Supplement to the Proceedings of the Cambridge Philological Society* (1998). Swanwick's translation was published as *The Agamemnon of Aeschylus as Performed at Cambridge November*

16–21, 1900 (Cambridge, Cambridge University Press, 1900) and had Greek and English on facing pages.

26 Quoted in Bruce, *Anna Swanwick*, pp. 108–14, 107. This acceptance by the academic establishment was publicly marked when Swanwick became one of the first women to receive a Doctors' degree – the Hon. LLD of the University of Aberdeen.

27 Quoted in Bruce, *Anna Swanwick*, pp. 88–9.

28 'Capacities of women', *Westminster Review*, 84 (1 October 1865), pp. 352–80. The article reviewed: Bessie Rayner Parkes, *Essays on Woman's Work* (London, Alexander Strachan, 1865); *The Agamemnon, Choephori and Eumenides of Aeschylus*, translated into English verse by Anna Swanwick (London, Bell and Daldy, 1863); Frances Power Cobbe, *Studies; New and Old of Ethical and Social Subjects* (London, Trübner/Boston, Crosby Nichols and Co., 1864) plus idem *Religious Duty* (London, Trübner, 1864); *The Cities of the Past* (London, Trübner, 1864) and *Essays on the Pursuits of Women* (reprinted from Fraser's & Macmillan's *Magazines*, London, Emily Faithful, 1863).

29 George Stillman Hillard, *North American Review* (July 1842), pp. 201–18 and see also Charles A. Bristed's reference to Barrett's genius 'utterly unaided by art [is] continually running wild … but where scholars cannot agree, ladies may be excused mistranslating': C. A. Bristed, 'English poetry and poets of the present day', *The Knickerbocker* (1845), pp. 534–42.

30 The reviewer concludes by expressing satisfaction that 'if the study of Greek is declining in colleges and schools, it is pursued to such good purpose by ladies like Mrs. Webster and Miss Swanwick, worthy followers in this respect of Lady Jane Grey': *The Athenaeum*, no. 2135, 26 September 1868. The reviewer was probably J. M. Millard, Headmaster of Magdalen College School. Edith Hall has recently argued that interest in *Medea* was stimulated by the Divorce Act of 1857 which prompted new productions of the play in the years which followed. I am grateful to Dr Hall and Dr Fiona Macintosh for discussing their work on *Medea* with me in advance of publication.

31 'Capacities of women', p. 353.

32 'Capacities of women', pp. 360, 364, 367.

33 'Capacities of women', pp. 370–1.

34 'Capacities of women', p. 367.

35 Walter E. Houghton *et al.* (eds), *The Wellesley Index to Victorian Periodicals 1824–1900* (Toronto, University of Toronto Press, 1966–90), vol. III.

36 According to Mary Bruce, Newman converted to Christianity at the age of 92, supposedly under Swanwick's influence.

37 Bruce, *Anna Swanwick*, p. 40.

38 Newman emphasised that Homer was a product of an oral culture and tried to find correspondences for its popular elements, hence the attack by Matthew Arnold in *On Translating Homer* (1861) in which Arnold argued that an objective or 'innocent' language was possible and hence translation should transcend linguistic and cultural differences rather than point to them. He also claimed that only scholars who both knew Greek and could appreciate poetry were qualified to comment on translations. In contrast, the German tradition developed by Schleiermacher proposed the creation of a special sub-language for translation only, aiming to show the peculiarity of the original. Schleiermacher also influenced F. W. Newman, Carlyle and William Morris who all aimed at conveying a sense of the worth of the original combined with a conscious archaising. Arnold called this 'Newmanising'. For discussion of Newman and Arnold see Lawrence Venuti, *The Translator's Invisibility: A History*

of Translation (London and New York, Routledge, 1995), esp. pp. 118–47, and S. Bassnett-Maguire, *Translation Studies* (London and New York, Methuen, 1980), pp. 68–72.

39   Swanwick, *Aeschylus*, p. xxviii. Contrast the twentieth-century translator Richmond Lattimore who uses the term 'citizen'.

40   See translation by R. Lattimore, *Eumendies* (Chicago and London, Chicago University Press, 1953), ll. 658–61.

41   See R. Lattimore, *Eumenides*, ll. 269–75.

42   See G. Beckerlegge, 'Professor Friedrich Max Müller and the missionary cause', in John Wolffe (ed.), *Religion in Victorian Britain* (Manchester, Manchester University Press, 1997), vol. V, pp. 177–220; Daniel L. Pals, 'Max Müller, E. B. Taylor and the intellectual origins of the science of religion', *International Journal of Comparative Religion and Philosophy*, 1:2 (1995), pp. 16–26; D. Wiebe, 'Religion and the scientific impulse in the nineteenth century: Friedrich Max Müller and the birth of the science of religion', *International Journal of Comparative Religion and Philosophy*, 1:1 (1995), pp. 76–97; N. C. Chaudhuri, *Scholar Extraordinary: The Life of Professor the Rt. Hon. Friedrich Max Müller, PC* (London, Chatto and Windus, 1974). I am grateful to Dr Gwilym Beckerlegge for advice on this part of my investigation.

43   *Saturday Review*, 23 July 1893, p. 119ff. This volume on the poets from Homer to Tennyson and Browning was dedicated to James Martineau. It included chapters on Roman Literature, Dante, Spencer, Shakespeare, Racine, Corneille, Molière, Goethe, Schiller, Elizabeth Barrett Browning, Hugo and Arnold and represents evidence of Swanwick's considerable learning and intellectual range.

44   *Iliad*, xxii, pp. 484–507.

45   *Odyssey*, xxiii, pp. 239–40. Swanwick does not use the term reverse simile, but in their precision her observations in other respects anticipate Helene P. Foley's influential article '"Reverse similes" and sex roles in the *Odyssey*', in J. Perradotto and J. P. Sullivan (eds), *Women in the Ancient World: The Arethusa Papers* (Albany, SUNY Press, 1984), pp. 59–78.

46   Swanwick, *Poets*, p. 29.

47   Swanwick, *Poets*, p. xxxvi.

48   Lucretia Mott's account is recorded in Frederick B. Tolles (ed.), 'Slavery and "the woman questions": Lucretia Mott's diary of her visit to Britain to attend the World's Anti-Slavery Convention of 1840', Supplement no. 23 (1952) to *The Journal of the Friends' Historical Society*, Haverford, Friends' Historical Association, and London Friends' Historical Society. For discussion of the impact of the anti-slavery movement on the language and ideas of feminists see P. Levine, *Victorian Feminism 1850–1900* (London, Hutchinson, 1987), p. 62.

49   Quoted in Bruce, *Anna Swanwick*, p. 159.

50   Catalogue of the Archives of Bedford College, University of London, 1849–1985, AR 201/l; see also Levine, *Victorian Feminism*, ch. 2.

51   Details are in the Pfeiffer archive at Girton and in the Recollection by Sir Joshua Fitch, quoted in Bruce, *Anna Swanwick*, p. 257.

52   Quoted in Bruce, *Anna Swanwick*, p. 34.

53   Bruce, *Anna Swanwick*, p. 55; M. J. Tuke, *History of Bedford College for Women 1889–1937* (Oxford, Oxford University Press, 1939), p. 59.

54   Her father was a naval officer and as a child she moved round to his various postings, even spending time on board ship (although mainly in Chichester Harbour). The romantic and/or feminist expectations raised by Webster's naval background are satirised by Vita Sackville-West, 'The women poets of the seventies',

in H. Granville-Barker (ed.), *The Eighteen Seventies: Essays by Fellows of the Royal Society of Literature* (Cambridge, Cambridge University Press, 1929).

55 Perhaps Webster provided an ironic counter to the claim of Sarah Sewell, *Women and the Times We Live In* (London, 1865; 2nd edn 1869) that 'Women who have stored their minds with Latin and Greek seldom have much knowledge of pies and puddings', quoted in Levine, *Victorian Feminism*, p. 26.

56 Augusta Webster, *A Housewife's Opinions* (London, Macmillan, 1879), pp. 178, 71.

57 For example, the parallel between her appreciation of the male citizens' discourse used in Euripides' *Medea* in Medea's speech on the condition of women to the women of Corinth (Webster, *Medea*, line 207ff., Euripides, line 213ff.) and her arguments in her essay 'Parliamentary franchise for women ratepayers'. In both cases, male misogynists were exposed by the logic of their own arguments appropriated and applied to a woman's situation.

58 Webster, *Housewife's Opinions*, pp. 61–5, 66–79, 66.

59 For discussion of this issue, see Yopie Prins, 'E. B., R. B. and the difference of translation', *Victorian Poetry*, 29:4 (1991), pp. 435–51 and Herbert Sussman, *Victorian Masculinities* (Cambridge, Cambridge University Press, 1995), esp. ch. 2 which discusses Browning and the problematics of a masculine poetic.

60 Webster, *Housewife's Opinions*, pp. 77, 78, 79.

61 See Angela Leighton and Margaret Reynolds (eds), *Victorian Women Poets: An Anthology* (Oxford, Blackwell, 1995); Angela Leighton, *Victorian Women Poets: Writing Against the Heart* (Hemel Hempstead, Harvester, 1992); Mermin, *Godiva's Ride*.

62 C. Rossetti, Letters 97, 175, in W. M. Rossetti (ed.), *Family Letters* (London, Brown, Langham, 1908). Gladstone was not the only excluder of Webster's poetry. For example, in the first edition of A. H. Miles's anthology *The Poets and Poetry of the Nineteenth Century*, 10 vols (London, 1891–97) a few of Webster's lyrics were included but *none* of her socially committed work. The second edition, 12 vols (London, George Routledge & Sons, 1907), included two volumes of women's poetry with more substantial extracts from Webster and an introduction by Mackenzie Bell which suggested that her most penetrating treatment of women's emotions could be comprehensible only to women (p. 108).

63 A. Webster, *Portraits* (London, Macmillan, 1870).

64 The final sentence of Lilian Doherty, *Siren Songs: Gender Audiences and Narrators in the Odyssey* (Ann Arbor, University of Michigan Press, 1995) could also serve as a testimony to Webster: 'I would be a Circe with a difference; one who puts the once and future reader on guard against the Siren Songs of the Homeric Text itself'. For political analysis of literary 'silences', see Erika Hulpe, 'Cultural constraints: a case of political censorship', in H. Kittel and A. P. Frank (eds), *Interculturality and the Historical Study of Literary Translations* (Berlin, Erich Schmidt Verlag, 1991), pp. 71–4.

65 Webster's use of distancing techniques in the dramatic monologue is discussed in Susan Brown, 'Determined heroines: George Eliot, Augusta Webster, and closet drama by Victorian women', *Victorian Poetry*, 33 (1995), pp. 89–109. A new dimension is added when these techniques are brought to bear on themes and subjects from the ancient world. I hope to explore this aspect in detail in a future study of Webster.

66 There were of course other aspects to their authority. For example, Theodore Watts-Dunton, in the *Athenaeum*, 3490, 15 September 1894, p. 355, referred to 'the noble band represented by George Eliot, Mrs. Webster and Miss Cobbe, who, in

virtue of lofty purpose, purity of soul and deep sympathy with suffering humanity, are just now far ahead of the men'. But this was Webster's obituary. Nietzsche's perspective on this was rather different – 'little moralistic females à la Eliot', *The Twilight of the Idols* (1888) (in the *Portable Nietzsche*, pp. 515–16). Nietzsche was particularly interested in the way loss of conventional Christian faith could be associated with a strongly developed morality and regarded this as a particularly English phenomenon.

67 See F. M. Turner's discussion of 'amateur' scholarship in 'The triumph of idealism in classical studies', in idem, *Contesting Cultural Authority*, pp. 322–61. The general breadth of intellectual debate fostered by and in periodicals and reviews and Open Lectures at least until the 1860s is summarised by Gilmour, *The Victorian Period*, pp. 7–8.

'I love my sex': two late Victorian pulpit women[1]

Susan Mumm

By the mid-1880s Catherine Mumford Booth and Jane Ellice Hopkins were two of the best-known and most reviled women in England. Both had developed careers and a high degree of notoriety in one of the sacred preserves of male privilege: the pulpit. While female preachers had not been unknown in the eighteenth and very early nineteenth centuries, women preachers with national reputations were few, and disappeared almost entirely after the end of the Napoleonic Wars. Hopkins and Booth were in the forefront of the late Victorian resurgence of women who enjoyed international reputations as preachers and who published professionally and with authority on the subject of religion. Their work and experiences highlight issues of professionalisation, privatisation, and how women could reformulate the moral boundaries of behaviour in one of the professions most sturdily resistant to female infiltration.

Problems of professionalisation and marginalisation were particularly acute when Victorian women claimed religion as an area especially appropriate for female involvement. In one sense, the role of women in religion was not problematic at all, if they confined themselves to the experiential, the personal and the interior – both domestic and psychological. For the Victorians, dissonance occurred when women began to claim the right and the expertise to interpret and publicise the sacred texts for themselves, and to spread their conclusions in the form of public religious teaching. Systematic reinterpretation of the sacred text was considered to be beyond the capacity of women: theology, 'the queen of the sciences', remained an all-male preserve.

Both the content of religion as a theoretical system, and the form in which it was expressed, were believed to be beyond the limits of female capacity. Booth and Hopkins used avenues for spreading their religious ideas and engaging in controversy that had long histories of acceptability and authority when used by men, but whose use by women was still contested. These were preaching and publication – the sermon and the printed controversial pamphlet – long considered the most authoritative forms of theological and moral education for a secular audience.[2] Because of their activities in this prohibited sphere, both occupied debated and problematic liminal space as women who rejected the gendering of religious authority and revelation, and who colonised male religious territory, claiming the ability, and the right, authoritatively to interpret the scriptures.

They entered this all-male preserve through a manipulation of accepted gendering of authority: the traditional female concern with morality and sexual behaviour was the key that these women used to open up wider issues of female competence, responsibility and capacity as religious authorities. Both adopted moral issues, traditionally seen as more appropriate for women, as a way into their re-visioning of Protestant theology. Crucially, both used their 'reforms' of conventional religious teaching to demand the transformation of their society, especially with regard to its treatment of women and its attitude toward sexual behaviour.[3] This demand culminated with the 'Maiden Tribute' crusade of the 1880s. Nominally a demand to raise the age of consent to sixteen, it was in reality something more important. It marked a repudiation of the idea that moral and sexual purity were gendered, and an indignant rejection of the common belief that men could not be expected to take responsibility for their sexuality. Men and women (but, crucially, not children who were the beneficiaries of the Act) were portrayed as equally capable of taking full responsibility for their own sexual conduct, and in doing so the crusade put an axe to the root of the sexual double standard.

Booth, who claimed that she had never envisaged a life more public than that of a minister's wife, began preaching in Methodist chapels in the north-east in 1860. She left Methodism and, together with her husband, was to form a new denomination which became known as The Salvation Army, in part because of the Methodist refusal to recognise her vocation as a preacher. Booth relied on appeals to the intuitive and personal to justify her jettisoning of much of the traditional Christian teaching on the subordination of women. She forged a successful career as preacher and writer with the newly-formed Salvation Army, requiring, in the process, equality for women as well as salvation for all.

The Anglican Hopkins was notorious both as the leader of the male chastity group known as the White Cross Army, which demanded that men take responsibility for their own sexual behaviour, and for her reformulation of Christian theology, which equated the oppression of Victorian womankind with the suffering of Christ. She applied the language and methods of science (she was educated by her mathematician father) to a re-examination of conventional Christian teaching, radically reinventing her Christianity as a result. Both women devoted much of their adult lives to the spreading of their messages, communicating their beliefs through their own books, speeches and sermons, as well as through skilful manipulation of the public press.

I have chosen this particular pair of women evangelists out of a number of potential candidates because despite very different backgrounds, biographies, denominational affiliations and religious beliefs, both travelled a similar professional and spiritual pathway. They began as religious enthusiasts, in love with the sacred and the sublime; but both discovered that their encounter with the sacred forced them into an encounter with the sordid, in particular with the issues of the sexual double standard and the sexual abuse of children. For both this became the defining issue of their social and religious teaching, and both used issues of sexual control and protection to justify the enlargement of the public role of women.

Hopkins started her public career preaching to working-class men in Cambridge around 1865. One American observer had described Hopkins's preaching at the very outset of her public career, long before she became a celebrated speaker:

> I have listened to the most eminent revivalist preachers in America, and to many of the most impressive ministers in England; but I never heard an address more calculated to melt an audience of common men than hers; and I never saw an audience more deeply moved. In diction and argument it was beautiful and powerful; but in fervour and pathos it was indescribable.[4]

Within weeks of commencing her spectacularly successful public ministry, she was under attack from the clergy who criticised her presumption in preaching to hundreds of working men, a task they considered improper for a woman. She was fully aware of the sexism underlying their condemnation of her, writing, 'It was hard that the power which would have been a glory to me if I were a man, should be held a shame and disgrace to me because I was a woman.'[5] It was this that jolted her out of her rather conventional evangelical Christianity: criticised for teaching the Bible to men, she found herself radicalised by her search for a Biblical defence of her behaviour. Hopkins was forced to repudiate Biblical teaching on the subordination of women in order to justify her inward call. She came to reject all claims that the Bible could be understood as inerrant and ahistorically true, and instead argued that the Bible must be reinterpreted for each age, and that this applied specially to its strictures on women. She condemned the clergy for their complacent chauvinism and unthinking conformity, especially 'their old foolish tendency to stick to the letter of Scripture, and, too, to sin against its divine, progressive spirit, to bind women, after nineteen centuries of freedom, with precisely the same worn-out bandages and restrictions which were necessary to preserve social order when first the great truth of the equality of the sexes was proclaimed'.[6]

Conventionally pious Victorians were scandalised by Hopkins's insistence that the message of the gospel must be reinterpreted for every generation and society, and that any Biblical teaching that had ceased to be morally and socially liberating should be jettisoned. Over time, she moved to a rejection of the entire idea of personal salvation and by the 1880s she was arguing that the purpose of Christian belief is not personal salvation, but the service and protection of the weak and helpless; this was her 'theology of altruism', based in part upon the writings of James Hinton whose biographer she was. (Hinton was a surgeon and philosopher of altruism, reviled by many of his contemporaries for his cautious advocacy of free love.) Hopkins's interpretation of altruism was summarised in *Touching Pitch*: 'Surely the great central fact of Christianity is not personal salvation, not saving our own soul, not just getting to heaven, but a life poured out for the good of the world ...'[7] Despite this heterodox rejection of the primacy of personal salvation, she remained actively Anglican throughout her life. Like Booth, she came to believe that her experience of religion overrode traditional interpretations of women's place, but, unlike Booth, she saw herself as an exception to her sex in general, rather than as an exemplar of female religious leadership. Particularly in the earlier stages of her career, she did not always advocate the appropriation of religious authority by other women; but by the end of her life she had become a convinced advocate of the active ministry of women.

What makes Hopkins unusual is not her rejection of Biblical authority; plenty of educated men (and a few educated women) had reached this point before her. Hopkins's unique contribution was her democratisation of such ideas, especially her demand to be permitted to spread her revision of scripture to working-class men and to women of all classes. Few among even the most radical Broad churchmen advocated the diffusion of their ideas beyond a male elite: Hopkins took it upon herself to popularise critical views of Biblical interpretation, but always in a strong moral context. Already theologically maverick, Hopkins's social opinions radicalised when she began working with young prostitutes in Brighton in 1866. She was horrified by the futility of the work, trying to rehabilitate 'fallen' and damaged women while male demand for sexual services was allowed to continue unabated. It was her experiences in Brighton that determined her to start a national assault on the sexual double standard.

Hopkins's creative writing

During a long period of invalidism in Brighton she wrote her only novel, *Rose Turquand*, which enjoyed a highly sensational plot, including a woman who was 'a mother but no wife', disguised love in a monastery, and a mysterious being confined to a crumbling wing of a country house. Despite its lurid narrative, it introduced many of the ideas about suffering, altruism and sexuality that were to dominate her later work; it also contained Hopkins's first sustained explication of her maternalist feminism. The novel sold well and was well reviewed. Her second book of poetry, *Autumn Swallows*, also published during this period, deals very explicitly with the issues that Hopkins was to concentrate on in her theological writing, especially the mystic relationship between the crucified Saviour and the fallen woman. *Swallows* too was favourably reviewed, and both it and *Turquand* indicate Hopkins's utter absorption in the problems of suffering, especially suffering caused by social or sexual inequality. She gave up literary writing when she devoted herself to the cause of righting the sexual injustice embedded in Victorian society, remarking sadly, 'Nature made me a singing-bird, but man has made me a sewer-rat.' [8]

Hopkins as platform woman

Hopkins's greatest short-term achievement was undoubtedly the organisation that she founded in 1882, the White Cross Army. This organisation recruited mostly working-class men as soldiers in the army of social purity and social equality: the tens of thousands of men who enrolled under her urging dedicated themselves to the rejection of the sexual double standard and the raising of women's status in society. She travelled throughout Britain holding mass meetings where men were urged to 'take the pledge' of chastity until marriage: more than 100 local branches of the White Cross Army were formed in its first year. Initially, Hopkins emphasised her reluctance to encourage other women to join her as social purity campaigners: 'I have a great terror of setting the fashion of women speaking in public to men on this subject ... I am only "holding the fort" till the men come up ...' [9] Her views on female religious leadership did change over time: tellingly, her last major book (1899) was entitled *The Power of Womanhood*. Unlike Booth's simultaneous campaigns, her speaking tours placed great emphasis on quietness and the avoidance of sensationalism. Hopkins was acutely sensitive to accusations of vulgarity and of pandering to titillation and sensation-seeking male audiences, although how discreet a woman notorious for advertising her lectures as 'For Men Only' could have been is open to question. Hopkins's platform style was quiet, almost subdued, but extremely intense. Contemporary auditors described it as overpowering in its emotional impact: she was tremendously effective in conveying her anger at the injustice of the sexual double standard to her all-male audiences, who (as with the medical students in Edinburgh and Glasgow) often came to jeer, but went away committed to her vision of purity for men and justice for women. She described her first lecture to Edinburgh undergraduates as an ordeal, but one that ended in triumph. After the Bishop of Durham refused to speak because he believed the audience was uncontrollable, Hopkins took the platform; she listened:

> with sinking heart to the noise going on, roaring, stamping, and whistling, and knew I had to control it somehow. It was an awful moment when I advanced to the edge of the platform, and stood opposite that roaring scene of young faces, many of which meant mischief. I simply cast myself on our Lord, and held them transfixed for forty minutes, through the most hard-hitting, home-thrusting address I ever gave. I thought I would do it thoroughly when I was about it! [10]

Polemical publications

Hopkins used the White Cross Army as a medium to publicise her demands for purity and equality as widely as possible amongst working-class men. Even more important to her reformist agenda were her publications, especially the White Cross Series, published by Hatchards in the 1880s, which spread her ideas widely in a cheap and popular form. She preferred the pamphlet to longer books, feeling that the brief and cheap form was more likely to reach working-class homes. In Hopkins's hands, they were essentially printed substitutes for platform lectures. The pamphlets' brevity also allowed her to produce written 'sermons' on a large number of themes, which could be published independently of one another: of the almost eighty titles by Hopkins that I have identified, more than half are in pamphlet form. Her best-selling pamphlet, *True Manliness*, sold more than three hundred thousand copies within a year of publication, and continued to be distributed in large numbers into the twentieth century. Like many other women who initially published anonymously (Hopkins signed the pamphlet JEH), she suffered the annoyance of having a friend assure her that 'everyone knew' that the book had been written by a prominent man of the day. Hopkins's books and pamphlets were widely read; some titles went into anything from twenty to seventy-five editions, with a few remaining in print until the 1940s. By her death in 1904, well over two million copies of her works had been distributed. She did not profit financially from these enormous sales, as she gave the proceeds to further the work of the White Cross Army.

She wrote for two distinct audiences: for working-class men she authored a large number of pamphlets arguing the case of justice and equality between the sexes; one of the most interesting and successful of these was *Damaged Pearls* (1884), which denounced the double standard as a form of class oppression. Her other audience was composed of middle-class women: these publications were dedicated to transforming middle-class women into activists in the cause of social purity. Some were aimed at advising mothers on how to teach children (especially boys) about purity and the proper attitude toward women: these must be some of the earliest pamphlets advocating explicit sex education for children.

In preparation for her public work as lecturer and writer she had devoted herself to the study of Puritan theologians, the writings of John Bunyan and the sermons of contemporary Evangelicals such as Charles Spurgeon, very much as Catherine Booth was doing. She scoured ancient and modern authors for racy anecdotes, telling examples, and memorable stories to convey attractively the message of social purity to a late Victorian audience. Unsurprisingly, given her scientific education, many of her most telling examples were drawn from geology and zoology. She employed different kinds of scientific argument for her two audiences: the pamphlets and sermons aimed at recruiting working-class men to the causes of purity and justice were based on homely metaphors and examples from nature. For example, in *Is It Natural?* (1885) she finds lessons among the animal species that co-operate in rearing their young, arguing that it was 'unnatural' for men to father children and then take no further responsibility for them. When writing for her other major audience, middle-class women, she tended to use statistics and demographic arguments to make the point that national racial decay, as well as individual moral degeneration, would be the inevitable result of the double standard. She believed women needed knowledge and she exhorted them to demand it and use it for the benefit of all women: 'My sisters, I say it urgently and solemnly, we have let men impose their views on us too long on this subject. We must act and think for ourselves ... Women must insist on knowing – refuse to acquiesce any longer in the babyish ignorance that unfits [us] for the care of [our] own sons ...'[11]

Hopkins's language is terse and earthy, and her style reflects her hatred of what she termed Pulpit English and denounced as 'the most vicious English in existence'. She believed that because women were educated in English rather than spending their childhoods writing Latin verses, they made better preachers and writers than men, for 'women never wrong their thoughts with pulpit English, but preserve the strength and sweetness of their mother tongue ... they speak not from theological systems but from the heart and the life'.[12] Over time Hopkins's rhetoric became more radical, and she abandoned the stereotypes and religious cant that disfigure some of her earlier writing. However, she always wrote with enormous passion; even today the emotional impact of her writing comes through clearly to the reader. She herself rejected most devotional literature, finding it unreal, sentimental and incapable of addressing the real problems of the Christian life.

Even though her writing style was generally vigorous, she was constrained by the orthodoxies of publishing and frustrated by conventional boundaries of decency. Much of what she wanted to convey could not be put in print without offending Victorian decorum. She came to prefer lectures to writing: 'In everything one publishes, one is tormented by the sense that one has to stop just short of the useful.'[13] Even her audiences sometimes found her speeches too shocking to be acceptable; after a long debate, the Norwich branch of the Ladies' Association for the Care of Friendless Girls rejected her as a potential speaker, because 'many people considered her to be far too plain spoken to be generally acceptable': this from a branch of an organisation she had herself founded.[14] By the middle of the 1880s, her name, if daringly mentioned in polite society, 'was spoken in a whisper and heard with a shudder'.[15] Her radical rhetoric barely remained within the constraints of her society, as she savaged the double standard and demanded a re-examination of the central truths of Christianity. She wrote less in the 1890s as her health again declined; the decade of non-stop speaking and writing had taken its toll, leaving her with a repetitive stress injury which made it difficult for her to hold a pen. By the time of her death in 1904, she had been largely forgotten except by women reformers such as her loyal secretary and only biographer, the activist Rosa Barrett, although her writings continued to circulate in large numbers and the White Cross Movement was flourishing. It is painful to notice that the male-dominated White Cross Army ungratefully described her not as founder, but as their 'first lady associate' in their obituary notice; while another group inspired by Hopkins, the National Union of Women Workers, gave her full credit for her role as founder of the White Cross.[16]

Catherine Booth has entered the historical record more successfully than Hopkins; as co-founder, with her husband William, of the Salvation Army, she is an important figure in mid and late Victorian nonconformity. Her memory (and some of her papers) have been preserved as part of the Army's heritage, and many adoring and largely uncritical biographies have been issued. A successful preacher, revivalist and religious writer, her determination to participate on equal terms within a religious movement shaped the last thirty years of her life. She campaigned tirelessly for the causes she believed in: the right of women to lead religious movements, social purity of a kind very similar to Hopkins's and, above all, for the salvation of souls.

Her father, a coachbuilder's assistant, married into a gentry family (who duly cast their daughter off) while he was working as a Methodist lay preacher. Shortly thereafter Mr Mumford lost his faith; he became an alcoholic during Catherine's early childhood. In this divided household, mother and daughter formed an alliance that was to shape Booth's life, centred around religion and temperance. Unlike Hopkins, her formal education was scanty; she spent two years at a school in her early teens and the rest was provided at home by her well-educated mother, who kept her completely isolated from other children. It was an episode of illness in her late teens that provided Mumford with her real education; confined to her sofa for almost two years, she devoted herself to the study of theology, reading mostly Puritan and eighteenth-century divines. Typical of many working-class writers of the Victorian age, she was profoundly influenced by the ideas and language of John Bunyan.

So far we have followed a life that might have ended in the profound obscurity of mid-Victorian conventional wifehood and motherhood. But Mumford refused to contemplate marrying any man who did not believe that women were the intellectual, as well as moral, equal of men. In the early 1850s she met a struggling evangelist, William Booth. The long courtship, conducted largely by letter, was unconventional in a number of respects, and allowed Mumford to prepare herself for her future career. During the engagement of three years she wrote a weekly sermon for William to deliver, and in her voluminous letters she formed his ideas and opinions.[17] Her better education (William had formerly been an apprentice pawnbroker in Nottingham) made her intellectual leadership easier than it might otherwise have been. The couple married in 1855.

In 1859 an obscure independent clergyman, Mr Rees, published a pamphlet denouncing women who preached, a wholly conventional polemic on the subject. The pamphlet, originally a sermon, enraged Catherine, who was incredulous that a congregation had tolerated it: 'would you believe that a congregation half composed of ladies could sit and hear such self-deprecatory rubbish?'.[18] Booth wrote her reply in December 1859, completing it a week or two before the birth of her fourth child. The reply, too, is conventional in its arguments, save that it is saturated with Booth's conviction that women are genuinely equal to men. She argues that this equality is intellectual as well as moral, and that attempts to suppress women's abilities are unchristian as well as absurd. She concludes that only women themselves can make the decision to speak, and that decision should be made in the confidence of God's love, rather than in the fear of man. Women must learn to be bold and assured, rather than diffident and 'servile': 'If she have the necessary gifts, and feels herself called by the Spirit to preach, there is not a single word in the whole book of God to restrain her, but many, very many to urge and encourage her.'[19]

Booth as pulpit woman

While Booth was defending the right of women to preach in print, she failed to apply this to her own situation for some months longer. Her respect for Methodist tradition, coupled with her profound shyness, made her reluctant to take a step on which her conscience was becoming increasingly insistent. She later described herself as being at the point of breakdown in the months before her first sermon. She reasoned that if the Bible were true, people were dying and being damned. Some of them might be converted and saved through her preaching, if she would only begin. Confident of her ability, she was unable to dismiss her sense of personal responsibility for the souls of others, and could find no comfort in hiding behind conventional notions of women's sphere. While recovering from her daughter's birth, the sleepless nights she spent thinking about the condition of the lost and her unused talents 'drove' her into preaching.[20] One Sunday in the spring of 1860, she sat struggling with profound depression and fear in the pew while her husband preached in the Methodist chapel he served. She rose to her feet and told the congregation of almost a thousand that she wished to speak. This first sermon was extempore, prophetic and autobiographical, three elements that remained consistently part of her rhetorical strategy throughout her career.

Aged 31, and with four children, ranging in age from four years to four months, Booth immediately ratified her new status by accepting an invitation to preach a series of sermons in Methodist chapels in Gateshead. William stayed at home with the children: so novel was this role reversal that one newspaper depicted Booth as preaching in her husband's clothes.[21] Her only episode of revulsion based on conventional ideas of female behaviour was her startled reaction to first seeing her name emblazoned in large letters on posters. Despite her dismay, she was persuaded that she had given her name to God along with the rest of her, and if the novelty factor helped to attract listeners who would not otherwise dream of attending a sermon, so much the better. It seems she became accustomed to the publicity. Later posters shouted, 'Come and hear a WOMAN preach!'[22]

The only hiatuses in Booth's preaching after the spring of 1860 were a few months after the birth of each of her subsequent children (she and William had a family of eight). She made sermon notes while nursing her babies at night, the only period of quietness and solitude in her life. She preached from these brief outlines scratched in pencil, or entirely

spontaneously. However, Booth seems never to have doubted the importance of her words, nor of the rewards they had brought her, later writing
of that first sermon and what followed it:

> I think I can say that from that day – and it is about 19 years and 9
> months since – He has never allowed me to open my mouth without
> giving me signs of his presence and blessing ... while the Devil kept me
> silent, he kept me comparatively fruitless; now I have ground to hope
> and expect to meet hundreds in Glory, whom God has made me in-
> strumental in saving.[23]

But she did feel anger at the lack of practical support she received from
the Methodists, complaining that if they wanted her to preach, they should
provide enough money to allow her to hire someone else to do her sewing.
In 1861 the Booths left the New Connexion, the branch of Methodism to
which they belonged. In response, Methodist pulpits were closed to them
in 1862, the cause given being 'the perambulations of the male and
female'.[24]

Because Methodist pulpits were shut to her, Catherine preached in
music halls, skittle-alleys, dancing rooms and circuses, as well as in the
chapels of other nonconformist denominations. What began as expediency
proved to be an important factor in the success of what was to become the
Salvation Army, allowing Booth to spread her message to populations who
shunned churches. Booth proved to be a skilled evangelist. All those years
of sitting silently in congregations had familiarised her with the techniques,
verbal style and discernment of crowd response required for successful
evangelism. She was good at drawing numbers, at crowd control, and at
eliciting conversions. During the eighteen months of the Cornish campaign
alone, she made 7,000 converts.[25] It was while in Cornwall that she
pioneered her highly successful series of meetings for women only. Booth
loved preaching, and was proud of her success. Her letters repeatedly make
the point that she was in her element on the platform, and felt more at
home there than anywhere else. Despite her personal success as a preacher,
she felt resentment that women were so poorly received in the role,
convinced that the press conspired to marginalise them.

> I despise the attitude of the English press toward woman. Let a man make
> a decent speech on any subject, and he is lauded to the skies Whereas,
> however magnificent a speech a woman may make, all she gets is, 'Mrs.
> So-and-so delivered an earnest address'! I don't speak for myself. My
> personal experience ... has been otherwise. But I do feel it keenly on
> behalf of womankind at large, that the man should be praised, while the
> woman, who has probably fought her way through inconceivably greater
> difficulties in order to achieve the same result, should be passed over
> without a word![26]

Booth resented this gendering of praise and public acclaim, and she was concerned that women's words were being lost, due to under-reporting by a biased press. Not all coverage, even of Booth, was positive. A review of her preaching in *The Christian World* (15 February 1867), disapproved of her unfeminine intelligence and force, writing 'She evidently bestows a good deal of pains upon the arrangement of her composition. Throughout the appeal is to the intellect and never once to the affections.' Worst of all, Booth was described as using 'language which is rather strong for feminine lips ...' It is clear that this critic was unaware that the sermon he heard, as with almost all of her public utterances, was preached extempore.

Like most other late Victorian platform women, but very unlike Hopkins, Booth understood the power of spectacle and exploited melodrama in order to make her message as effective as possible. At the end of her lengthy addresses, she often collapsed and was carried off the platform by her eldest son. This moment of high drama was exploited to the full, both as evidence of her earnestness and as testimony to the importance of the occasion. Her admirers claimed that Booth was a better speaker than Gladstone or Spurgeon, the famous evangelist.[27] But unlike other platform women, Booth could not permit herself any respite from her public work. Her sense of responsibility for the eternal destiny of her auditors meant that she laid a burden of unending public work upon herself, for every rejected opportunity to speak meant that she might be responsible for the damnation of those who would otherwise have responded to her message that night. Unlike Hopkins, she remained unsure of the efficacy of the printed word to change hearts. Writing of her first sermon, she remarked with some sadness, 'I never imagined the life of publicity it was going to lead me into, and of trial also; for I was never allowed to have another quiet Sabbath, when I could speak or stand up ...'[28]

Booth actively encouraged other women to join her in the ministry of preaching. The Salvation Army was thus giving equal opportunities to women before it had either its name or its constitution; male and female preachers alike celebrated communion, until the sacraments were eliminated in 1883.[29] Unlike Hopkins, who initially discouraged other women from sharing her public role as a purity lecturer, Booth urged other women to preach, using her own experience to encourage them and exhibiting herself as exemplar and model: 'Never mind trembling. I trembled. Never mind your heart beating. Mine beat nearly through. Never mind how weak you are. I have gone many a time from the bed to the pulpit and back from the pulpit to bed.'[30] While Hopkins appealed to 'the mother in all women' to join in the work of social purity, Booth concentrated her maternalism on encouraging women within the Salvation Army. A recent historian of Booth's role in the Salvation Army argues that the most innovative aspect of her work was its rejection of female exceptionalism: 'her assertion that women could possess spiritual authority as women and could preach as Christian women in their own voices as part of the natural order'.[31]

Booth's insistence on the duty and right of women to work for God resulted in the Salvation Army being the only Victorian denomination sending out young women, usually former domestic servants, as preachers, evangelists and local heads. The number of women leaders in the movement grew rapidly. In the 1870 Whitechapel circuit, 5 of 13 preachers were female, as were 9 of 16 exhorters.[32] There were more than 70 women preachers in the Army by 1878, and two years later Hallelujah Lasses were in charge of 46 of the 118 corps. The Army employed nearly 380 women preachers in 1882, and growth continued to be rapid: it has been estimated that there were between 400 and 500 women officers in 1883. There was continued opposition to female religious leadership, however. In 1882 a total of 251 female Salvation Army officers were attacked in the streets; in the same year 15 were imprisoned for conducting open-air services.[33] The nurturing of women's abilities continued after Booth's death. Forty per cent of Army officers were women in 1900, owing largely to Booth's insistence that equal numbers of men and women be admitted to the Army's training courses, and promotion in the Army continued to be strictly on merit. Near the end of her public ministry, Catherine made the point of the uniqueness of the Army again:

> Where outside the Salvation Army is there any provision for the exercise of the spiritual gifts of women? And yet from the word of God, the history of the early churches, and from experience, we are convinced that the Holy Spirit uses women as effectively as men where he is allowed to do so! We allow him to choose his own instruments, and consequently He is developing a mighty force of saved and consecrated women officers who have no need to be ashamed of their calling. We have today nearly 2000 women warriors in the world's great harvest field.[34]

Polemical publications

Aside from numberless articles in Salvation Army periodicals such as the *War Cry*, which she co-edited, Booth published little other than sermons. When approached by a publisher who was interested in publishing her sermons, she initially refused, writing that 'she felt he overestimated her powers, and that her words were hardly worth printing'.[35] This refusal is linked to her conviction that she spoke under the influence of the Holy Spirit, and that much of the effectiveness of her words was due to this, rather than what was actually said. She was also sensitive about the general impression that her preaching was more effective than that of her husband. She was to come to regret this decision, seeing that only a tiny fraction of her sermons was ever preserved.[36] Later she consented to the proposal that a shorthand writer take down her sermons, which she then edited for publication. (This was never an entirely satisfactory solution, as the shorthand writers sometimes ended up kneeling in penitence at the seeker's bench, their note-taking function forgotten.) Because she was so peripatetic, writers had to be employed on a casual basis in the towns she visited, and their work varied in quality. It also caused problems at the editorial stage, as she seldom had adequate time to devote to the task of revision. However, almost all of the published volumes result from this kind of collaboration.

There is one important exception. Booth wrote *Papers on Practical Christianity* (1879) herself, rather than editing the transcripts of sermons. In these essays, she grasps the opportunity offered by writing for print rather than for delivery to make an impressive show of her scholarship. This is especially evident in the unpromisingly titled 'Worldly amusements and Christianity' which displays an extensive and sophisticated acquaintance with the writings of the early Church Fathers, Roman Catholic mystics and Puritan divines. In this sermon alone, she quotes from almost a dozen Puritan writers, as well as citing many eighteenth- and nineteenth-century authorities. Booth was always more reliant on authority in her writings than Hopkins, who tended to argue from nature and example. This may reflect Booth's self-consciousness over her lack of formal education, as well as her interest in appealing to a middle-class audience. However, in the thought of both women theology must always be ratified by experience, and is rejected if it fails that crucial test.

In a book of collected sermons, *Life and Death* (1883) Booth included one of her most important and suggestive addresses, 'Mercy and judgement'. In it she argues against an over-literal interpretation of scripture, in a line of argument designed to allow women access to the pulpit, as well as attacking theological systems such as predestination. Like Hopkins, she had come to see blind acceptance of the literal truth of scripture as a hindrance to her spiritual development, and to the services of women to religion. Here, too, we find perhaps her most interesting attack on those who forbade female preaching. She dismisses the few statements in the Pauline writings upon which the prohibition is based, saying: 'whole systems of theology have been built on some of these isolated paragraphs, as repugnant to our innate perceptions of rectitude and benevolence as they are inimical to the character of God'.[37] The characteristically autobiographical element of the sermon shows unusual freedom from the fetters of Biblical literalism for a nonconformist of the period, especially one still in her teens.

When I was fourteen years old, I rejected all theories about God and religion which contradicted my innate perceptions of right and wrong. I said, 'No, I will never believe any theory which represents that a course of procedure is good and benevolent in God which in men would be despicable and contemptible. I cannot receive it'.[38]

The sermons in *Popular Christianity* (1887) were first preached, and then revised by Booth. They show a widening of her understanding of faith, an almost ecumenical spirit, in contrast to her early eagerness to condemn those who thought differently from herself. Here, too, she argues for women's and men's absolute duty to work to purify society, morally and socially.[39] This collection should put to rest the assumption that Booth's conversionist religion was quietist and anti-radical. Booth envisioned the Day of Judgement not as an individual reckoning of personal sins, but as a day for the ultimate satisfaction of demands for social justice, especially for the righting of the wrongs of women and children. It was this anger over injustice that brought Booth into the 'Maiden Tribute' agitation in 1885, which nominally demanded the raising of the age of sexual consent to sixteen. While later commentators have condemned the movement as anti-sex and repressive, they have missed the point that what drove the agitation was a deep anger over the sexual double standard. Campaigners demanded not just protection for young girls, but equal treatment of the sexes in all matters of sexual behaviour and morality. Like Hopkins, there was a clear undertone of class issue in her rhetoric, despite her denials of having a class grievance. It is significant that she was the only speaker of working-class origin that I can identify at the Hyde Park demonstration, despite the crowds of 250,000 being largely composed of working people. In the previous year (1884) Booth had first publicly aligned herself with the social purity movement, publishing a sermon entitled *The Iniquity of State Regulated Vice*. In it she argues that political action as well as spiritual rebirth are necessary to deal with the issue of sexual justice: a position very untypical of the evangelical world-view, and one influenced both by Hopkins and Josephine Butler.[40] Booth spent twenty-eight years as a preacher-evangelist. One of the memorial sermons preached after her death in 1890 summarised her achievement in terms she would have relished: 'What John Wesley did for laymen, Mrs. Booth did for women. She emancipated them from the muzzle of the devil.'[41]

I would like to conclude by highlighting some of the shared experience of these two women, notorious in their own time, and largely forgotten in ours. Both used the demand for the sexual *single* standard as an important rationale for their public roles. Hopkins aimed to publicise the private sphere through her exposure of male sexual irresponsibility; she demanded male morality because she believed the sexual double standard oppressed women and degraded men. Booth, more traditionally, sought to bring more and more of the public sphere within the domain of private moral judgements, demanding a sexual single standard based on traditional Biblical morality. Hopkins founded her revision of the Victorian understanding of both faith and sexuality on arguments from science, nature and history; Booth sought to reform the religious and moral world by relying primarily on the authority of her own personal experience and inner testimony. Hopkins must be seen as more of a single issue reformer, who used her re-versioning of Christianity (based on exegesis) to demand sexual justice; Booth, while insisting that personal salvation was the goal of all her speaking and writing, worked on multiple issues under an umbrella of evangelical Christianity, however unorthodox and experience-based. Hopkins focused her campaigns on the provinces, especially the north and Scotland, while Booth concentrated on London, although the organisations these women founded were spread around the world by the times of their deaths. The middle-class Hopkins's most important contribution was the establishment of a men-only social purity group attractive to the working class, locally organised with only loose central administration; the working-class Booth preferred to minister to women, and in the highly centralised army she helped to found was considered to be the only Salvationist preacher capable of reaching middle-class audiences effectively. While Booth 'emancipated women from the muzzle of the Devil', Hopkins provided the moral ammunition that empowered women publicly to reject the sexual oppression inherent in the double standard.

Hopkins and Booth, in different ways, appropriated gendered forms of authority for the purposes of spiritual counsel. Both proclaimed the equality of the sexes, not simply before God, but demanding equality as a right on earth, and in this life. They used strategies of feminisation, maternalism and privatisation to legitimate their demands for male sexual responsibility and as a response to the social turbulence and moral questioning of the late Victorian period. Both, as women who claimed the right to preach, to function as religious authorities and as public arbiters of male behaviour and attitudes, outraged Victorian conventions. They sought to replace traditional theological anthropologies of male and female with a new interpretation of the gospel's meaning, of gender roles and sexual behaviours, all refracted through their re-reading of the gospel and negotiated through their redefinitions of public and private.

Notes

1   Thanks to the Salvation Army International Heritage Centre for their co-operation. The title of this essay comes from Booth's 1853 letter to her minister, Dr David Thomas, defending the right of women to preach.

2   Although women had a long tradition of writing devotional pamphlets and tracts, controversial works by women were rare.

3   For a discussion of the relationship between social purity movements and feminism, see Lucy Bland, *Banishing the Beast: English Feminism and Sexual Morality, 1885–1914* (London, Penguin, 1995). Judith Walkowitz discusses the role of the 'platform women' in *City of Dreadful Delight: Narratives of Sexual Danger in Late Victorian London* (London, Virago, 1992).

4   Elihu Burritt, preface to Jane Ellice Hopkins, *An English Woman's Work Among Workingmen* (New Britain, CT, John A. Williams, 1875), pp. 15–16.

5   Hopkins, *Work among Workingmen*, p. 43.

6   Hopkins, *Work among Workingmen*, p. 42.

7   J. E. Hopkins, *Touching Pitch* (London, Hatchards, [1885]), p. 4.

8   Hopkins to Frank Crossley, 17 September 1882, cited in Rosa M. Barrett, *Ellice Hopkins: A Memoir* (London, Wells Gardner, Darton [c. 1905]), p. 139.

9   Barrett, *Ellice Hopkins*, p. 143.

10   Barrett, *Ellice Hopkins*, pp. 171–2.

11   Jane Ellice Hopkins, *Work in Brighton, or, Woman's Mission to Women, with additions and a preface by Florence Nightingale* (London, Hatchards, 1877), pp. 40, 42.

12   Hopkins, *Work among Workingmen* [1879 edn], p. 79.

13   Jane Ellice Hopkins, *Grave Moral Questions Addressed to the Men and Women of England* (London, Hatchards, 1882), p. 39.

14   Norwich Record Office, SO 27/3, minutes of the Norfolk and Norwich Ladies Association for the Care of Girls, vol. III, May 1886.

15   Edward Bristow, *Vice and Vigilance: Purity Movements in Britain Since 1700* (Dublin, Gill & Macmillan, 1977), p. 5.

16   Barrett, *Ellice Hopkins*, pp. 248–9.

17   Catherine Bramwell-Booth, *Catherine Booth: The Story of Her Loves* (London, Hodder & Stoughton, 1971), p. 99.

18   Bramwell-Booth, *Catherine Booth*, p. 181.

19   Catherine Booth, 'Female ministry, or women's right to preach the gospel' (rev. edn), *Papers on Practical Christianity* (London, S. W. Partridge, [1879]), p. 111.

20   Booth, 'Witnessing for Christ', *Papers on Aggressive Christianity* (London, S. W. Partridge, [1881]), pp. 14–15. This autobiographical sermon is the best source for Booth's entry into public ministry.

21   Roger J. Green, *Catherine Booth: A Biography of the Cofounder of the Salvation Army* (Grand Rapids, Baker, 1996), p. 136.

22   Bramwell-Booth, *Catherine Booth*, p. 194; F. de L. Booth-Tucker, *The Life of Catherine Booth* (London, The Salvation Army, [1893]), vol. I, p. 382.

23   Booth, 'Witnessing', pp. 18–19.

24   Bramwell-Booth, *Catherine Booth*, p. 215.

25   Bramwell-Booth, *Catherine Booth*, p. 217.

26   Booth-Tucker, *Life*, I, p. 87.

27   Bramwell-Booth, *Catherine Booth*, p. 236.

28 Booth, 'Witnessing', p. 17.

29 Article XII of the 1870 Constitution of the Christian Mission, reprinted in Glenn K. Horridge, *The Salvation Army: Origins and Early Days, 1865–1900* (Godalming, Ammonite, 1993), p. 256; Green, *Catherine Booth*, pp. 196, 236–40.

30 Booth, 'Witnessing', p. 19.

31 Pamela J. Walker, 'Proclaiming women's right to preach', *Harvard Divinity Bulletin*, 23 (1994), p. 21.

32 Exhorters dealt with souls under the supervision of the local evangelist. The usage was probably borrowed from Methodism, where exhorters ranked above class-leaders.

33 Commissioner Railton, 'The Salvation Army following Christ', *Popular Christianity* (London, Salvation Army Book Depot, [1887]), p. 188.

34 Bramwell-Booth, *Catherine Booth*, p. 236.

35 Booth, Address at Exeter Hall, 4 May 1887, *All the World*, (June 1887), p. 159.

36 Bramwell-Booth, *Catherine Booth*, p. 236; Booth-Tucker, *Life*, vol. I, p. 420.

37 Catherine Booth, 'Mercy and judgement', *Life and Death* (London, Salvation Army, 1883), p. 29.

38 Booth, 'Mercy', p. 30.

39 Booth, 'Cowardly service versus the real warfare', *Popular Christianity* (London, Salvation Army Book Depot, [1887]), p. 96.

40 Catherine Booth, *The Iniquity of State-Regulated Vice* (London, Dyer Bros, [1884]), pp. 13–14.

41 G. T. Allpress, *The Late Mrs. Booth: A Memorial Sermon* (n.p., preached at Greengate Congregational Church, 19 October 1890), p. 3.

Postscript

Database

In association with the essays in this book, the Women in the Humanities Research Group at the Open University complied a modest database of biographical material relating to nineteenth-century women scholars and critics and their writings. On it we recorded basic life events as well as information about their work and networks of communication.

The database allowed us to consider how women's lives and experiences differed or changed over time and produced some interesting and sometimes unexpected results. For example, of the 150 or so women we recorded about a quarter of the total received their early education at home and about a quarter at school. Yet the proportion of women about whose early education we know nothing seems to increase rather than decrease over the nineteenth century. One reason for this may be that more women working later in the century received some form of higher education, which encouraged biographers to take less notice of their early education.

A particularly interesting finding is that the women working as scholars in the later period were much less likely to be married than those of the earlier period. Of the cohort born in the decade 1780–90 around 50 per cent married and 38 per cent never married, whereas of the cohort born in the decade 1860–70 no one married. Although the number of women in the sample is relatively small, we hope these preliminary findings are suggestive of possible shifts which a database is capable of indicating. It will also suggest further avenues of investigation. A copy of the database can be obtained from Anne Laurence, History Department, Arts Faculty, The Open University, Walton Hall, Milton Keynes, MK7 6AA.

Bibliography

Aikin, L., *Memoirs of the Court of Queen Elizabeth*, 2 vols, London, Longman, 1818.

Aikin, L., *Epistles on Women Exemplifying Their Character and Condition in Various Ages and Nations*, London, J. Johnson & Co., 1810.

Alexander, S., *Women's Work in Nineteenth Century London*, London, Journeyman, 1983.

Alison, A., *Essays on the Nature and Principles of Taste*, 6th edn, 2 vols, Edinburgh, D. Willison for A. Constable, 1825.

Allpress, G. T., *The Late Mrs. Booth: A Memorial Sermon*, n.p., preached at Greengate Congregational Church, October 19 1890.

Altick, R. D., *The Cowden Clarkes*, Oxford, Oxford University Press, 1948.

Arnold, M., *On Translating Homer*, London, Longman, Green & Roberts, 1861.

Arnold, M., *Matthew Arnold: Poetry and Selected Prose*, ed. M. Allott and R. H. Super, Oxford, Oxford University Press, 1986.

Asleson, R. (ed.), *A Passion for Performance: Sarah Siddons and Her Portraits*, Los Angeles, The Paul Getty Museum, 1999.

Aspinall, A., *Mrs Jordan and Her Family, being The Unpublished Letters of Mrs Jordan and the Duke of Clarence, later William IV*, London, A. Barker, 1951.

Barker, H., and E. Chalus (eds), *Gender in Eighteenth-Century England: Roles, Representations and Responsibilities*, Harlow, Longman, 1997.

Barrett, R. M., *Ellice Hopkins: A Memoir*, London, Wells Gardner, Darton, c. 1905.

Barry, J., *Inquiry into the Real and Imaginary Obstructions to the Acquisition of the Arts in England*, London, 1775.

Bassnett-Maguire, S., *Translation Studies*, London and New York, Methuen, 1980.

Beale, D., Girls' schools past and present, *The Nineteenth Century*, 23 (1888), 541–53.

Beckerlegge, G., Professor Friedrich Max Müller and the missionary cause, in J. Wolffe (ed.), *Religion in Victorian Britain Volume V*, Manchester, Manchester University Press, 1997.

Beckett, J. C., The Irish writer and his public in the nineteenth century, *The Yearbook of English Studies*, II (1981), 102–16.

Bland, L., *Banishing the Beast: English Feminism and Sexual Morality, 1885–1914*, London, Penguin, 1995.

Boaden, J., *Memoirs of Mrs Siddons*, 2 vols, London, Henry Colburn, 1827.

Boaden, J., *The Life of Mrs Jordan*, 2 vols, London, Henry Colburn, 1831.

Booth, C., Female ministry, or women's right to preach the gospel (rev. edn), *Papers on Practical Christianity*, London, S. W. Partridge, 1879.

Booth, C., Witnessing for Christ, *Papers on Aggressive Christianity*, London, S. W. Partridge, 1881.

Booth, C., Mercy and judgement, *Life and Death*, London, Salvation Army, 1883.

Booth, C., *The Iniquity of State-Regulated Vice*, London, Dyer Bros, 1884.

Booth, C., Address at Exeter Hall, 4 May 1887, *All the World*, (June 1887).

Booth, C., Cowardly service versus the real warfare, *Popular Christianity*, London, Salvation Army Book Depot, 1887.

Booth-Tucker, F. de L., *The Life of Catherine Booth*, London, The Salvation Army, 1893.

Bradley, A. C., *Oxford Lectures on Poetry*, London, Macmillan, 1909.

Bramwell-Booth, C., *Catherine Booth: The Story of her Loves*, London, Hodder & Stoughton, 1971.

Brink, C. O., *English Classical Scholarship*, Cambridge, James Clarke, 1985.

Bristed, C. A., English poetry and poets of the present day, *The Knickerbocker*, 1845, 534–42.

Bristow, E., *Vice and Vigilance: Purity Movements in Britain Since 1700*, Dublin, Gill & Macmillan, 1977.

Brown, S., Determined heroines: George Eliot, Augusta Webster, and closet drama by Victorian women, *Victorian Poetry*, 33 (1995), 89–109.

Bruce, M. L., *Anna Swanwick: A Memoir and Recollections 1813–1899*, London, T. Fisher Unwin, 1903.

Burritt, E., preface to Jane Ellice Hopkins, *An English Woman's Work Among Workingmen*, New Britain, CT, J. A. Williams, 1875.

Burstyn, J. N., *Victorian Education and the Ideal of Womanhood*, London, Croom Helm, 1980.

Burton, H., *Barbara Bodichon*, London, John Murray, 1949.

Butler, J., *Women's Work and Women's Culture*, London, Macmillan, 1869.

Butler, M., *Maria Edgeworth: A Literary Biography*, Oxford, Clarendon Press, 1972.

Butler, H. J., and H. E. Butler, *The Black Book of Edgeworthstown and Other Edgeworth Memories*, London, Faber and Gwyer, 1927.

Byron, G., *The Complete Poetical Works*, 7 vols, ed. J. McGann, Oxford, Oxford University Press, 1980–92.

Cairns, D., and S. Richards, *Writing Ireland: Colonialism, Nationalism and Culture*, Manchester, Manchester University Press, 1988.

Calder, J., *The Victorian Home*, London, Batsford, 1977.

Campbell, T., *Life of Mrs Siddons*, London, Effingham Wilson, 1834.

Canny, N., Identity formation in Ireland: the emergence of the Anglo-Irish, in N. Canny and A. Pagden (eds), *Colonial Identity in the Atlantic World, 1500–1800*, Princeton, Princeton University Press, 1987.

Carlyle, T., *Oliver Cromwell's Letters and Speeches with Elucidations by Thomas Carlyle*, London, J. M. Dent, 1907.

Chalmers, F. G., *Women in the Nineteenth Century Art World: Schools of Design for Women in London and Philadelphia*, London, Greenwood Press, 1999.

Chard, C., and H. Langdon (eds), *Transports: Travel, Pleasure, and Imaginative Geography, 1600–1830*, New Haven and London, Yale University Press, 1996.

Chaudhuri, N. C., *Scholar Extraordinary: The Life of Professor the Rt. Hon. Friedrich Max Müller*, London, Chatto and Windus, 1974.

Clarke, C. C., *Shakespeare – Characters*, London, Smith Elder, 1863.

Clarke, M. L., *Classical Education in Britain 1500–1900*, Cambridge, Cambridge University Press, 1959.

Clarke, M. C., *Letters to an Enthusiast*, ed. A. U. Nettleton, Chicago, A. C. McClurg, 1902.

Collet, C., *Educated Working Women. Essays on the Economic Position of Women Workers in the Middle Classes*, London, P. S. King, 1902.

Collins, K. K., and F. Williams, Lewes at Colonus: an early Victorian view of translation from the Greek, *The Modern Language Review*, 82 (1987), 293–312.

Colvin, H., *A Biographical Dictionary of British Architects 1600–1840*, 3rd edn, New Haven and London, Yale University Press, 1995.

Corrado Pope, B., The influence of Rousseau's ideology of domesticity, in M. J. Boxer and J. H. Quataert (eds), *Connecting Spheres*, New York and Oxford, Oxford University Press, 1987.

Cowden Clarke, M., *My Long Life: An Autobiograhic Sketch*, London, T. Fisher Unwin, 1896.

Croghan, M. J., Swift, Thomas Sheridan, Maria Edgeworth and the evolution of Hiberno-English, *Irish University Review*, 20:1 (1990), 19–34.

Cross, J. (ed.), *George Eliot's Life as related in her Letters and Journals*, 3 vols, Edinburgh, Blackwood, 1885.

Cunningham, C., *Alfred Waterhouse 1830–1905: Biography of a Practice*, Oxford, Oxford University Press, 1992.

Dabbs, T., *Reforming Marlowe*, Lewisburg, Pa., Bucknell University Press, 1991.

David, D., *Intellectual Women and Victorian Patriarchy*, Basingstoke, Macmillan, 1987.

de Staël, G. (Anne Louise Germaine de Staël-Holstein), *Corinne; ou, l'Italie*, 2 vols, ed. C. Herrmann, Paris, Des Femmes, 1979.

Deane, S. *Civilians and Barbarians*, Derry, Field Day, 1983.

Delamont, S., The contradiction in ladies' education, in S. Delamont and L. Duffin (eds), *The Nineteenth-Century Woman: The Cultural and Physical World*, London, Croom Helm, 1978.

Delorme, M., 'Facts not opinions' – Agnes Strickland, *History Today*, 38 (February 1988), 45–50.

Dunne, T., Maria Edgeworth and the colonial mind (O'Donnell Lecture), Cork, University College, Cork, 1984.

Dyhouse, C., *Girls Growing Up in Late Victorian and Edwardian England*, London, Routledge and Kegan Paul, 1981.

Eagleton, T., *Heathcliff and the Great Hunger: Studies in Irish Culture*, London, Verso, 1995.

Easterling, P. E., George Eliot and Greek tragedy, *Arion*, 3rd series, 1:2 (1991), 60–74.

Easterling, P. E., The early years of the Cambridge Greek Play: 1882–1912, in C. Stray (ed.), *Supplement to the Proceedings of the Cambridge Philological Society*, 1998.

Eastlake, C. L., *Hints on Household Taste*, 2nd edn, London, 1869.

Edgeworth, M., *The Absentee*, ed. W. J. McCormack and K. Walker, Oxford, Oxford University Press, [1812] 1988.

Edgeworth, M., *Castle Rackrent and Ennui*, ed. M. Butler, London, Penguin, [1800 and 1809] 1992.

Edgeworth, M., and R. L. Edgeworth, *Essay on Irish Bulls*, London, J. Johnson, 1802.

Edgeworth, M., and R. L. Edgeworth, *Memoirs of Richard Lovell Edgeworth, Esq. Begun by Himself and Concluded by His Daughter Maria Edgeworth*, 2 vols, London, R. Hunter, 1820.

Edwards, C. and M. Liversidge, *Imagining Rome: British Artists and Rome in the Nineteenth Century*, London, Merrell Holberton, 1996.

Ellsworth, E. W., *Liberators of the Female Mind: The Shirreff Sisters, Educational Reform and the Women's Movement*, Westport, CT and London, Greenwood Press, 1979.

Faithfull, E., *Shall My Daughter Learn a Business?*, London, Victoria Press, 1863.

Firth, C. H., obituary to Sophia Crawford Lomas, *History*, 14 (1929).

Foley, H. P., 'Reverse similes' and sex roles in the *Odyssey*, in J. Perradotto and J. P. Sullivan (eds), *Women in the Ancient World: The Arethusa Papers*, Albany, SUNY Press, 1984.

Fowler, R., On not knowing Greek: the classics and the women of letters, *Classical Journal*, 78 (1983), 337–48.

Froude, J. A. (ed.), *Letters and Memorials of Jane Welsh Carlyle*, London, Longmans, Green & Co., 1883.

Gere, C. and M. Whiteway, *Nineteenth Century Design*, London, Weidenfeld & Nicolson, 1993.

Gill, C., *Personality in Greek Epic, Tragedy and Philosophy: The Self in Dialogue*, Oxford, Clarendon Press, 1996.

Gilmour, R., *The Victorian Period: The Intellectual and Cultural Context of English Literature, 1830–1890*, London and New York, Longman, 1993.

Gleadle, K., *The Early Feminists: Radical Unitarians and the Emergence of the Women's Rights Movement*, London, Macmillan, 1995.

Goldstein, D. S., The organizational development of the British historical profession, 1884–1921, *Bulletin of the Institute of Historical Research*, 55 (1982), pp. 180–93.

Graves, A. and W. V. Cronin, *A History of the Works of Sir Joshua Reynolds PRA*, 4 vols London, published by subscription, 1901.

Green, M. A. E., *Lives of the Princesses of England*, 6 vols, London, Henry Colburn, 1849–55.

Green, M. A. E., Introductions to the *Calendar of the Proceedings of the Committee for Compounding 1643–60*, 5 vols, London, HMSO, 1889–92; *Calendar of the Proceedings of the Committee for the Advance of Money 1642–56*, 3 vols, London, HMSO, 1888; *Calendar of State Papers Domestic 1649–50*, London, HMSO, 1875.

Green, M. A. E., *Calendar of State Papers Domestic 1660–61*, London, HMSO, 1860.

Green, R. J., *Catherine Booth: A Biography of the Cofounder of the Salvation Army*, Grand Rapids, Baker, 1996.

Grey, M., *On the Education of Women*, Society of Arts, 31 May 1871.

Grier, L., *The Life of Winifred Mercier*, Oxford, Oxford University Press, 1937.

Gross, G. C., Mary Cowden Clarke, 'The girlhood of Shakespeare's heroines' and the sex education of Victorian women, *Victorian Studies*, 16:1 (1972), 37–58.

Havely, C. P., Saying the unspeakable: Mary Cowden Clarke and *Measure for Measure*, *Durham University Journal*, 87:2 (1995), 233–42.

Haweis, M. E., *The Art of Decoration*, London, Chatto & Windus, 1881.

Haweis, M. E., *The Art of Beauty*, London, 1878.

Haweis, M. E., *The Art of Housekeeping: A Bridal Garland*, London, Sampson Low & Co., 1889.

Haweis, M. E., *Beautiful Houses: A Description of Certain Well-Known Artistic Houses*, 2nd edn, London, Sampson Low & Co., 1882.

Haweis, H. R. (ed.), *Words to Women: Addresses and Essays* (with a memoir), London, Bernard & Isbister, 1900.

Hawis, O., *Four to Fourteen*, London, Robert Hale, 1939.

Hill, B., *The Republican Virago: The Life and Times of Catherine Macaulay, Historian*, Oxford, Clarendon Press, 1992.

Holmes, R., *Shelley: The Pursuit*, London, HarperCollins, 1994.

Hopkins, J. E., *Touching Pitch*, London, Hatchards, 1885.

Hopkins, J. E., *Work in Brighton, or, Woman's Mission to Women*, with additions and a preface by Florence Nightingale, London, Hatchards, 1877.

Hopkins, J. E., *Grave Moral Questions Addressed to the Men and Women of England*, London, Hatchards, 1882.

Horridge, G. K., *The Salvation Army: Origins and Early Days, 1865–1900*, Godalming, Ammonite, 1993.

Houghton, W. E. et al. (eds), *The Wellesley Index to Victorian Periodicals 1824–1900*, Toronto, University of Toronto Press, 1966–90.

Howe, B., *Arbiter of Elegance*, London, Harvill Press, 1967.

Howitt, M., *An Autobiography*, 2 vols, London, W. Isbister, 1889.

Hughes, K., *The Victorian Governess*, London, Hambledon Press, 1993.

Hulpe, E., Cultural constraints: a case of political censorship, in H. Kittel and A. P. Frank (eds), *Interculturality and the Historical Study of Literary Translations*, Berlin, Erich Schmidt Verlag, 1991.

Hurst, M., *Maria Edgeworth and the Public Scene*, London, Macmillan, 1969.

Ingleby, C. M., *Shakespeare's Centurie of Prayse; Being Materials for a History of Opinion on Shakespeare and his Works AD 1591–1693*, 2nd edn revised with many additions by Lucy Toulmin Smith, New Shakespere Society, series IV, no. 2 (1879)

James, H., *Notes on Novelists With Some Other Notes*, London, J. M. Dent & Sons Ltd, 1914.

Jameson, A., *Diary of an Ennuyée*, London, Henry Colburn, 1826.

Jameson, A., *Characteristics of Women, Moral, Political and Historical*, 2 vols, London, 1832.

Jay, E. (ed.), *The Autobiography of Margaret Oliphant*, Oxford, Oxford University Press, 1990.

Jay, E., *Mrs Oliphant: 'A Fiction to Herself'*, Oxford, Clarendon Press, 1995.

Jenkyns, R., *The Victorians and Ancient Greece*, Oxford, Blackwell, 1980.

Johnston, J., *Anna Jameson: Victorian, Feminist, Woman of Letters*, Aldershot, Scolar Press, 1997.

Jones, V. (ed.), *Women in the Eighteenth Century, Constructions of Femininity*, London, Routledge, 1990.

Keats, J., *Complete Poems*, ed. J. Barnard, Harmondsworth, Penguin, 1977.

Keats, J., *The Letters of John Keats 1814–1821*, ed. H. E. Rollins, Cambridge, Mass., Harvard University Press, 1958.

Kirkham, P. (ed.), *The Gendered Object*, Manchester, Manchester University Press, 1996.

Kowaleski-Wallace, E., *Their Fathers' Daughters: Hannah More, Maria Edgeworth and Patriarchal Complicity*, New York and Oxford, Oxford University Press, 1991.

Lawrence, V., *The Translators Invisibility: A History of Translation*, London and New York, Routledge, 1995.

Le Breton, P. H., *Memoirs, Miscellanies and Letters of the Late Lucy Aikin*, London, Longman, 1864.

Le Breton, P. H., *Memoir of Mrs Barbauld*, London, George Bell & Sons, 1874.

Leadbeater, M., *Cottage Dialogues Among the Irish Peasantry*, with Preface and a Glossary by M. Edgeworth, London, J. Johnson, 1811.

Leadbeater, M., *The Leadbeater Papers*, ed. R. D. Webb, 2 vols, London, 1862 (printed in Dublin).

Leighton, A., *Victorian Women Poets: Writing Against the Heart*, Hemel Hempstead, Harvester, 1992.

Leighton, A. and M. Reynolds (eds), *Victorian Women Poets: An Anthology*, Oxford, Blackwell, 1995.

Lennep, W. van (ed.), *The Reminiscences of Sarah Kemble Siddons, 1773–1785*, Cambridge, Mass., Widener Library, 1942.

Levine, P., *The Amateur and the Professional: Antiquarians, Historians and Archaeologists in Victorian England, 1838–1886*, Cambridge, Cambridge University Press, 1986.

Levine, P., *Victorian Feminism 1850–100*, London, Hutchinson, 1987.

Liebschner, J., *Foundations of Progressive Education: The History of the National Froebel Society*, Cambridge, The Lutterworth Press, 1991.

Liversidge, M. and C. Edwards, *Imagining Rome: British Artists and Rome in the Nineteenth Century*, London, Merrell Holberton, 1996.

Lynn Linton, E., *My Literary Life: Reminiscences of Dickens, Thackeray, George Eliot*, London, Hodder & Stoughton, 1899.

McClure, L., On knowing Greek: George Eliot and the classical tradition, *Classical and Modern Literature*, 13:2 (1993), 139–51.

Maitzen, R., 'This feminine preserve': historical biographies by Victorian women, *Victorian Studies*, 38:3 (1995), 371–93.

Marshall, M. P., *What I Remember*, Cambridge, Cambridge University Press, 1947.

Martineau, H., *Harriet Martineau's Autobiography*, 3rd edn, London, Smith Elder, 1877.

Matthew, H. C. G. (ed.), *The Gladstone Diaries*, VI, 1861–1868, Oxford, Clarendon Press, 1978.

Mermin, D., *Godiva's Ride: Women of Letters in England, 1830–1880*, Bloomington and Indianapolis, Indiana University Press, 1993.

Miles, A. H., *The Poets and the Poetry of the Nineteenth Century*, 2nd edn, London, George Routledge & Sons, 1907.

Mill, J. S., *Autobiography*, ed. H. Taylor, London, Longmans, 1873.

Misenheimer, H. E., *Rousseau on the Education of Women*, Washington, DC, University Press of America, 1981.

Montagu, E., *An Essay on the Writings and Genius of Shakespeare*, London, J. Dodsley et al., 1769.

Moore, J., *A View of Society and Manners in Italy*, 2nd edn, 2 vols, London, W. Strahan & T. Cadell, 1781.

More, H., *Strictures on the Modern System of Female Education*, 2 vols, London, T. Cadell & W. Davies, 1799.

Morgan, Lady Sydney, *Italy*, 3rd edn, 3 vols, London, H. Colburn, 1821.

Morgan, T. E. (ed.), *Victorian Sages and Cultural Discourse: Renegotiating Gender and Power*, New Brunswick and London, Rutgers University Press, 1990.

Oliphant, M., *The Literary History of England in the End of the Eighteenth Century and the Beginning of the Nineteenth Century*, London, Macmillan & Co., 1882.

Orton, D., *Made of Gold: A Biography of Angela Burdett Coutts*, London, H. Hamilton, 1980.

Pals, D. L., Max Müller, E. B. Taylor and the intellectual origins of the science of religion, *International Journal of Comparative Religion and Philosophy*, 1 (1995), 16–26.

Peck, W., *A Little Learning or, A Victorian Childhood*, London, Faber, 1952.

Penny, N. (ed.), *Reynolds*, London, Royal Academy of Arts, 1986.

Perrone, F., Women academics in England, 1870–1930, *History of Universities*, 12 (1993), 339–67.

Perry, G., Women in disguise: likeness, the Grand Style and the conventions of feminine portraiture in the work of Sir Joshua Reynolds, in G. Perry and M. Rossington (eds), *Femininity and Masculinity in Eighteenth Century Art and Culture*, Manchester, Manchester University Press, 1994.

Perry, G., 'The British Sappho': borrowed identities and the representation of women artists in late eighteenth century British Art, *Oxford Art Journal*, 18:1 (1995), 44–57.

(Phipps, C. H.), Marquis of Normanby, *The English in Italy*, 3 vols, London, Saunders and Otley, 1825.

Piozzi, H. L., *Observations and Reflections Made in the Course of a Journey through France, Italy, and Germany*, 2 vols, London, A. Strahan & T. Cadell, 1789.

Pope-Hennessy, U., *Agnes Strickland: Biographer of the Queens of England*, London, Chatto & Windus, 1940.

Porter, G., *Annals of a Publishing House*, Edinburgh, Blackwood, 1898.

Prins, Y., E. B., R. B. and the difference of translation, *Victorian Poetry*, 29:4 (Winter 1991), 435–51.

Prior, M. (ed.), *Women in English Society 1500–1800*, London, Methuen, 1985.

Purvis, J., *A History of Women's Education in England*, Milton Keynes, Open University Press, 1991.

Rich, R. W., *The Training of Teachers in England and Wales During the Nineteenth Century*, Bath, Cedric Chivers, [1933] 1972.

Ritchie, A., *From the Porch*, London, Smith, Elder & Co., 1913.

Ronge, J., and B. Ronge, *A Practical Guide to the English Kindergarten*, London, Hodson, 1855.

Rossetti, W. M. (ed.), *Family Letters*, London, Brown, Langham, 1908.

Royde-Smith, N., *The Private Life of Mrs Siddons*, London, Gollanz, 1933.

Runte, R., Women as muses, in S. Spencer (ed.), *French Women and the Age of Enlightenment*, Bloomington, Indiana University Press, 1984.

Ruskin, J., *Sesame and Lilies, II Of Queen's Gardens* (Lectures delivered at Manchester in 1864), London, J. M. Dent, 1907.

Sackville-West, V., The women poets of the seventies, in H. Granville-Barker (ed.), *The Eighteen Seventies: Essays by Fellows of the Royal Society of Literature*, Cambridge, Cambridge University Press, 1929.

St Clair, W., *The Godwins and the Shelleys: The Biography of a Family*, London, Faber, 1990.

Shelley, M. W., *Collected Tales and Stories*, ed. C. E. Robinson, Baltimore and London, Johns Hopkins University Press, 1976.

Shelley, M. W., *Letters*, 3 vols, ed. B. T. Bennett, Baltimore and London, Johns Hopkins University Press, 1980–88.

Shelley, M. W., *Frankenstein*, ed. J. Rieger, Chicago, Chicago University Press, [1818] 1982.

Shelley, M. W., *Journals 1814–1844*, 2 vols, ed. P. R. Feldman and D. Scott-Kilvert, Oxford, Clarendon Press, 1987.

Shelley, M. W., *The Last Man*, Lincoln, University of Nebraska Press, [1826] 1993.

Shelley, P. B., *Posthumous Poems*, ed. M. Wollstonecraft Shelley, London, J. and H. L. Hunt, 1824.

Shelley, P. B., *The Collected Poems of Coleridge, Shelley, and Keats: Complete in One Volume*, Paris, A. and W. Galignani, 1829.

Shelley, P. B., *Collected Poems*, 4 vols, ed. M. Wollstonecraft Shelley, London, Edward Moxon, 1839.

Shelley, P. B., *Essays, Letters from Abroad, Translations and Fragments*, 2 vols, ed. M. Wollstonecraft Shelley, London, Edward Moxon, 1840.

Shelley, P. B, *The Complete Poetical Works of Percy Bysshe Shelley*, 4 vols, ed. with a memoir by G. E. Woodberry, London, Kegan Paul, 1893.

Shelley, P. B., *Poems*, ed. T. Hutchinson, London, Oxford University Press, 1907.

Shelley, P. B., *Letters*, 2 vols, ed. F. L. Jones, Oxford, Clarendon Press, 1964.

Shelley, P. B., *Complete Poetical Works of Percy Bysshe Shelley*, vol. 2, ed. N. Rogers, Oxford, Clarendon Press 1975.

Shelley, P. B., *Shelley's 'Adonais': A Critical Edition*, ed. A. D. Knerr, New York, Columbia University Press, 1984.

Shelley, P. B., *The Poems of Shelley Vol. 1 1804–1817*, ed. G. Matthews and K. Everest, London, Longman, 1989.

Shirreff, E., *Intellectual Education and its Influence on the Character and Happiness of Women*, London, John Parker, 1858.

Shirreff, E., *The Kinder-garten: Principles of Froebel's System*, London, 1876.

Shirreff, E., *A Sketch of the Life of Friedrich Froebel*, London, 1877.

Shirreff, E., *The Kindergarten at Home*, London, 1882, 3rd edn, W. H. Allen & Co. Ltd, 1894.

Shirreff, E., *Moral Training*, London, Philip & Son, 1892.

Smalley, D. (ed.), *Trollope, The Critical Heritage*, London, Routledge & Kegan Paul, 1969.

Smith, J. S., *Elsie de Wolfe*, New York, Athenaeum, 1982.

Snodin, M., and M. Howard, *Ornament: A Social History Since 1450*, New Haven and London, Yale University Press, 1996.

Somerville, M., *Personal Recollections from Early Life to Old Age of Mary Somerville and With Selections from her Correspondence*, by her Daughter, Martha Somerville, London, J. Murray, 1873.

Stephen, B., *Emily Davies and Girton College*, London, Constable & Co., 1927.

Sterne, L. '*A Sentimental Journey*' with '*The Journal to Eliza*' and '*A Political Romance*', ed. I. Jack, Oxford, Oxford University Press, 1984.

Stocking, G. W., *Victorian Anthropology*, New York, The Free Press, 1987.

Straub, K., *Sexual Suspects: Eighteenth Century Players and Sexual Ideology*, Princeton, NJ, and Oxford, Princeton University Press, 1992.

Stray, C. A., *Reconstructing Classics: Schools, Universities and Society in England 1830–1960*, Oxford, Oxford University Press, 1998.

Strickland, A., *Letters of Mary Queen of Scots and Documents Connected with her Personal History*, 3 vols, London, Henry Colburn, 1842–43.

Strickland, A., *Lives of the Queens of England*, 10 vols, London, Henry Colburn, 1845.

Strickland, A., *Lives of the Queens of England*, 12 vols, London, Henry Colburn, 1848.

Strickland, J. M., *Life of Agnes Strickland*, Edinburgh, Blackwood, 1887.

Sussman, H., *Victorian Masculinities*, Cambridge, Cambridge University Press, 1995.

Swanwick, A., *The Agamemnon, Choephori and Eumenides of Aeschylus Translated into English Verse*, London, Bell & Daldy, 1863.

Swanwick, A., *Books, Our Best Friends or Our Deadliest Foes*, An address at a celebration meeting held in the Bethnal Green Free Library, London, printed privately, 1886.

Swanwick, A., *An Utopian Dream and How It May Be Realised*, London, Kegan Paul & Co., 1888.

Swanwick, A., *Poets, the Interpreters of their Age*, London, G. Bell & Sons, 1892.

Swanwick, A., *Evolution and the Religion of the Future* (reprinted, with additions, from the *Contemporary Review*), London, P. Green, 1894.

Swanwick, A., *The Agamemnon of Aeschylus as Performed at Cambridge November 1900*, pp. 16–21, Cambridge, Cambridge University Press, 1901.

Swinburne, H., *Travels in the Two Sicilies in the Years 1777, 1778, 1779, and 1780*, 2 vols, London, 1783–85.

Taylor, G., *Reinventing Shakespeare*, London, Hogarth, 1990.

Taylor Allen, A., Spiritual motherhood: German feminists and the kindergarten movement, 1848–1911, *History of Education Quarterly*, 22:3 (1982), 319–39.

Thirsk, J., The history women, in M. O'Dowd and S. Wichert (eds), *Chattel, Servant or Citizen: Women's Status in Church, State and Society* (Belfast, Institute of Irish Studies, The Queen's University of Belfast, 1993).

Thompson, E. P., *William Morris: Romantic to Revolutionary*, London, Lawrence & Wishart, 1955.

Tolles, F. B. (ed.), Slavery and 'the woman question': Lucretia Mott's diary of her visit to Britain to attend the World's Anti-Slavery Convention of 1840, Supplement no. 23 (1952) to *The Journal of the Friends' Historical Society*, Haverford Friends' Historical Association, and London Friends' Historical Society.

Tomalin, C., *Mrs Jordan's Profession: The Story of a Great Actress and a Future King*, London, Penguin, 1995.

Toulmin Smith, L. (ed.), *Lench's Trust: Copies of the Original Deeds*, Birmingham, privately printed, 1869.

Toulmin Smith, L., *Manual of English Grammar and Language for Self Help*, London, Ward Lock, 1885.

Toulmin Smith, L. (ed.), *The Itinerary of John Leland in or about the Years 1535–1543*, 5 vols, London, George Bell, 1907.

Toulmin Smith, J. T. and L. Toulmin Smith, *English Gilds. The Original Ordinances of More than One Hundred English Gilds*, edited, with Notes by the late Toulmin Smith Esq … with an Introduction and Glossary, &c. by his daughter Lucy Toulmin Smith, London, Early English Text Society, 1870.

Trivedi, H., *Colonial Transactions: English Literature and India*, Delhi, Papyrus, 1993.

Tuke, M. J., *History of Bedford College for Women 1889–1937*, Oxford, Oxford University Press, 1939.

Turner, F. M., *The Greek Heritage in Victorian Britain*, New Haven and London, Yale University Press, 1981.

Turner, F. M., Antiquity in Victorian contexts, *Browning Institute Studies*, 10 (1982), 1–14.

Turner, F. M., Why the Greeks and not the Romans in Victorian Britain?, in G. W. Clarke (ed.), *Rediscovering Hellenism: The Hellenic Inheritance and the English Imagination*, Cambridge, Cambridge University Press, 1989.

Turner, F. M., The triumph of idealism in classical studies, in F. M. Turner, *Contesting Cultural Authority*, Cambridge, Cambridge University Press, 1993.

Varikas, E., Gender and experience, *New Left Review*, 211 (1995), 89–104.

Venuti, L., *The Translator's Invisibility: A History of Translation*, London and New York, Routledge, 1995.

Vicinus, M., *Independent Women*, London, Virago, 1985.

Wake, R. and P. Denton, *Bedales School, The First Hundred Years*, London, Haggerston Press, 1993.

Walker, P. J., Proclaiming women's right to preach, *Harvard Divinity Bulletin*, 23 (1994), 21.

Walkowitz, J. R., *Prostitution and Victorian Society*, Cambridge, Cambridge University Press, 1980.

Walkowitz, J., *City of Dreadful Delight: Narratives of Sexual Danger in Late Victorian London*, London, Virago, 1992.

Wark, R. R., *Mrs Siddons as the Tragic Muse*, Henry E. Huntingdon Library and Art Gallery, Pasadena, California, The Castle Press, 1965.

Wassyng Roworth, W., Kauffman and the art of painting in England, in W. Wassyng Roworth (ed.), *Angelica Kauffman: A Continental Artist in Georgian England*, London, Reaktion Books, 1992.

Watts, R., Knowledge is power – Unitarians, gender and education in the eighteenth and early nineteenth centuries, *Gender and Education*, 1:1 (1989), 35–50.

Webb, T., *The Violet in the Crucible*, Oxford, Oxford University Press, 1976.

Webster, A., *The Prometheus Bound of Aeschylus*, Literally translated into English verse, ed. T. Webster, London and Cambridge, Macmillan & Co., 1866.

Webster, A., *Dramatic Studies*, London and Cambridge, Macmillan & Co., 1866.

Webster, A., *A Woman Sold and Other Poems*, London and Cambridge, Macmillan & Co., 1867.

Webster, A., *The Medea of Euripides*, Literally translated into English verse, London and Cambridge, Macmillan & Co., 1868.

Webster, A., *Portraits*, London and Cambridge, Macmillan & Co., 1870.

Webster, A., *Essays on Suffrage*, London, The Women's Suffrage Union, 1878.

Webster, A., *A Housewife's Opinions*, London, Macmillan & Co., 1879.

Webster, A., *In a Day. A Drama*, London, Kegan Paul, Trench & Co., 1882; London, Macmillan & Co., 1893.

Webster, A., *The Sentence; A Drama* (in three acts and verse), London, T. Fisher Unwin, 1887; London, Macmillan & Co., 1893.

Webster, A., *Mother & Daughter. An Uncompleted Sonnet-Sequence*, Introductory note by W. M. Rosetti, London, Macmillan & Co., 1895.

White, R. G., 'On reading Shakespeare', in idem, *Studies in Shakespeare*, London, Sampson Low, 1885.

Widdowson, F., *Going up into the Next Class: Women and Elementary Teacher Training, 1840–1914*, London, Women's Research and Resources Centre, 1980.

Wiebe, D., Religion and the scientific impulse in the nineteenth century: Friedrich Max Müller and the birth of the science of religion, *International Journal of Comparative Religion and Philosophy*, 1:1 (1995), 76–97.

Williams, M., *Margaret Oliphant, A Critical Biography*, London, Macmillan, 1986.

Wollstonecraft, M. and W. Godwin, *A Short Residence in Sweden and Memoirs of the Author of 'The Rights of Woman'*, ed. R. Holmes, London, Penguin, 1987.

Wood, M. A. E., *Letters of Royal and Illustrious Ladies*, 3 vols, London, Henry Colburn, 1846.

Woodham Smith, P., History of the Froebel Movement in England, in E. Lawrence (ed.), *Friederich Froebel and English Education*, London, Routledge and Kegan Paul, 1969.

Woolf, D. R., A feminine past? Gender, genre, and historical knowledge in England, 1500–1800, *American Historical Review*, 102:3 (1997), 645–79.

Woolf, V., *The Three Guineas*, Harmondsworth, Penguin, 1977.

Wu, D., *Romanticism: An Anthology*, Oxford, Blackwell, 1994.

Yeo, E. J., *The Contest for Social Science: Relations and Representations of Gender and Class*, London, Rivers Oram Press, 1996.

Zemon Davis, N., Gender and genre: women as historical writers 1400–1820, in P. H. Labalme (ed.), *Beyond Their Sex: Learned Women of the European Past*, New York, New York University Press, 1980.

Biographies

Aikin, Lucy (b. Warrington, Cheshire, 1781, d. Hampstead, London, 1864)

Daughter of Dr John Aikin, Unitarian physician and writer and editor of the *Athenaeum*. Niece of Anna Lætitia Barbauld. Educated largely by her father. Author of *Memoirs of the Court of Queen Elizabeth* (1818) 2 vols; *Memoirs of the Court of King James I* (1822) 2 vols; *Memoirs of the Court of King Charles I* (1833) 2 vols; *Life of Addison* (1843), as well as poetry and children's books. Spent most of her life living with relatives. Moved in Unitarian and intellectual circles, was a close friend of Joanna Baillie, Sarah Austin (translator of Von Ranke's work into English), and of the Bentham and Mill circle in London. In her latter years developed a close epistolary friendship with the American evangelist William Channing. Believed in better education for women to teach them to think, but saw their fundamental role as that of wife and mother rather than aspiring to economic or intellectual autonomy. In politics she was a Whig, in favour of reform but out of sympathy with demands for greater popular participation in political life.

Beale, Dorothea (b. London, 1831, d. Cheltenham, 1906)

Born into the large family of eleven children of a London surgeon and was educated at home and at a school in Shalford, Essex, before attending lectures at Gresham College. Sent to a Paris finishing school, but her stay was curtailed when the school was forced to close by the Revolution of 1848. Became one of the first students at Queen's College, Harley Street. (Frances Buss (q.v.) was an evening student while Beale attended in the daytime so their paths did not coincide.) Employed as teacher of mathematics there from 1849 to 1856. In 1857 appointed headmistress of the Clergy Daughters' School at Casterton, Westmoreland (which the Brontë girls had attended), but her demands for reforms forced her resignation. In 1858, at the age of 27, became Principal of Cheltenham Ladies College (founded 1854). Increased the size of the school (from 82 pupils to 500 in 1880), established its own nursery department and St Hilda's Teacher Training College (for secondary school teachers), St Helen's (for elementary school teachers) and a system of training kindergarten teachers in the Ladies' College itself; and founded St Hilda's Hall, Oxford, in 1892 to allow trainee teachers a year at the University. Forbade competitive sport and competitive work in the College. The curriculum, however, was broadened and academic standards high and these factors enabled the 'ladies' to enter the professions which were beginning to be opened to them. Appeared before the Schools' Inquiry Commission in 1866 and gave a full account of the curriculum at her school – a curriculum which included innovatory methods of mathematics, history and language teaching based on reason and her observation of how children and (in her view) especially girls learnt. President of the Headmistresses' Association from

1895–97. Awarded the honorary degree of LL. D. by Edinburgh University in 1902. Her *Work and Play in Girls' Schools* (1898) remains an interesting study of her approach to the education of girls.

Booth, Catherine Mumford (b. Ashbourne, Derbyshire, 1829, d. Clacton-on-Sea, 1890)

Daughter of John Mumford, a coach builder and Wesleyan lay preacher before lapsing into agnosticism and alcoholism. Educated largely by her mother, a well-educated woman of fervent religious feeling. Also had two years of formal education, 1841–43. Converted in 1844, she joined the Wesleyan Methodists, but was expelled by them in 1848 and joined the New Connexion. Became engaged to William Booth in 1852 and married in 1855; they had eight children. She entered public life as a preacher and writer in 1860. In 1865 the Booths moved to London where they founded the organisation that was to take the name of the Salvation Army. An active preacher for the remainder of her life. Involved in the 1855 agitation for The Criminal Law Amendment Act. Promoted the right of women to preach and was adamant that women were the intellectual as well as moral equals of men. Died of breast cancer. Generally considered to be the primary theological force that shaped the beliefs of the Salvation Army. Publications include: *Papers on Practical Religion* (1879), *Aggressive Christianity* (1880), *Life and Death* (1883), *The Salvation Army in Relation to the Church and State* (1883), *The Iniquity of State Regulated Vice* (1884), *Female Ministry or, Woman's Right to Preach the Gospel* (n.d.).

Buss, Frances Mary (b. London, 1827, d. London, 1894)

Daughter of Frances (née Fleetwood) and Robert William Buss. Her mother was a hard-working schoolmistress (who had been trained at the Home and Colonial Institute and who kept a small school of her own) and her father an improvident painter-etcher. Educated at schools in London. Aged eighteen, she opened a school with her mother in Kentish Town. Took courses at Queen's College, London. In 1850 started her North London Collegiate School for Ladies (later Girls). It became a public school in 1871. Renowned for its academic and competitive ethos, this school became the prototype for the Girls' Public Day School Trust. In December 1863 the school put forward 25 pupils to take the first Cambridge local examination open to women. She was in agreement with Emily Davies (q.v.) that women should compete on an equal footing with men and was one of the signatories of the memorial asking Cambridge University to make the access to local examinations permanent. Also allied with Davies in petitioning that the Schools' Inquiry Commission investigate girls' schooling and was one of the women called to give evidence (and opinion) by the Commission in 1866. Nervously gave information about education in her own school (which had 201 day girls and 118 boarders), outlining the curriculum, the poor preparation of the girls who came to her, the need for financial assistance and the shocking shortage of trained teachers. A founder member of the Council for Teacher Training, the Training College for Women Teachers (which opened in Cambridge in 1886), and the Association of Headmistresses, of which she was first President. Held in high regard and personal affection by her former pupils.

Collet, Clara Elizabeth (b. London, 1860, d. 1948)

Second daughter and fourth of the six children of Jane and Collet Dobson Collet. Her father was editor of the *Diplomatic Review*; her mother ran a small laundry in North London. From 1873–78 attended the progressive North London Collegiate school run by Frances Mary Buss (q.v.). Expected to work for her living. She began by carrying messages in connection with her father's job. Her world, and his, was the world of Grub Street. Associated with the Marx family and became close friends with Eleanor Marx and Clementina Black. From 1879 taught at Wyggeston Girls' School, Leicester. Combined her teaching with studying for her B.A. at London externally. Hoping to get over disappointments in her personal life, threw herself into her studies. Obtained an M.A. in moral and political philosophy, psychology and economics at University College London. Began work as an investigator into women's work and female education for Charles Booth in 1888; also worked for Graham Balfour, when he was preparing his Battersea enquiry, and for Booth's study of the Poor Law Unions. The quality of these contributions was very high. Elected a Fellow of the Royal Statistical Society in 1893, she became a Fellow of University College, London in 1896. A governor of Bedford College. In 1903, on Booth's recommendation, moved to the Labour Department of the Board of Trade as a Labour Correspondent. Her recent book *Educated Working Women: Essays on the Position of Women Workers in the Middle Classes* (1902) recommended her. Became an expert on the work of women, varied as it was. Found that, as a civil servant, could not speak her mind and in 1910 she threatened resignation. She did retire early.

Cowden Clarke, Mary Victoria (b. London, 1809, d. Genoa, 1898)

Eldest daughter of the eleven children of Mary (née Hehl) and Vincent Novello. Her half-Italian father was a celebrated organist and musical editor who founded the London musical publishing firm which eventually provided comfortable wealth under the directorship of their son Alfred. Her mother was the daughter of a German father who held minor posts at various lesser European courts and an Irish mother. She published essays and children's stories, educated all her children and supervised their tutors when specialised instruction was needed. Many of the children followed artistic careers: Edward became a respected painter; Clara became an internationally renowned soprano; another sister became an actress. Eminent writers and artists frequented the family home, and Mary Lamb gave Mary lessons in Latin and poetry. At the age of fifteen Mary went to school in Boulogne. After a year returned to take up a post as a governess for a short time. In 1828 left to marry Charles Cowden Clarke, now best known as Keats's early mentor. His background was liberal, republican and dissenting with Unitarian connections. He and the Novellos were friends and supporters of the radical journalist Leigh Hunt, and their circle included Keats, Byron, the Lambs, Haydon, Edgeworth, Bentham, James Mill, the Shelleys, Hazlitt and Godwin. The couple had no children, but a large close-knit family and many friends. Following her marriage, Mary published a few trivial articles as a contribution to the family budget, then began work on her *Complete Concordance to Shakespere* (sic), which was eventually published in 1844. This was the first thorough and reliable concordance to Shakespeare's dramatic works. It was a monumental achievement which brought her immediate international acclaim. The Bibliography included in her autobiography *My Long Life* (1897) lists over 60 items, plus joint publications with her husband, in some of which hers was the largest share. Some of her most noted publications were *Shakespear Proverbs, or The Wise Saws of our Wisest Poet Collected in a Modern Instance* (1847); ten articles in *Sharpe's London Magazine* 1848–51 'On Shakespeare's individuality in his characters'; another series on Shakespeare's women characters in *The Ladies Companion* 1849–50 and 1854, and in the same journal from 1851–53 a further series on 'The woman of the writers' (Chaucer, Cervante, Spenser and Richardson); *Girlhood of Shakespeare's Heroines* (1850); *World-Noted Women; or, Types of Womanly Attributes of All Lands and Ages* (1858); a complete edition of Shakespeare's plays (published in America in 1858), and, with Charles, *Illustrated Shakespeare* published by Cassell in weekly parts from 1864–68, and *The Shakespear Key* (1879). In middle age the Cowden Clarkes moved to Italy to be close to her parents and sister Clara's family. Mary remained there after Charles's death in 1877.

Davies (Sarah) Emily (b. Southampton, 1830, d. Hampstead, 1921)

Daughter of a clergyman. Largely self-educated, her father also trained her to work in the parish when they moved to Gateshead. Through her brother, Rev. Llewellyn Davies, Rector of Christ Church, Marylebone, met and came under the influence of Frederick Denison Maurice, founder of the Working Men's College. In 1859 met Elizabeth Garrett Anderson, Barbara Leigh Smith (Madame Bodichon) and Bessie Rayner Parkes. Their friendship gave her desire to aid the women's movement a sense of direction and she was employed by them as editor of *The English Women's Journal.* After her father's death in 1861 moved to Cunningham House, near Langham Place, and began to campaign for women's rights to higher education. Integral to Davies's campaign was the belief that women should compete with men on the same terms and study for the same qualifications. Pressed successfully for the inclusion of female education in the Schools Inquiry Commission. In 1865, gave evidence before this commission, arguing for improved education for girls, better teacher training, and exhibitions and scholarships to finance these. A founding member and, for 22 years, Secretary of the Schoolmistresses' Association. Regarded as the genius behind the establishment of Girton College. This first opened, after much campaigning and fund-raising, in October 1869 at Benslow House at Hitchin, Hertfordshire. In 1873 Hitchin was incorporated as Girton College and in 1874 moved to Girton, Cambridge. For a short time Emily was Mistress. Resigned in 1875, but retained the position of Secretary for the next thirty years. An active suffragette: in 1866 helped prepare the petition for the suffrage which J. S. Mill presented to Parliament; in 1906 led a deputation to Parliament demanding votes for women. Author of *The Higher Education of Women* (1866) and *Thoughts on Some Questions Relating to Women 1860–1908* (1910). In 1919 made her last public appearance – at the Girton Jubilee.

Edgeworth, Maria (b. Black Bourton, Oxfordshire, 1767, d. Edgeworthstown, County Longford, 1849)

Daughter of Anna Maria (née Elers) – who died in 1773 – and Richard Lovell Edgeworth. Attended boarding schools in Derby and London, before joining her family at their estate in Ireland in 1782. Her father encouraged her intellectual development and trained her in the affairs of the Edgeworthstown estate. Lived at Edgeworthstown until her death. Heavily involved in the running of the estate and in the education of her younger siblings. (R. L. Edgeworth married a further three times, and had twenty-two children in total.) She, her father and some of her stepmothers collaborated on various educational projects, some of which provided material for subsequent books on education. Through her father became acquainted with literary and scientific figures such as Thomas Day and Erasmus Darwin. Later formed her own circle of notable friends. Through correspondence, and in person during her visits to England, Scotland and the Continent, knew writers including Anna Laetitia Barbauld, Elizabeth Hamilton, Elizabeth Inchbald, Jane Marcet and Walter Scott. Scott acknowledged Edgeworth as the originator of regional fiction, stating that he would never have thought of writing Scottish novels if he had not read her Irish works. (Mary Leadbeater (q.v.) and Anna Maria Hall also cited her as a major influence.) Her interest in the future of Ireland led to correspondences with economists and politicians such as David Ricardo and Thomas Rice Spring. Her publications fall into five main groups: Irish fiction, including *Castle Rackrent* (1800), *Ennui* (1809), *The Absentee* (1812) and *Ormond* (1817); English fiction, such as *Belinda* (1801), *Patronage* (1814) and *Helen* (1834); fiction for children, such as *Moral Tales for Young People* (1801); writings on education, including *Practical Education* (1798) and *Professional Education* (1809) (both with R. L. Edgeworth); satirical essays such as *Letters for Literary Ladies* (1795) on war between the sexes and, with R. L. Edgeworth, *Essay on Irish Bulls* (1802) on Anglo-Irish relations and stereotyping.

Green, Mary Anne Everett (b. Sheffield, 1818, d. London, 1895)

Daughter of Robert Wood, Wesleyan minister in Lancashire and Yorkshire, moving to London in 1841. Educated at home and by her own reading at the British Museum. Author of *Letters of Royal and Illustrious Ladies of Great Britain* (1846) 2 vols (as Mary Anne Wood). In 1846 married George Pycock Green, a painter. Spent her early married life in Paris and Antwerp where she worked in archives and libraries. Returning to England, she had to support the family of three daughters and a son when her husband became disabled. Wrote *Lives of the Princesses of England* (1849–55) 6 vols, and journalism in the *Athenaeum*, the *London Review* and the *Gentleman's Magazine*. Editor of *Diary of John Rous 1625–1642* (1856) Camden Society 66, and of 41 volumes of calendars for the Public Record Office, chiefly for the late sixteenth and seventeenth centuries. Niece Sophia Crawford Lomas her assistant in her later years. Close friendship with bibliomaniac Sir Thomas Phillips.

Haweis, Mary Eliza (b. 1818, d. Bath, 1898)

The eldest daughter of Thomas Musgrove Joy, an only moderately successful portrait painter. Childhood spent partly in Pimlico, and partly with relatives in the countryside of Kent and Surrey. Her talent for drawing and painting was encouraged by her father. Her mother introduced her to the British Museum where she copied illuminated manuscripts. Also studied in the newly-opened South Kensington Museums. Her first Royal Academy picture was exhibited in 1866. In 1867 she married Reginald Haweis (pronounced Hoyce), a curate in their parish of St James the Less Westminster. He was soon appointed to the crown living of St James Westmoreland Street, where his musical ability and theatrical preaching brought considerable popularity and fame. He was also a writer and editor. They had four children, but one died in infancy. Her friends included Oscar Deutsch, the Semitic scholar, Sir Lawrence Alma Tadema and Colonel Godwen Austen, who even proposed she elope with him. Fulfilled her role as mother and home-maker with much creativity. Designed her own and her children's clothes (much to her daughter's disgust). She also took a keen interest in their education. Failing to find suitable editions of the classics, she made and illustrated a version of Chaucer. Also illustrated her husband's publications. Partly to improve the family income, she embarked on a career as a writer on decoration and dress. Publications include: *The Art of Beauty* (1878), *The Art of Decoration* (1881), *Beautiful Houses* (1882). The family moved to increasingly expensive homes, all of which were decorated to Mary's designs. From 1878 they lived in St John's Wood Road, then from 1884 in Rossetti's former home, Queen's House, Chelsea. She was deeply involved in the League of Mercy for Animals and the suffrage movement, the inspiration for the novel she published in 1897. Became increasingly ill after 1887. Her husband was involved in lecture tours that left her frequently alone, and the partnership began to show signs of pressure by the 1890s. This in turn damaged Mary's relationship with her elder children, particularly with her daughter. The Chelsea House was given up in favour of one in Marylebone. Meanwhile her husband's flirtations had caused some scandal and loss of patronage, which further exacerbated the problems though they remained married.

Hopkins, Jane Ellice (b. Cambridge, 1836, d. Brighton, 1904)

Daughter of Caroline (née Boys) and William Hopkins, a Cambridge mathematician and geologist. Educated by her father. Entered public life around 1856, preaching to navvies in Cambridge. Her first publications were in 1865, and much of her adult life was spent as a chronic invalid due to a bungled surgery at about that time. Following death of her father, she moved to Brighton with her mother. In 1872 met James Hinton who gave her a thorough medical training and launched her on her lifework of agitation for social purity and sexual equality. Involved in active reform work between 1875 and 1885, preaching purity as the founder of the White Cross Army. Responsible for the 1880 Amendment to the Industrial Schools Act which attempted to protect children from commercial sexual exploitation. Also credited with inspiring the first women's trade union in Britain. Her activism culminated in the reform to the 1885 Criminal Law Amendment Act. An invalid after 1888, she continued to write on reform issues until her death. Her many publications include: *Idylls, and Other Poems* (1865); under pseudonym of Jane Ellice: *Home Thoughts for Mothers and Mothers' Meetings* (1868); *The Visitation of Dens, An Appeal to the Women of England* (1874); *An English Woman's Work Among Workingmen* (1875); *Work in Brighton, or, Woman's Mission to Women* (1877) with preface by Florence Nightingale; *Grave Moral Questions Addressed to the Men and Women of England* (1882); *England's Law for Women and Children* (1883); *God's Great Gift of Speech Abused* (1883); *Per Angusta Ad Augusta* (1883); *The White Cross Army* (1883); *Drawn unto Death: A Plea for the Children Coming Under the Industrial Schools Act Amendment Act, 1880* (1884); *Purity the Guard of Manhood* (1885); *The Present Moral Crisis: an Appeal to Women* (1886); *True Manliness* (1886); *The National Purity Crusade* (1904).

Jameson, Anna (b. Dublin, 1794, d. London, 1860)

Daughter to Dennis Brownwell Murphy, an Irish miniature painter, and his English wife Anna. The family moved to England in 1798. Educated by a governess, she became one herself at the age of sixteen to help support her family. Worked for several employers, including the Rowles family, with whom she travelled to France and Italy in 1821–22, after the collapse of her love affair with Robert Jameson, a barrister. Her *Diary of an Ennuyée* (1826), based on this European tour, launched her literary career. She married Jameson in 1825, but her relations with him remained troubled. Her many subsequent books included other accounts of travel, in Europe and in Canada, as well as guidebooks to galleries and art history. Her iconographic studies of religious art, in particular, established her reputation as a literary and scholarly figure. (Her own religious inclinations appear to have been Anglican.) *Sacred and Legendary Art* (1848–64) was published in four parts; the final part completed after her death by her friend Lady Eastlake. Her wide circle of friends included Lady Byron, Mrs Gaskell, the Brownings and Fanny Kemble. Long interested in the advancement of women, she welcomed the growth of the women's movement in the 1850s and supported Bessie Rayner Parkes and Barbara Bodichon. For the most part she lived separately from her husband, and struggled to support herself through her writings, while nonetheless gaining valuable independence from her status as a married woman. In 1860 she fell ill and died, after working long hours at the British Museum.

Jordan, Dorothy (b. London, 1761, d. Saint-Cloud, near Paris, 1816)

Daughter of Irish father (Francis Bland) and Welsh mother (Grace Phillips). Both worked on the Dublin stage. Although unmarried her parents had a large family. Francis abandoned them to marry an heiress when Dorothy was thirteen. She became the main breadwinner, working in a hat shop, but soon followed her mother on to the stage. Became pregnant by the Dublin theatre manager Richard Daly, but soon left with her mother for Yorkshire where she was given work by Tate Wilkinson. Adopted the stage name 'Mrs Jordan'. Her daughter Fanny born in 1782. Spent three years touring in Wilkinson's company. Soon began to acquire a reputation for her acting abilities. In 1785 offered a contract at Drury Lane where she was an instant success, renowned for her skills in speaking verse, singing, comic timing and physical movement. Gained particular fame for her role as Peggy in David Garrick's *The Country Girl*, as Viola in Shakespeare's *Twelfth Night* and as Hippolita in Colley Cibber's comedy *She Would and She Would Not*. Her popularity provoked a so-called 'Jordan-mania' in London, with many of her performances sold out. Worked for the next twenty-four years as one of the stars of the Theatre Royal Drury Lane, enjoying a high salary. During this period she was painted by many famous portraitists, among them Hoppner, Romney and Beechey. In 1786 Richard Ford, a young lawyer, became her lover. Their child, Dora Ford, born 1787. By 1790 Jordan was being wooed by Prince William, Duke of Clarence, whom (according to her own account) she kept at bay for a year, eventually parting from Ford because he had been unable to commit to marriage. In 1791 she began a relationship with the Duke which was to last twenty years. Continued working on the stage, helping to support the Duke. In 1797 they moved into an estate near Hampton Court, Bushy House. They had three children. Under pressure from the royal family, he eventually decided to marry a young heiress in 1811, when Jordan was fifty and their youngest child only four. She accepted the loss of her lover and her home with dignity, but never recovered from the blow. Continued to work in order to support her children, but suffered tragedy at the end of her life. She was cheated by a son-in-law whose debts she became liable for and was treated cruelly by the Duke's advisers. Forced to flee to France, where she died alone and in relative poverty.

Leadbeater, Mary (b. Ballitore, County Kildare, 1758, d. Ballitore, 1826)

Daughter of Elizabeth (née Carleton) and Richard Shackleton, who ran a boarding school at Ballitore (established in 1726 by her grandfather Abraham Shackleton soon after he left Yorkshire to settle in Ireland). She had a good education and received personal tuition from Aldborough Wrightson, who had been a student at Ballitore school. In 1784 she travelled in England with her father, staying in London and Yorkshire. Visited Edmund Burke, a student at Ballitore school under Abraham Shackleton, and through him met Sir Joshua Reynolds and George Crabbe. Raised as a Quaker, her faith remained important to her throughout her life. William Leadbeater, of Huguenot descent, obtained admission to the Society of Friends before marrying Mary in 1791. He was a farmer and housebuilder. She kept the village post office. They had three children and their marriage lasted until her death. She corresponded with Edmund Burke, Maria and R. L. Edgeworth, George Crabbe and Melusina Trench. (Assisted Trench in her philanthropic work among her tenants at Ballybarney.) Interested in prison reform and opposed to the death penalty and the slave trade. Used informal networks of Quaker women to distribute anti-slavery literature around Ireland. During the revolutionary and violent 1790s, she combined enthusiasm for the Quaker principle of Peace with support for radical local members of the United Irishmen. *Extracts and Original Anecdotes for the Improvement of Youth* (1794), published anonymously, was her first work. It combined didacticism and entertainment in an attempt to make instructive writing for young Quakers more appealing. Under her married name published a collection of poems (1808). *Cottage Dialogues Among the Irish Peasantry* (1811) was intended for the improvement of the poor in Ireland. Maria Edgeworth (q.v.) wrote an Advertisement and Glossary for the English edition. Further publications include: *Tales for Cottagers* (1814), with Elizabeth Shackleton; *Cottage Biography, being a Collection of the Lives of the Irish Peasantry* (1822); *Biographical Notices of Members of the Society of Friends in Ireland* (1823). Her 'Annals of Ballitore' covered the period 1766 to 1824 and ranged from domestic traditions to the impact on Ballitore of the 1798 Uprising. It was published in 1862, along with some of her correspondence, as *The Leadbeater Papers* (edited by R. D. Webb).

Morgan (Lady) Sydney (b. Dublin, 1783 (disputed), d. London, 1859)

Daughter of Jane (née Mill) and Robert Owenson, an actor-manager. Attended schools in Dublin, but spent much of her youth backstage in her father's theatrical company. In order to ease his financial difficulties, she worked as a governess in her youth. Published her first book of poems in 1801 and her first novel *St Clair* in 1803. Her third novel *The Wild Irish Girl* (1806) – strongly nationalistic in sentiment – established her literary reputation.

Romantic nationalism suffused her Irish tales, novels and verses, which won her the praise of Walter Scott and savage reviews in the Tory periodicals. A financially successful writer, she moved in fashionable circles in Dublin. In 1812 married Sir Charles Morgan, a moderately prosperous English doctor, just after he had received a knighthood. *Italy* (1821) was her second travel book, and confirmed the reputation for political liberalism that she had already gained from her writings on Irish matters. The book, admired by Byron, was attacked in the *Edinburgh Magazine* and the *Quarterly Review*, and banned in the Papal States, Austria and Germany. In 1837 became the first woman to receive a pension for 'services to the world of letters'. Moved to London in 1839.

Oliphant, Margaret (b. near Edinburgh, 1828, d. Windsor, Berkshire, 1897)

The youngest child and only daughter of the lower middle-class family of Margaret Oliphant and Francis Wilson who moved from Scotland to Liverpool when she was ten years of age. Educated by her active and intelligent mother, who encouraged her hopes of becoming a writer. (The mother maintained contact with relatives in Scotland and through them had access to the Blackwoods of Edinburgh, the publishing family.) In 1852 she married her cousin Francis (Frank) Oliphant and thus came to bear the somewhat unusual, full name of Margaret Oliphant Wilson Oliphant. In seven years of marriage she had six pregnancies, though only three children survived infancy. Her husband, a stained-glass artist, was unsuccessful in his business and she supplemented the family income by writing. She wrote regularly and prolifically over a period of fifty years. In 1859 he was diagnosed as suffering from tuberculosis. They moved to Italy where he died that year, leaving her with two young children and about to give birth to another. Returned to Britain without any financial resources and entirely dependent on her own efforts. After some initial difficulties established a lasting and financially advantageous working relationship with the Blackwoods while maintaining links with other important publishers. In 1864 her eldest child and only daughter died suddenly, aged ten. None of Oliphant's male relatives appears to have been reliable or supportive. She took responsibility for an alcoholic brother living in Rome and after 1868 when her other brother suffered financial ruin and nervous collapse she supported him and his three children. Had great social ambitions for her two sons, educating them at Eton and Oxford, but neither succeeded in establishing careers and remained dependent on her. Both predeceased her.

Robinson, Mary (b. Bristol, 1758, d. Windsor Park, Berkshire, 1800)

Born Mary Darby to an American merchant father and a mother descended from the Seys of Beverton Castle, Wales. Her two brothers became merchants. She received her first schooling from Hannah More's two sisters in Bristol. Her father was often away on ill-conceived financial schemes, took up with another woman, and became increasingly remote. The family moved to London where she was taught by a well-educated woman called Lorrington, and learnt several foreign languages. She and her mother started their own ladies' boarding school in Chelsea. Forced to close the establishment under pressure from Mr Darby. Mary was soon recommended to the dancing master of Covent Garden for her remarkable ability for 'dramatic exhibitions'. In 1774, aged only fifteen, married Thomas Robinson, an articled clerk. Subsequently regretted this union. Her daughter Maria was born the same year. In 1775 he was confined to the Kings Bench Prison for bankruptcy as a result of his profligate and reckless life within fashionable society. She sought her own income by publishing her poems in 1775, which attracted the attention of Georgiana, Duchess of Devonshire. Took up acting with support of David Garrick and Richard Brinsley Sheridan. Debut as Juliet in 1776 was a huge success. Soon became an acclaimed actress renowned for her beauty and her feckless husband. After a royal command performance as Perdita in *A Winter's Tale* she was pursued by the young Prince of Wales, with whom she became involved in 1780. Robinson separated from her husband and gave up her stage career. By 1783 when the affair was over she had been painted by many famous portraitists, including Reynolds, Romney and Gainsborough, and her private life had been featured regularly in the satirical press. Subsequent affairs with politicians Charles James Fox and Baron Tarleton were often discussed scurrilously in the press. Despite developing a serious illness of rheumatic gout in the 1780s, she continued writing poems, plays and novels. During her last decade produced a pamphlet on women's rights. Although the relationship with Tarleton had lasted over fifteen years, and she had supported him, it came to a dramatic end when he married an heiress. Left sad and exhausted by her work, her health deteriorated and she died two years later.

Shelley, Mary Wollstonecraft (b. Somers Town, London, 1797, d. London, 1851)

Born Mary Wollstonecraft Godwin to Mary Wollstonecraft (who died within days of giving birth) and William Godwin. Eloped with Percy Bysshe Shelley in 1814, married 1816. Mother of unnamed girl (born February 1815, died March 1815), William (born 1816, died 1819), Clara (born 1817, died 1818), Percy Florence (born 1819, died 1889). Stepsister of Claire Clairmont (mother of Clara Allegra Byron, born 1817, died 1822). Her works and published *Letters* and *Journals* testify to her learning, which included being fluent in Italian, Latin and Greek, but all her education was acquired at home and by travelling. After elopement and marriage travelled extensively in France and Italy then, after Shelley's death in 1822, returned to England to live in something close to poverty in Harrow and London until Percy Florence inherited the Shelley baronetcy in 1844. Earned money by writing novels, stories and journalism, and editing the works of Shelley. Author of *Six Week's Tour* (1817), *Frankenstein* (1818), *Matilda* (1819, but unpublished until 1959), *The Last Man* (1826), *Valperga* (1823), *Perkin Warbeck* (1830), *Lodore* (1835), *Falkner* (1837), *Lives of the most Eminent Literary and Scientific Men of Italy, Spain and Portugal*, vols 1–2 (1835), *Lives of the most Eminent Literary and Scientific Men of France*, vols 1–2 (1838–9) – both for Lardner's *Cabinet Cyclopedia* – *Poetical Works of Shelley* (1839), *Essays and Letters of Shelley* (1840), *Rambles in Germany and Italy* (1844). In addition she wrote two mythological dramas, *Proserpine* (1820, published 1832), *Midas* (for children, 1820, unpublished until 1922). Through Godwin, Shelley and her own circle was acquainted with most of the literary world of the day including especially Byron, Thomas Love Peacock, Leigh Hunt, Thomas Moore, the Novellos including Mary Cowden Clarke (q.v.). Also a friend of and assisted the writer Mary Diana Dods (pseudonym David Lyndsay) who later assumed a masculine identity as Walter Sholto Douglas and lived abroad as the husband of Isabel Robinson Douglas.

Shirreff, Emily Anne (b. 1814, d. London, 1897) and Grey, Maria Georgina Shirreff (b. 1816, d. London, 1906)

Emily was the fourth and Maria was the fifth child (and they were the second and third daughters respectively) of Elizabeth (née Murray) and Captain (later Rear-Admiral) William Shirreff. Mainly educated at home by a French-Swiss governess. Spent only a brief and unsuccessful time at school in Paris in 1826. In the 1820s and early 1830s they and their family lived in Avranches (Lower Normandy), Gibraltar and Tangiers. Together they published *Letters from Spain and Barbary* (1835). By this time they were in England to escape the cholera epidemic in Gibraltar. Formed close relations with the family of their father's sister, the honourable Mrs Grey, who was married to a brother of Earl Grey, the prime minister. Her son, their cousin William, guided the reading and conversation of the two sisters – encouraging them to read Bacon and Locke. Lord Gage, a cousin of their father, invited them to stay at his house in Firle, Sussex, and gave them the run of his library. In 1841 Captain Shirreff took up a position at Chatham. Promoted to Rear-Admiral, he took command of the Portsmouth Dockyard in 1847, but died in the same year. The sisters were friends with Sir Richard Napier and his wife; Sir William Grove, lawyer, judge and scientist; Mary Somerville, Britain's premier woman scientist; Sir Charles Lyall and his family; Lord Wrottesley, President of the Royal Society and the British Association; and Sir George Biddell Airy, astronomer royal. They had discussions with Frederick Denison Maurice, Herbert Spencer, Thomas Huxley, Benjamin Jowett and other prominent intellectuals. In 1841 Maria married William Thomas Grey. From 1847 the couple shared a house with Emily in London. The sisters collaborated to write *Thoughts on Self-Culture Addressed to Women* (1850) and a novel *Passion and Principle* (1854). Both Emily and Maria spent much of their lives as carers, nursing numerous relatives through long periods of ill-health. Maria's novel *Love's Sacrifice* (1868) explored the caring relationship between heroine Maria and her husband. While at first the sisters accepted the domestic role of women, they came to seek female liberation and fulfilment through education. They made significant contributions to education as a discipline. Emily was involved in campaigning for Froebelian Kindergartens in Great Britain. She wrote of Froebel's ideas and how they should be applied both in schools and in the home. Maria urged the development of women's intellect alongside family responsibilities; she saw education not only as academic but as fulfilment of individual potential. Her initiative was behind the National Union for the Improvement of the Education of Women of All Classes (known as the Women's Education Union (WEU)) (1871) and the Girls' Public Day School Company (formed 1872). Important offshoots of the WEU were the *Journal of the Women's Education Union* (launched 1873); local branches of WEU; the Teachers' Training and Registration Society (TTRS) (started in 1876 to found a training college for women); the Evening College for Women, Bloomsbury and the Brompton Evening College for Women (established 1878) and the Governesses' Registration Agency (1880). The TTRS founded the Skinner Street Training College in 1876. This was to provide women with a lengthy period of education between school and work, to strengthen character and improve knowledge, and to study education as a science in theory and practice. Women were to be tested at the end of the course by independent examiners. Many of the ideas behind the teacher training initiative derived from Emily, who had been acting Mistress of Hitchin in 1869 and who wrote a paper, 'On the training of teachers'. The College, when it moved to Fitzroy Square, was renamed the Maria Grey Training College. Maria was also involved in the work of the COS and in autumn 1871 she stood for election to Chelsea School Board. A member of the central society of the suffrage movement. Author of *Is the Exercise of the Suffrage Unfeminine?* (1870). The sisters spent lengthy periods in Italy during the 1870s and 1880s. They were members of a lively Anglo-American circle in Rome, which included Mary Cowden Clarke (q.v.). A severe riding accident ended Maria's public prominence. Both sisters remained intellectually active almost to the end.

Siddons, Sarah (b. Brecon, 1755, d. London, 1831)

Daughter of Roger Kemble Kemble, a provincial actor and manager of a travelling theatre company. Mother and maternal grandfather also provincial actors. Eight of her brothers and sisters went on to the stage, of which John and Charles were the best known. Most of her childhood was spent travelling with the company. At the age of eighteen she married the actor William Siddons, with whom she worked in the provinces. After being spotted by David Garrick, she first appeared at Drury Lane in December 1775, although her contract was not renewed for the following season. In her own memoirs she recalls the hardships and disappointments of those early years when she continued working in poor health 'for the sake of my poor babies'. By 1782 she already had four children (a fifth had died in infancy) and had become established as the leading actress of the Bath theatre company. Accepted a contract from the dramatist Richard Brinsley Sheridan to return to the Drury Lane stage in London for the 1782–83 season. Soon established her reputation as the leading tragic actress of her day. Achieved particular renown for her performances as Isabella in Thomas Southerne's Restoration drama *The Fatal Marriage*, Belvidera in Otway's *Venice Preserv'd*, and the title role in Rowe's *The Tragedy of Jane Shore*. Her performances had a powerful impact on her audiences. Her biographer James Boaden recorded that during her performance as Isabella about to plunge a dagger into her bosom 'literally the greater part of the spectators were too ill themselves to use their hands in her applause'. Later she became famous for her performances in the part of Shakespeare's Lady Macbeth, which she played for her farewell appearance in June 1812. Respected for her intelligence and 'moral' character. Became a close friend of Dr Johnson, Horace Walpole and Sir Joshua Reynolds. Painted by many successful portraitists, among them Gainsborough, Beechey, Romney, Lawrence and Reynolds, whose famous portrait *Mrs Siddons as the Tragic Muse* of 1784 has helped to establish her status as one of Britain's greatest tragic actresses. Had seven children, although four girls died in infancy. Many younger members of her family established successful careers on the stage, including her son Henry and her niece Fanny Kemble.

Strickland, Agnes (b. London, 1796, d. Southwold, Suffolk, 1874)

Second daughter of Elizabeth (née Horner) and Thomas Strickland of Reydon Hall, Essex, manager of Greenland Docks. Educated at home by her father. Attempted to make a living writing poetry after her father lost his fortune, but was more successful with children's books. Her father's death made earning a living more pressing and she and her sister Elizabeth (editor of the *Court Magazine*) published *Lives of the Queens of England* (1840–48), 12 vols, a series of royal lives which had originally appeared in the magazine. Between the 1820s and the 1870s the two sisters published numerous historical works, notably *Queen Victoria from Birth to Bridal* (1840), 2 vols; *Letters of Mary Queen of Scots* (1842–43), 3 vols; *Lives of the Bachelor Kings of England* (1861); *Lives of the Last Four Princesses of the Royal House of Stuart* (1872), though most came out under Agnes's name alone as Elizabeth much disliked publicity. Agnes also published poetry, novels and children's stories, and journalism in *New Monthly Magazine*; *Juvenile Scrapbook*; and *Pic-nic Papers*. In 1870 she received a civil list pension from Queen Victoria. Although Agnes wrote a good deal about the joys of visiting historic sites and the excitements of making discoveries in manuscripts, most of the research for their books was done by Elizabeth. Agnes was ardently royalist, Anglican and Jacobite and, in so far as she noticed women's causes, was hostile to them.

Swanwick, Anna (b. Liverpool, 1813, d. Tunbridge Wells, 1899)

Daughter of Hannah (née Hilditch) and John Swanwick, a merchant. Her Liberal and Unitarian family had a bust of Charles Fox on display and got up in the middle of the night to celebrate news of passing of 1832 Reform Bill. Educated at a girls' school in Liverpool (left at thirteen). Attended Rev. James Martineau's lectures on mental and moral philosophy. Studied ancient Greek, Hebrew, German and philosophy in Berlin 1839–43. Had an independent income. First publications were translations into English of Goethe and Schiller, then turned to Greek. Aeschylus' *Oresteia* (1865), with lengthy Introduction; complete works of Aeschylus (1873), illustrated by Flaxman. Translation of Aeschylus' *Agamemnon* performed as the Cambridge Greek play, 1900. Also published *Books, Our Best Friends or Our Deadliest Foes* (1886), *An Utopian Dream and How It May Be Realised* (1888), *Poets, the Interpreters of their Age* (1892), *Evolution and the Religion of the Future* (1893). Awarded an Hon. LL. D, University of Aberdeen. Her network included Rev. J. Martineau, F. W. Newman, F. D. Maurice, Rev. P. H. Wickstead, Frances Power Cobbe, W. Gladstone, Tennyson,

R. Browning, and Prof. F. Max Müller. Committed to the advancement of women, especially through increased educational opportunities. In 1838 held evening classes for poor girls in her home in London. Separate classes for young men, from which Morley College developed. In 1849 involved in foundation of Queen's College and Bedford College. Became a chaperone to female students and attended scientific lectures. Member of Bedford College Council 1857–61 and first woman Visitor 1884–89. Active in development of Somerville College, Oxford and Girton College, Cambridge. Extensive committee work for the Pfeiffer Bequest, channelling funds into women's university and teacher training colleges, and colleges which accepted women students. A signatory to the 1865 Petition for Women's Suffrage. Attended suffrage meetings and in later life spoke publicly in support (1873).

Toulmin Smith, Lucy (b. Boston, Massachusetts, 1838, d. Oxford, 1911)

Daughter of Martha (née Jones Kendall) and Joshua Toulmin Smith, Unitarian reformer, writer and editor of the *Parliamentary Remembrancer*, whose great aim was to further knowledge of local government and the principles of democracy. Educated largely by her father whose assistant she became for his later historical works, such as *English Gilds*. *The Original Ordinances of More than One Hundred English Gilds* (1870) edited by the late Toulmin Smith with an Introduction and Glossary by his daughter Lucy Toulmin Smith, Early English Text Society. After her father's death in 1869 she started work on her own account, and edited various volumes for the Camden Society and the New Shakespere Society, often taking over the work of male editors whose assistant she had been. Editor of the standard edition of *The Itinerary of John Leland In or About the Years 1535–43* (1907–10), 4 vols. Also author of *A Manual of the English Grammar and Language for Self-Help* (1885), which she wanted to be used for the education of working people. In 1894 appointed librarian of Manchester College, Oxford (a Unitarian college) and was the first woman to be head of a public library in Britain. Remained there until her death.

Webster, Augusta (b. Poole, Dorset, 1837, d. Kew, London, 1894)

Daughter of Julia (née Hume) and Vice-Admiral George Davies. Following her father's career moves, spent much of her childhood aboard ship in Chichester Harbour, then Banff Castle in Scotland, then Cambridge. Educated at Cambridge School of Art, Paris and Geneva. Fluent in French. Taught herself other languages, including Greek. In 1863 married Thomas Webster, fellow of Trinity College, Cambridge. He became a solicitor in London. They had one daughter. Moved in literary circles. Knew George Eliot, Browning and the Rossetti family. Published translations from the Greek, novels, poetry, plays, essays and reviews (mainly in the *Athenaeum* and the *Examiner*). Publications include: *Blanche Lisle and Other Poems* (1860); *Lilian Grey* (1864) (both under pseudonym Cecil Home); (then under married name) *Dramatic Studies* (1866), *A Woman Sold and Other Poems* (1867), *Portraits* (1870), the sonnet sequence *Mother and Daughter* (1895). Translations of Aeschylus' *Prometheus Bound* (1866), Euripides' *Medea* (1868). Verse dramas include *Disguises* (1879), *The Sentence* (1887), *In a Day* (1893). Collected essays *A Housewife's Opinions* (1879). From the 1860s active in local government. Elected to the London School Board in 1879 and 1885. Public speaker. Published essays on women's education. Thought higher education for women would lead to women's time being more valued. 1878 article on 'Parliamentary franchise for women ratepayers' issued as a pamphlet by Women's Suffrage Union.

Index

Where references are given in italics, the page range shown includes one or more illustrations; 'n.' after a page reference indicates a note number on that page.